WALKS IN EAST ANGLIA

II CAMBRIDGESHIRE & ESSEX

WALKS IN EAST ANGLIA

II. CAMBRIDGESHIRE AND ESSEX

Bruce Galloway

THE BOYDELL PRESS

Published by
Boydell Press, an imprint of
Boydell & Brewer Ltd, PO Box 9, Woodbridge, Suffolk IP12 3DF

British Library Cataloguing in Publication Data

Galloway, Bruce
Walks in East Anglia.
2: Cambridgeshire and Essex
1. East Anglia (England) – Description and travel – Guide-books
I. Title
914.26′0486′8 DA670.E14

ISBN 0-85115-163-9

Printed in Great Britain by
St Edmundsbury Press, Bury St Edmunds, Suffolk

CONTENTS

ACKNOWLEDGEMENTS

This book belongs not to the author alone but to all the people who made it possible. I owe a debt of thanks to all the walkers I did not see, to the ramblers who keep the paths in existence, and to the writers of articles and booklets on whose work I have partly relied in drawing up my networks of walks. And a further debt is owed to every landowner who has not obstructed or obliterated a right of way.

Particular thanks are, however, due to the large number of people I met to discuss the best walks in each part of Cambridgeshire and Essex. I would like to thank George Smith, Henry Bridge, Dr and Mrs Moreton, Mr and Mrs Gillian, Mike Kelly, Trevor Noyes, Janet Laws and the former mayor of Ramsey for help in Cambridgeshire; Brian Offin, Edwin Amos, Michael Easter, Ted Pickett, Andy Cocks, George Hands, Mr and Mrs Tursland, Bob Carpenter, John Dowding, Fred Matthews and Dr Rudd for similar assistance in Essex; and John Andrews and Dr Dony for help with the Icknield Way. I would also like to acknowledge the help of footpaths officers and other county council officials.

Finally, I must also express my debt to those outside the walking community: my publishers, for their untiring work; and my wife and friends, for their equally unflagging support.

BRG

LEGAL DISCLAIMER

The author has gone to great lengths to ensure that the paths included on the maps in this book are open to public use, and that the route directions are accurate. Nevertheless, it is entirely possible that he has made mistakes in both departments. He cannot, however, accept responsibility for any allegations of trespass which might arise out of using the book.

EQUIPMENT and THE LAW

Walks in East Anglia I: Norfolk & Suffolk contains key information on recommended equipment for walking, and on the law as it relates to footpaths and their use, which should be read by all intending to walk in the four counties of East Anglia.

Introduction

This book is a detailed look at walks and walking in Essex and Cambridgeshire, a companion volume to *Walks in East Anglia I: Norfolk and Suffolk*.

Those who have used the Norfolk and Suffolk volume will find a great deal in this book that is familiar, including the arrangement of the contents: each county is divided into a number of areas, concentrating on those where there is regular walking or footpaths of particular interest or beauty. These divisions generally follow natural boundaries – geological or geographical – and are based on a convenient centre. The chapters on each area contain a general description, a gazetteer to places of interest, maps based on the Ordnance Survey 1:50 000 series with footpaths added (see Key and Abbreviations), Recommended Walks with route directions, and a list of Other Suggested Routes. This list is divided into short walks, medium walks, day walks and (for the really energetic) weekend hikes. The last chapter looks at the long-distance footpaths in Essex and Cambridgeshire, and includes a full introduction with mapping to the author's Icknield Way, a hundred-mile route connecting the Peddars Way in Norfolk to the Ridgeway at Ivinghoe Beacon in Buckinghamshire. My book does not claim to be exhaustive. There are some good paths which are not in this book, usually because they are not in good walking areas. The only thing totally exhausted is the author, and those who have helped him compile the book.

Some people may feel that Essex and Cambridgeshire are not good walking country. This allegation is, I think, adequately rebutted by the book, and needs no further comment. Throughout the two counties, there is a wealth of walking to be found among pleasant, often beautiful, and in a few places even spectacular, countryside, along excellent (and in many cases historic) tracks.

Of the two counties, Cambridgeshire is perhaps the less walked, or known. Outsiders may often say that the county is one big fen. This is not the case; but the Fens, in the north and east of the shire, are undoubtedly the most remarkable feature. In the southern fenlands medieval farms and abbey ruins jostle with drainage ditches cut by the Romans and dried-up river courses once used by boats on their way to Ely, Wisbech, Reach and Cambridge. The Fens can be dauntingly lonely, or suddenly and unexpectedly beautiful. The finest walk I have ever had was down a frozen, snowy bridleway near Willingham, north of Cambridge; the finest picture I have ever taken was of sunset on the New Bedford River at Earith. For those who like droves, birdlife and river banks, this is the place.

The uplands of southern Cambridgeshire are very different: a string of villages follows the line of the river valleys, clumps of woodland stand on gently rolling hills; and the chalk upland stretching from Royston to Newmarket carries the myriad tracks of the Icknield Way, the great chalk spine of England beginning in Wiltshire and continuing through west Norfolk to Lincolnshire. An area of little water, few people and enormous fields, this chalk belt is rich in antiquity, with major archaeological sites. Old Huntingdonshire and the Soke of Peterborough are for the most part fairly even and depopulated clay farmlands, with only the meadows of the Great Ouse and Nene to break the monotony, but around Barnack in the west of the Soke are some handsome stone-built villages set in more rugged and hilly, wooded country.

The county of Essex is basically clay, here as elsewhere, heavily forested until comparatively recent times. Epping and Hatfield Forests are now the principal remains of this cover, but there are also thousands of lesser woods throughout the centre of the county, where the landscape is one of gently rolling hills divided by surprisingly steep little valleys, each with its own stream. Such pleasant country has always attracted settlers and there are many small villages and hamlets with a wealth of footpaths between them, making interesting but sometimes difficult walking country. No other area in England has as many footpaths or green lanes as central Essex; few have so much mud.

The valleys of the Chelmer, Roding and Colne dominate the county geographically, but the Dengie and Rochford Hundreds, in south-east Essex, a lonely and beautiful coastline, dominate the walker, who, trudging along the sea wall between saltmarsh and sea, faces a landscape as bleak as anything on the Yorkshire Moors.

Using this book the walker can find both the well-known and scenic routes, and the rural backwaters where paths are used mainly by local people. The construction of the M11 and the possible expansion of Stansted Airport both point to increasing development in Essex and, to a lesser extent, Cambridgeshire. East Anglia is, we are told, a growth area. In the meantime rights of way must be preserved, and no doubt, after the dust has settled, there will still be many fine places to visit, and the same unassuming but charming views to see. By walking the paths in these two counties, the rambler keeps this heritage alive for those who follow him – as well as enjoying it himself.

It is possible that a revised edition of this book may be brought out at some later stage. The author would therefore welcome any comments by readers on the footpaths contained in it, or suggested alternatives with details of their condition and, if possible, directions concerning the route.

KEY TO MAPS, ABBREVIATIONS

—+—	Described route
— — —	Selected rights of way
• • •	Long-distance footpaths
o o o	Permissive paths, or paths where right of way difficulties may exist

VHR	Very Highly Recommended
HR	Highly Recommended
IW	Icknield Way
SPW	St Peter's Way
HW	Harcamlow Way
FW	Forest Way
TFW	Three Forests Way
EW	Essex Way

1 EAST CAMBRIDGESHIRE

Soham to Wandlebury Ring; Newmarket to Linton

The area examined in this chapter is a diamond-shaped region bounded by the river Cam, Devil's Dyke, the Suffolk border and the great Roman road from Colchester to Cambridge, the so-called Via Devana. The towns at its corners are Cambridge, Soham, Newmarket and Linton. It is in my view one of the most interesting areas to walk, for it is an area of great history: several of the best green lanes and other paths in the whole of East Anglia are found here – the Devil's and Fleam Dykes, Street Way, the track followed by my own Icknield Way from Willingham Green to Balsham, and of course the Roman road itself – and in each case these routes relate to the area's historical geography.

There are two obvious districts to be considered. The first is the area of the southern Fens east of the river Cam and including the villages on the edge of the Fens along the open belt of low-lying chalkland. The second is the more easterly line of villages along the forested claylands of south-east Cambridgeshire.

The Fens occupy a large area of very low-lying ground and are subject to chronic problems of flooding and drainage. In north Cambridgeshire the ground is mainly silt deposited by the incursions of the sea over the centuries, but elsewhere in the Fens, and in east Cambridgeshire generally, the soil is peat. Originally, the district was forested land lying just above the water level. Subsidence during the Neolithic period meant a gradual flooding of the Fens, mostly by the rivers of the interior rather than by marine intrusion. The forests rotted, leaving the huge stumps known as bog oaks to annoy future farmers. A thick layer of peat grew up from the rotting vegetation, covered by shallow freshwater meres and marshes. The Fens remained thus throughout the prehistoric period, such settlement as existed being on the fen islands of clay, like Ely. The first major attempt to turn them into useful agricultural land was made by the Romans, who constructed three of the five main drainage channels, or lodes. The channels were also important commercially, for most of them were large enough to accommodate substantial river traffic. The maintenance of these dykes, however, required something very like central co-ordination, and with the collapse of Roman rule the drained fen reverted for the most part into its previous swampy state. It is also likely that there was a further subsidence in the level of the land at this point – for the whole of England is gradually tipping about a central axis, the west being raised up and the east sinking.

Anglo-Saxons tended to ignore the Fens, except again for the islands like Ely where monastic orders in search of solitude established religious foundations that soon gained great temporal as well as spiritual power. This state of affairs continued during the middle ages; the traditional practices of fowling, fishing and eeling ruled the Fens, with only piecemeal attempts at drainage at the fen edge and around the 'islands' of higher ground. The place-name ending -ey derives from the Anglo-Saxon for island, as in Ely and Stuntney. The great change came in the 17th century with the resurrection of earlier Tudor ideas for the complete drainage of the Fens. The project was financed by the Earl of Bedford and other 'Adventurers', planned by the Dutch engineer Vermuyden, contracted out to 'Undertakers', completed by navvies – and fiercely resisted by many of the dwellers in the Fens, the so-called Fen Tigers. The drainage was interrupted by the Civil War, but eventually completed during the 1660s. For a few decades, the Fens seemed to be tamed; but the drying out of the peat caused it to shrink, bringing about a further subsidence, and renewed flooding. In an attempt to prevent this, large floodbanks were raised about the major rivers like the Cam; in the 18th century it became necessary to install series of windmills to pump water up from the drainage lodes out into the river; further shrinkage in the 19th century soon rendered windmills inadequate, and they were gradually replaced by steam engines. Now, diesel or electric engines predominate. The dereliction and flooding of some fens was marked even in our own times, notably at Burwell where the local landowners saw more profit out of fowling and fishing than arable agriculture, but generally, this is now changed and the Fens have become prime arable farmland.

The chalk belt along the edge of the Fens has been settled since around 2000BC. The wealth of Bronze Age round barrows east of Great Wilbraham is an indication of this early settlement; an even more famous example stands on Wandlebury Ring, the Iron Age hill fort. There are several contributory reasons. First, the chalk ground of the belt provided the water essential for an occupied site. Second, the proximity of the Fens provided settler farmers with fertile soil along the edges. Third, after the construction of the lodes, the fen edge villages could engage in river trade as well as growing subsistence crops. However, the fen edge was also crossed by a maze of tracks (many lost during the enclosures of the 18th-19th century), mostly trending NE-SW, and making up the Icknield Way belt, whose impact on the history of the area cannot be doubted. The existence of these led to the construction of the two largest defensive earthworks built by the Anglo-Saxons of East Anglia against their neighbours, Devil's Dyke and Fleam Dyke, which ran from the swampy fens to the impenetrable forests of the claylands.

The open chalkland was widely used for sheep grazing during the middle ages, but after the great 17th-century drainage it became increasingly arable in nature. The fen edge villages then became small agricultural ports, not losing their important river trade until the coming of the railways in the Victorian period. Today, they remain a remarkably populous line of large farming villages with fine churches and old buildings.

The clay land of the south-east has a different history. Here, there was almost no settlement until the middle ages; Domesday Book shows a district almost entirely covered in forest. The few villages were primarily in the east, settled from the Suffolk side – an assumption made from the recurrent West to be found in their names. Similarly, the -ley ending to many of the village names implies that they were formed in forest clearings along the chalk/clay edge. The original settlements were small, and remain so today – agricultural backwaters without any of the commercial importance of the villages on the fen edge. For that reason, they are often much less spoilt by subsequent development. There are many more streams than in the chalk belt, and more woods, particularly south of the villages – one of the better features of this upland landscape.

Soham to Wandlebury Ring

There is some pasture to be found around the rivers and lodes, but for the most part the Fens are now prime arable farmland: dark earth and enormous rectangular fields separated not by hedges but by drainage ditches. Apart from the Nature Reserve at Wicken and Adventurers' Fen (*see below*), there is very little other landscape within the district. Walking here is generally easy, for the few paths that do exist follow well-established paths along floodbanks of the Cam or the lodes. It is almost entirely depopulated, and extremely wild. The fen edge has few paths, but those few are mainly very good. The great mass of little tracks that once existed were rationalised out of existence during the great parliamentary enclosures of the 18th and early 19th centuries. The paths remaining include some major green lanes, a lot of good headland walking and some ploughed field. There are wide views across rolling land, with little sign of human settlement except on the fen and forest edges.

Burwell Church of St Mary the Virgin is the largest and finest 'glasshouse' in old Cambridgeshire. To the W of the church stands Burwell castle mound. The castle was to have been one of a string of fen-edge castles built during Stephen's reign to contain the rebellion of Geoffrey de Mandeville, the great raider from Ely, who died attempting to capture the unfinished castle.

River Cam The lower Cam can be divided into two distinct stretches. Between Cambridge and Clayhythe the river and countryside have a gentle, civilised appearance. The first four miles to Bait's Bite Lock belong to nothing wilder than the University boat clubs. The boat races or May Bumps are held here in June, and here too the Cambridge Eight practise for the Boat Race against Oxford. The towpath is narrow and metalled, beside pollarded willows. Below Clayhythe, the river and landscape become wilder. The fields are flatter, darker, and hugely rectangular. The Cam flows between tall grassy banks, which stand back from the river to contain floods. Bottisham, Reach and Swaffham Bulbeck lodes, connecting their villages to the river, form the basic drainage of the southern Fens. Their current importance as drains goes back well before the 17c and Vermuyden's overall fen drainage. There is evidence that all three lodes were constructed by the Romans as part of their drainage schemes; Reach Lode in particular has thrown up a wealth of Romano-British pottery. Their function was dual: as drainage, they followed the same principle as that applied in the 17c on a far larger scale by the construction of the Bedford Rivers – that is, they diverted the rivers flowing off the uplands by a quick route to the natural outlet, in this case the Cam; they also, however, had a commercial function, even in Roman times. This dual use as drain and trade route remained well into the 19c.

Clayhythe As the name implies, this was a harbour on a little spur of solid clay, a major Roman river port, on the junction of the Cam with Car Dyke (see Chapter 2). In the middle ages, it served Waterbeach. Nothing is here now except the Bridge inn and the yachting club.

Devil's Dyke A stupendous Anglo-Saxon earthwork: a ditch 12-15ft below ground level, a bank or vallum sloping upwards at an angle of 36 degrees measuring 60ft on the slope, a horizontal width of some 45yd. It runs almost straight from Reach SE across the open chalkland to the forested boulder clay S of Stetchworth, 7½ miles away. Its purpose was almost certainly defensive; its sheer size suggests a military function. It makes a magnificent walk: a thin strip of chalk downland covered in short grass, with thickets of hawthorn, sloe and wild roses along the ditch and slope. There are many rare downland butterflies in the open section N of the A11. Further S, the Dyke is covered with sycamore, oak and hornbeam trees, as well as conifers. The dyke is an excellent vantage point from which to watch racehorses exercising on Newmarket Heath.

Fen Ditton Toward the river are thatched cottages, the Plough beside the Cam, and St Mary's church. The road connecting the church to the main Cambridge road lies along the line of the Fleam Dyke. Unlike its namesake to the SE, this is a prehistoric earthwork. Fen Ditton and Horningsea lie on a little tongue of higher land between the river on the one side and Quy and Teversham Fens upon the other. This peninsula was settled very early, and made even more defensible by the construction of the dyke across its landward neck.

Fulbourn The church is notable for its wealth of good late medieval and 17c brasses. Fleam Dyke, south of Fulbourn, is one of a series of defensive earthworks built to resist hostile pressure from the south-west, of which the largest is Devil's Dyke. Originally, it would have run in a straight line NW-SE from the boggy ground at Fulbourn Fen to the forests of the clay land east of Balsham. Now, something under 3 miles survive, mostly wooded and always a splendid path. There are a number of Bronze and Iron Age round barrows in the vicinity, notably Mutlow Hill tumulus just north of the A11 upon the dyke.

Horningsea The name (Island of Horn's People) records its former isolation. The village has given its name to a fine grey paste pottery produced in the Iron Age and Romano-British period, found throughout the county. Magnificent beamed inn, the Plough and Fleece.

Lode Anglesey Abbey (NT) built in late 12c. The last owner, Lord Fairhaven, owned a stud at Newmarket. Anglesey Abbey houses his collection of topographical paintings, snuff boxes, Italian mosaics, bronzes, statuary, tapestries and furniture. Open: afternoons, April to mid-October, Tuesday, Wednesday, Thursday, Saturday and Sunday. Friendly inn, the Three Horseshoes.

Newmarket A useful railway station for ramblers, on the Cambridge-Ipswich line. Ramblers are allowed to walk across the Heath provided there are no horses being exercised.

Reach Archaeological finds in the vicinity have included a hoard of no less than 55 Late Bronze Age (1000-450BC) artefacts, including spears, swords, gouges and axeheads. Visible remains of Reach's waterborne trade (in stone, corn and wool) include the foundations of warehouses and a series of silted up private wharves. Reach's annual fair survived into the Victorian age for horse-trading and amusements. Excellent pub, the Dyke's End, east of the green (no sign).

Soham Soham stands on a little promontory of chalk surrounded by fen. A large pagan cemetery has been found here. In the 7c St Felix founded a monastery here which rivalled Ely until its destruction by the Danes in 870. In the middle ages, it stood on one of the two causeways to Ely, an important town and minor port. There remain narrow, twisting lanes, many old cottages and an imposing church whose 15c tower is a landmark throughout the surrounding fens. Within is a fine array of arches and arcades, medieval woodwork in the stalls, the screen and the carved angels on the roof. Between Wicken and Soham once lay Soham Mere, the second largest expanse of open water in the Fens after Whittlesey Mere. It was a haven for eels, wildfowl and disease. The small fields in the area reflect the piecemeal intrusions upon the Mere made by centuries of farmers before the eventual concerted drainage in 1664.

Stow-cum-Quy The church is mainly 14c, with 19c chancel and upper reaches of the tower. Quy means Cow Island – another of the isolated Anglo-Saxon settlements.

Swaffham Bulbeck St Mary's church is predominantly 14c; carved wooden benches with figures of real and mythological creatures, travelling altar. The open chalkland east of the village around Middle Hill has produced more Bronze Age finds.

Swaffham Prior Fine windmill, and two churches in one yard. Grave of the poet Edwin Muir in the cemetery of St Mary's.

Upware A major Roman port stood here, confirming the commercial importance of Reach Lode. It remained an important stopping point for boats and barges until the river trade ended in the late 19c with the coming of the railways. In those days, it supported two public houses, including the Lord Nelson with its slogan 'Five Miles from Anywhere – No Hurry'. In the 19c a group of undergraduates declared Upware a republic, with themselves in the leading public positions of Consul, President, Minister of Education, Professor, and Tapster. Samuel Butler, author of *Erewhon*, was a member of the Upware Republic Society. Both pubs have now gone. The woods and pools of Commissioner's Pit, a small nature reserve north of Upware on the path to Dimmock's Cote, stand in old clay diggings.

Wicken A pleasant pub, the Maid's Head, behind the green, and a simple late medieval church. Inside the church are brasses and monuments of several members of the Cromwell family. One is Henry Cromwell, the Protector's best son. After being Lord Lieutenant of Ireland in the 1650s, he was stripped of public position and estates upon the Restoration, and retired to Spinney Abbey as a plain farmer: Charles II visted him once unexpectedly, after racing at Newmarket.

Wicken Fen belongs to the National Trust. It is one of the most interesting places in the entire county. It is not natural fen landscape; rather, it represents the various stages through which fen passes once the water level has fallen to a state of semi-drainage. In such a state, vegetation builds up below the water, mainly of reeds and sedge. Thus a platform of dry land is gradually established, building up the level of the peat until there is no surface water. The reed and sedge then give way to thick scrub, known as carr. The growth of this carr was checked for centuries, both here and throughout the semi-drained fens, by the annual cropping of the reeds and sedge for thatching and animal bedding. The general conversion of the surrounding countryside to arable during the later 19c rendered this unnecessary; the peat in the arable areas dried out and shrank, leaving Wicken Fen higher than the rest of the area. The end of the river as a major communications route is both a cause and a result of this abandonment of sedge cultivation. Wicken Fen supports both carr and sedge; the sedge droves are still annually cropped and shipped out along Wicken Lode. Elsewhere, the fen is growing out into woodland. To maintain the semi-drained state of Wicken Fen it is now necessary to pump water *into* the fen, a task performed by a re-sited 19c windmill. Open: daily. **Adventurers' Fen** is part of the reserve, but not open to the public. The name refers to the 17c Adventurers who put up the money for the drainage of the fens. During the Second World War Adventurers' Fen was reclaimed by Alan Bloom. The tale of his appalling struggles at Priory Farm, against bog oaks, bureaucracy and non-existent drainage, is told in his book *The Farm in the Fen*. Burwell Lode and Wicken Lode were constructed in the 17c as part of the general drainage, and have no Roman links. The construction was violently resisted by the men of Burwell and Wicken, who saw the drainage as threatening their traditional pursuits of fowling, fishing and eeling. A document in the Public Record Office in London records the reception given by Wicken to the officers despatched to enforce the drainage in 1637:

> The people came out with pitchforks and poles, and gathered around a place where great heaps of stones were laid. Amongst them, John Moreclark, a principal rioter, was charged to obey the Council's warrant. When the messengers approached him, he pushed at them with his pike. The people prepared to assist him, and the women got together to the heaps of stones to throw at the messengers, who were scoffed at and abused by the whole multitude.

Great and Little Wilbraham Wilbraham Temple's name comes from the Knights Templar, who owned Great Wilbraham during the middle ages. At Little Wilbraham there is a good pub, some pleasant cottages and a little river that winds past Fulbourn Fen into Quy Water. East of the Wilbrahams is Hare Park, with its large cluster of Bronze Age barrows lying on either side of **Street Way**, the excellent green lane from Fulbourn to the Devil's Dyke. Recent research has shown that Street Way's twists and turns can be related to parish boundaries, and that it was therefore presumably a turnpike road laid down after the enclosure of the commons within each parish in the 19c, rather than the prehistoric route it was previously thought to be.

Contd p. 39

Contd pp. 16-17

Contd p.15

Contd p.31

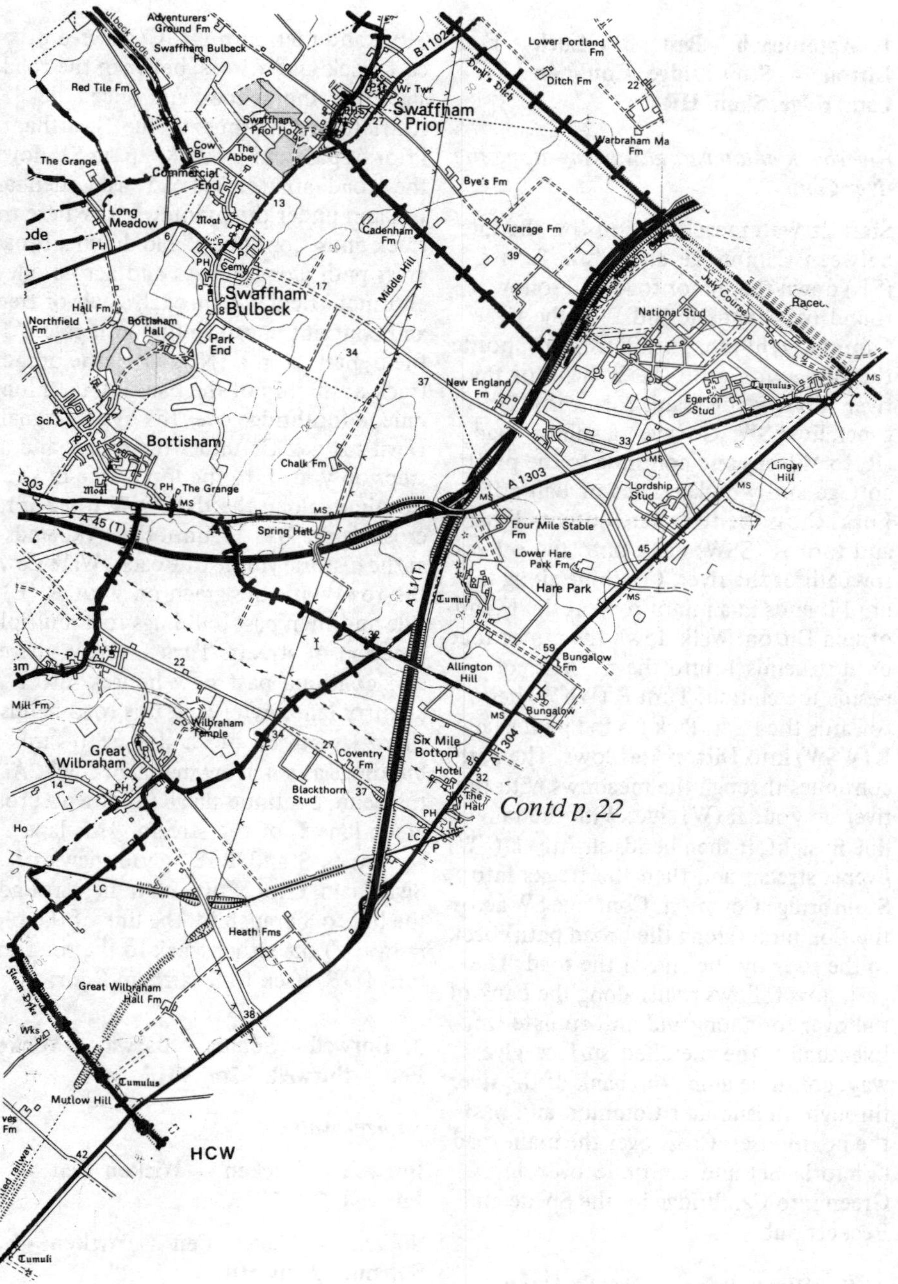

Adventurers' Ground Fm
Swaffham Bulbeck Fen
Red Tile Fm
The Grange
Commercial End
Cow Br
Long Meadow
Swaffham Prior Ho
The Abbey
Swaffham Prior
Wr Twr
B1102
Devil's Ditch
Lower Portland Fm
Ditch Fm
Warbraham Ma
Bye's Fm
Cadenham Fm
Vicarage Fm
Middle Hill
Swaffham Bulbeck
Cemy
Moat
Hall Fm
Northfield Fm
Bottisham Hall
Park End
National Stud
July Course
Racec
New England Fm
Egerton Stud
Tumulus
Sch
Bottisham
Chalk Fm
The Grange
Lingay Hill
Lordship Stud
A 1303
A 45 (T)
Spring Hall
Four Mile Stable Fm
Lower Hare Park Fm
Hare Park
A 11 (T)
Tumuli
Allington Hill
Bungalow Fm
Bungalow
A 1304
Mill Fm
Wilbraham Temple
Great Wilbraham
Coventry Fm
Six Mile Bottom
Hotel
The Hall
Blackthorn Stud
Heath Fms
Great Wilbraham Hall Fm
Fleam Dyke
Wks
Tumulus
Mutlow Hill
HCW
Tumuli

Contd p.22

RECOMMENDED WALKS

1. Waterbeach – Bait's Bite Lock – Fen Ditton – Stourbridge Common – Cambridge. 5½m. HR.

Riverbank and pastoral walking along the river Cam.

Start at Waterbeach station (on the line between Cambridge and Ely). Turn L (SE) down the minor road and follow it round two bends R and L to the river Cam at Clayhythe. Turn R (SSW) opposite the Bridge inn onto the W bank of the river. Follow this bank for nearly 2m generally SSW. Go over a minor road (R, to Milton) and continue to the pretty cottage and wooden gates of Bait's Bite Lock. Cross the river here onto its E bank and turn R (SSW) back onto the other towpath of the river. Continue along this until it ends in a minor road at the N end of Fen Ditton. Walk down the minor road until it bends L into the main street, beside the church. Turn R (WNW) here, towards the river. Pick up the path again L (WSW) into Ditton Meadows. The path continues through the meadows with the river on your R (W) side. With the railway line in sight, it then bends slightly L (SW) over a stream and then the tracks into Stourbridge Common. Continue SW across the Common (along the broad path) back to the river by the end of the road. The path now follows roads along the bank of the river for a long and unfortunate ½m. Eventually, the metalled surface gives way; continue along the bank of the river through Midsummer Common and past the boathouses. Cross over the main road (Victoria St) and continue over Jesus Green into Cambridge by the Spade and Beckett pub.

2. Swaffham Prior – Devil's Dyke – Reach – Swaffham Prior. 8½m. HR.

An excellent walk, with a great deal of archaeological interest.

Start at Swaffham Prior church. Walk SSW down the village street (B1102) for 30yd and then turn L (SE) down a broad cart track under trees, between the road signs for the school and speed de-restriction. Continue to the Swaffham Prior bypass and cross. Keep on SE down the broad farm track ahead past Cadenham Fm and under the pylon wires. Where the track ends, continue ahead down a broad grass path along hedges and across one enormous field. Go through a belt of trees and continue ahead to the farm gate. At the bypass, turn L (NE) along the broad track at the top of the bank. After a long mile, a footbridge over the bypass signals Devil's Dyke. Go under the bridge and up steps on your L to the top of the dyke. Continue along the dyke NW for 2½m, crossing the B1102, until the dyke ends at the historic village of Reach. Walk down the road with the green on your R (E) side and then past buildings to a multiple junction of streets. Turn L (WSW) here and continue past new houses into a country lane. After ½m, this road bends sharp R, and crosses a stream to farm buildings as a narrow metalled track. At the bend, continue ahead (S) down a broad green lane E of the stream. This lane continues S and ESE (good views of Swaffham Prior's two churches) round the hill to a branch by the line of the old railway. Take either track to the road and turn R (S) back to Swaffham Prior.

3. Burwell – Soham – Barway – Wicken Fen – Burwell. 17m. VHR.

Shorter walks:

Burwell – Wicken – Wicken Fen – Burwell. 7m. VHR.

Soham – Wicken Fen – Wicken – Soham. 12½m. HR.

A walk for the long-distance enthusiast fascinated by the history and geography of the Fens. A bleak and wild atmosphere with the interest of Wicken Fen and the old towns of the fen edge, Soham and Burwell.

Start in North St, Burwell, at the E end of Burwell Lode. Continue NNE down the road past side roads R and L and out of the village along the No Through Road. After ¾m, turn L (N) by Burwell sewage works down a signposted gravel track. Follow this track all the way to the bank of the New River and turn L (W). Go past Hundred Acres Fm on your L (S) side. ¼m later, cross the bridge over the river under the pylon lines. (If on the short walk, however, continue on the S bank for a long ½m until the river bends sharp L (SSW) with a wood on the N bank; cross over the little bridge at this point and turn N into Wicken. Walk WNW through the village and down the side road posted to Wicken Fen.) Continue up an excellent cart track to the A1123 and pick up a signposted green track upon the other side. This soon curves R (ESE) as a green lane. Follow broad tracks NNE and then due N for 1½m to Soham Mills; ignore a crossing track after ½m and a broad track L (W) after 1m. Turn L at the footpath signpost S of Soham Mills; skirt the lode, cross the railway and turn briefly R onto the S floodbank of the lode. Continue along the bank of the lode for over 3m to the point where it flows into the Gt Ouse. At this point, turn L (SSW by S) along the E bank of the river. At the Fish and Duck, continue S along the E bank of the Cam. After a long mile, the bank swings L (ESE) away from the river and terminates in a minor road W of High Fen Fm. At the end of the bank, turn R (S) down a broad unmade track. Continue to the A1123 and pick up an excellent green lane upon the other side. The route continues down this for ¾m, and then turns L (E) along a division between crops to the minor road. (The leaving point is difficult to describe; it is, however, close to the second telegraph pole before the little copse on your R (W), which is Commissioner's Pit.) Cross the road, go over the gate and continue down the broad grassy bank ESE along the N edge of Wicken Fen. Follow the bank and edge round a bend L (NNE) and continue past the end of the trees on your R to a bend in a broad track. Turn R (SE) down this broad green lane until it ends in a minor road. For a visit to the nature reserve, allow at least an hour. Cross onto the E bank of Wicken Lode and walk SSW down it between the lode and the trees. Where New River flows into the lode, turn briefly L (E) to the bridge, cross and regain the lode bank. Continue past the mere on Adventurers' Fen to the junction of Wicken and Reach Lodes. Turn L (ESE) here along the N bank of Burwell Lode for 1¼m. Cross the lode by the bridge SW of Priory Fm and continue along the S bank back into Burwell.

OTHER SUGGESTED ROUTES

Day Walks

1. Cambridge – Newmarket via Upware (Part 1 of the Weekend Walk). 15m.

2. Cambridge – Horningsea – Lode – Swaffham Prior – Devil's Dyke – Newmarket. 13m.
A variable walk along the villages of the fen edge.

3. Reach – Upware – River Cam – Clayhythe – Lode – Swaffham Prior – Reach. 14m.
An easy fen walk.

4. Gt Wilbraham – Street Way – Devil's Dyke – Swaffham Prior – Lode – Quy Water – Lt Wilbraham River – Lt Wilbraham. 15m.
This may be reduced to 13m by taking the Cadenham Fm track rather than Devil's Dyke.

5. Burwell – Wicken Fen – Commissioner's Pit – Upware – Reach Lode – Reach – Burwell. 12m.
A good walk taking in the interest of Wicken Fen.

Medium Walks

1. Reach – Reach Lode – Upware – River Cam – Swaffham Bulbeck Lode – Swaffham Prior – Reach. 9½m.

2. Waterbeach – Lode – Cow Bridge – Swaffham Bulbeck Lode – Clayhythe. 9½m.
Some heavy walking. Can be divided into two 7m walks by using the paths and road at Bottisham Lode.

3. Wicken – Wicken Fen – Commissioner's Pit – Upware – Priory Fm – Wicken. 6½m.
An interesting, easy and enjoyable walk.

4. Wicken – Adventurers' Fen – Priory Fm – New River – Soham Mere – Wicken. 8m.
Easy fen tracks.

Short Walks

1. Wicken – Reach Lode – Priory Fen – Wicken. 4m.
Easy.

2. Wicken – Wicken Fen – Commissioner's Pit – Upware – Wicken Lode – Wicken. 5m.
An excellent walk – if you get further than exploring Wicken Fen.

3. Wicken – Soham Mere – New River – Wicken. 4½m.
Less interest.

4. Waterbeach – Bait's Bite Lock – Horningsea – Waterbeach. 5m.
Substantial road work.

5. Lode – Stow-cum-Quy Fen – Quy Water – Lode. 4m.
Makes an excellent combination with a visit to Anglesey Abbey.

6. Lode – The Grange – Bottisham Fen – Lode. 4m. *Fen tracks.*

7. Reach – Railway Cutting – Devil's Dyke – Reach. 3m.
Easy: some good views.

8. Fulbourn – Hawk Mill Fm – Lt Wilbraham River – Fernleigh Fm – Fulbourn. 5½m.
The river is delightful with some rare wildlife, but is heavy walking.

Newmarket to Linton

The landscape is varied and there are many more paths than in other parts of east Cambridgeshire. There are however few of the broad and well-used footpaths to be found elsewhere; much of the walking is firmly arable, and on a particularly heavy clay soil at that. Signposting is reasonably good throughout the area, but a map and compass should be taken at all times.

Balsham The south end of Fleam Dyke lies just to the north, close to West Wratting Grange. The famous Balsham Massacre probably occurred during the early 10c in a clash between Danes and English soldiers of Edward the Elder. A century later still, a new Danish invasion swept through the village, murdering it to a single man who defended himself upon the steps of the church tower, and survived. The Saxon origin of the church has been confirmed by a coffin lid discovered here. The broad green lane marked Icknield Way, west of Willingham Green leading to Balsham is possibly an 18c formalisation of a maze of archaic paths along the traversable chalk belt, and not the prehistoric track it was once thought to be.

Brinkley Among meadows and trees. The church retains the battered Jacobean pulpit and soundly patriotic squire's pew, with its Union Jack, royal arms and crown. Park Wood to the south-west was a medieval deer park, with the moated site of the original hall just to the north-east of the wood itself; a right of way passes both.

Burrough Green Bull inn can be recommended (real ale).

Hildersham One of the group of closely-spaced Saxon settlements in the river valley which survive today as villages on the A604. It is mainly a street-village, aligned SW-NE (at right angles to the river): one of many such alignments that confirm the historic importance of the Icknield Way routes before the later NW-SE valley roads. All Saints' treasure is its two oak effigies, of a 13c knight and his lady.

Kirtling Green The land west of Kirtling Green is part of the original boulder clay forest never cleared during the centuries of gradual medieval settlement. Kirtling is a long street-village with several old thatched barns and brick houses, and a duckpond. Of the Tudor manor house, Kirtling Towers (built by the first Lord North) nothing remains except a remarkable gatehouse

Linton A large and bustling village with many shops and pubs, including my favourite, the Dog and Duck. The wooded hills to the north-east of the village are delightful, commanding some good views. Linton, as you would expect from its position, is an ancient settlement; besides having an important cemetery of Anglo-Saxon date, there have also been discovered several hut sites of pre-Roman Celtic times.

Stetchworth An excellent pub at the main T-junction. Plain church with dim 13c chancel in park of Stetchworth House.

Via Devana This is without doubt the most famous footpath in Cambridgeshire, known simply as the Roman road. Its name is, however, much more recent, and spurious: an 18c antiquarian looking at the map decided that it must have gone through to Chester, or Deva; in fact, it ran from Colchester only a little beyond Cambridge, to join Ermine Street at the Roman town of Godmanchester. It used to be thought that the road was built upon a previous partially levelled prehistoric earthwork similar to the Iron Age dyke at Fen Ditton, but excavations in 1920-1 showed that this was not the case. Bronze Age round barrow on Copley Hill.

Wandlebury Ring is the most famous, and enigmatic of the prehistoric sites along the Roman roads. The earthwork lies in woods at the peak of the Gog Magog hills, and was described by Camden's *Britannia* as 'girt with a threefold rampire'. Two of the ramparts still survive in the form of low banks with an intervening ditch, circling an inner enclosure 1000ft in diameter. The innermost bank levelled in 18c when the second Earl of Godolphin constructed a country house here: a piece of archaeological vandalism made the more ironic by the subsequent demolition of the house. Villagers nearby talk of giant chalk figures beneath the grass, similar to the Uffington White Horse and the Cerne Giant, a belief fostered by the name of the hills: Gogmagog, according to the Arthurian chronicler Geoffrey of Monmouth, was a giant overthrown by the first human settlers of the country. Claims to have detected the shapes of such figures remain the subject of controversy, but what is in no doubt is the importance of the hill-fort during the Early Iron Age. An even earlier artefact, a Neolithic axehead, was discovered in the author's presence in 1978.

Weston Colville Two interesting brasses in the church contrast sharply: the 15c Robert Leverer is a knight in armour, his wife is a lady in a graceful gown; Abraham Gates and his spouse kneel soberly at a prayer desk, in the best religious manner of the 1630s. The inn can be recommended.

Woodditton Surrounded by beautiful woods and fields. Church still has original 15c font and screen. West of church is Dane Bottom, a fine broad track whose name suggests some bloody encounter during the later Anglo-Saxon period. The track and Devil's Dyke to the west both end at Ditton Green.

RECOMMENDED WALKS

1. **Ditton Green – Dane Bottom – B1061 – Devil's Dyke – Ditton Green. 5m. VHR.**

The easiest of walks with the beauty and interest of Devil's Dyke as its central feature.

Start in Ditton Green. Walk WSW down the road and round a sharp bend R (NW). Where the road bends sharp L (SW) almost immediately afterwards, by the water tower, continue ahead down a broad cart track with the water tower on your R. Continue through the farm and past the stables along this broad and easy cart track, called Dane Bottom. At the minor road, cross and pick up the track again on the other side. Continue for a further mile until the lane ends in the B1061. Turn L (SSW) here for a long ¼m until the unmistakable line of Devil's Dyke intersects the road, as a tall wooded

Contd p. 17

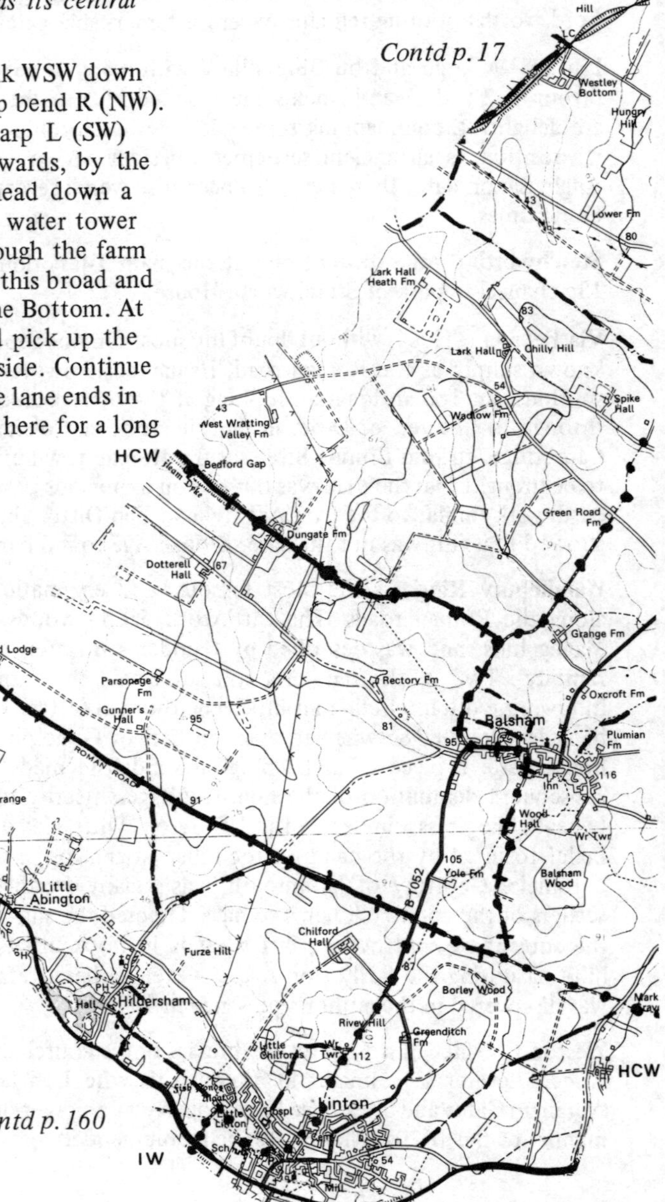

Contd p. 160

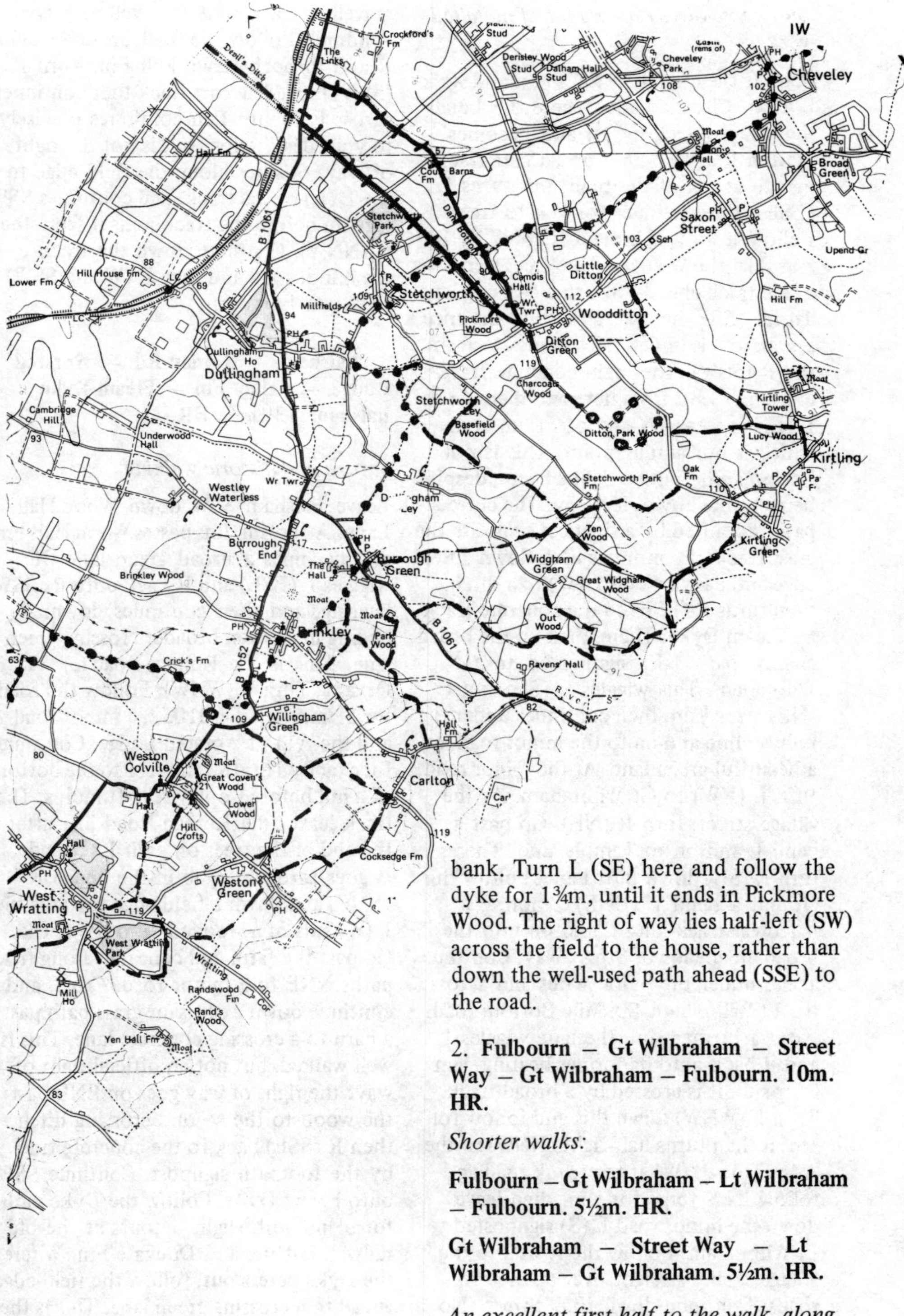

bank. Turn L (SE) here and follow the dyke for 1¾m, until it ends in Pickmore Wood. The right of way lies half-left (SW) across the field to the house, rather than down the well-used path ahead (SSE) to the road.

2. Fulbourn – Gt Wilbraham – Street Way – Gt Wilbraham – Fulbourn. 10m. HR.

Shorter walks:

Fulbourn – Gt Wilbraham – Lt Wilbraham – Fulbourn. 5½m. HR.

Gt Wilbraham – Street Way – Lt Wilbraham – Gt Wilbraham. 5½m. HR.

An excellent first half to the walk, along green lanes and broad tracks; the return journey involves rather a lot of metalled work.

Start at the church in Fulbourn and walk E down Church Lane. Where this bends sharply L (NNE by N) and becomes Station Rd, pick up a broad cart track just to the R of the road; this turns L (ESE) and continues for ¼m to trees. Follow it around a bend R (SSW by S) and skirt the W edge of the trees (ignoring a side track ahead ESE) to a crossing lane. Turn L (ESE) here. After a short distance, a grass track under trees comes in from the R (SSW). The main concrete track continues ESE from here and then bends L (ENE) to the N end of Fleam Dyke, which is our aiming point. This is not however a definitive right of way, despite being walked by everybody. The correct path is pointed by a signpost opposite the grass track; it continues ENE down a field edge and past a wood L (W) to a ditch, then turns R (ESE) to the concrete track by Fleam Dyke. There, pick up the broad chalky path NE, signposted to Gt Wilbraham. This wiggles R (SE) and L (NE) after ⅓m, then continues under the railway line and on to the minor road, as a beautiful green lane. At the minor road, turn L (NW) to Gt Wilbraham. At the village street, turn R (NE). Go past a bend L and on to Temple End. There, turn R (SE) down Butt Lane. Follow this around a bend L (ENE), ignoring a narrower track ahead, and on into the broad green lane of Street Way. Continue ahead under the pylon wires and across the Lt Wilbraham-Six Mile Bottom road. After a further ¼m, the lane wiggles L and R back onto its former bearing. ½m later still, it is crossed by a broad track. Turn L (WNW) down this and follow for 1m; it then turns half-right (NNW) to the A45. Turn L (W) at the trunk road and follow its S verge for ½m, then leave down the minor road L (S) signposted to Lt Wilbraham. Follow the road into the village, going straight over at the cross-roads. Continue down High Street (No Through Rd) WSW and then turn L (SW) at the footpath signpost down a broad gravelled track past the well-preserved windmill. Follow the track around a bend R and through Hawk Mill Fm. Turn L (SSW) here. The cart track that continues across Fulbourn Fen continues precisely to your destination, but is not the right of way; this lies along the field edge to the L (E) of the track, and continues SSW for ¼m before the track joins it from the R (NNW). Continue down the track to the minor road and turn R (W and SSW) back into Fulbourn.

3. **Balsham – Roman Rd – Worsted Lodge – Valley Fm – Fleam Dyke – Balsham. 13½m. VHR.**

Superb and historic walking.

Leave Balsham SSW down Wood Hall Lane. After ½m, this passes Wood Hall Fm and becomes a broad green lane. It wiggles L (ESE) and R back onto its SSW bearing, and then continues downhill, ending in an even broader crossing green lane. This is the Roman Road or Via Devana. Turn R (WNW). Follow the road for 5½m, over the B1052, a minor road and the A11 at Worsted Lodge. Continue for exactly 1m after the A11 to the bottom of a hill before Copley Hill Tumulus. The track leaves the Roman Road just after the end of the trees on your L (W) side. It goes through a gap in the hedge R (NNE) and down a field edge towards the L (W) side of a wooded farm site ahead. Go past the farm and continue along field paths NNE to a minor road. Cross, and continue down a pleasant grass path past a barn to a crossing concrete lane. This is well walked, but not an official right of way: the right of way goes on ENE past the wood to the second crossing ditch, then R (SSE) back to the concrete track by the footpath signpost. Continue SSE onto Fleam Dyke. Follow the Dyke path for 3½m, with slight detours at the old railway cutting and Dungate Fm. Where the Dyke peters out, follow the field edge ahead to a crossing green lane. This is the Icknield Way. Turn R (SSW) back into Balsham.

OTHER SUGGESTED ROUTES

Weekend Walk

Cambridge – River Cam – Upware – Reach Lode – Devil's Dyke – Newmarket (overnight stop); Newmarket – Icknield Way – Roman Road – Wandlebury – Cambridge. Day 1: 15m. Day 2: 20m.

Long distances, but easy tracks and a wealth of interest.

Day Walks

1. Burrough Gn – Out Wood – Kirtling Gn – Ditton Gn – Dane Bottom (or Devil's Dyke) – Icknield Way – Burrough Gn. 11m.
Some heavy but very pleasant walking in the wooded clay lands.

2. Brinkley – Spikehall Plantation – Six Mile Bottom – Street Way – Devil's Dyke – Icknield Way – Brinkley. 16m.
A mixture of easy tracks and arable.

3. Balsham – West Wratting – Weston Gn – Carlton – Park Wood – Burrough Gn – Icknield Way – Balsham. 12½m.
Likewise.

4. Balsham – Fleam Dyke – Gt Wilbraham – Six Mile Bottom – Icknield Way – Balsham. 11½m.
Excellent.

Medium Walks

1. Balsham – West Wratting – Weston Colville – Icknield Way – Balsham. 8m.
The outward journey is arable, the return magnificent.

2. Linton – Hildersham – Roman Rd – Water Tower – Linton. 6¼m. *Good tracks.*

3. Burrough Gn – Out Wood – Gt Widgham Wood – Marmer's Wood – Icknield Way – Burrough Gn.
Arable walking in wooded country.

4. Stetchworth – Marmer's Wood – Ten Wood – Kirtling Gn – Lucy Wood – Woodditton – Icknield Way – Stetchworth. 8m.
Two 6½m walks can be made out of this by using the short cut via Ditton Pk Wood and Devil's Dyke.

Short Walks

1. Burrough Gn – Ten Wood – Longacre Gn – Out Wood – Burrough Gn. 5m.
Views and woods.

2. Burrough Gn – Ten Wood – Marmer's Wood – Burrough Gn. 3½m.
Takes in part of the Icknield Way.

3. West Wratting – Weston Gn – Gt Coven's Wood – West Wratting. 4½m.
Mostly arable.

2 SOUTH CAMBRIDGESHIRE & THE ISLE OF ELY

South-west of Cambridge; Fen Drayton to Ely

The river valleys were settled early in the south of Cambridgeshire. Hauxton, for instance, was important in the Iron Age, and the Romans used the crossing too in their progress westwards. Settlement of the district as a whole continued under the Anglo-Saxons and into the early middle ages. The many small villages were often outlying lands of religious foundations, for whom the mainly serf population worked themselves to an early death while achieving the unprecedented agricultural prosperity of the early 1300s. The enclosures of the early 16th century, coupled with outbreaks of plague, saw an end to all that, with a particularly marked effect in this part of Cambridgeshire where several villages entirely disappeared, leaving just a name or a church. Towards the end of the century agricultural prosperity began a revival that lasted through the reversals of the Civil War to the mid-19th-century enclosures, when many old tracks were lost, leaving to this day a scarcity of rights of way, although there are many little-used roads.

North of Cambridge political considerations played a more important role. Settlement on the Isle of Ely had fluctuated according to the severity of the flooding in the low-lying land by which it is surrounded. Only with the coming of the Romans was any sustained attempt at drainage undertaken, but with the collapse of Roman rule this ceased. Ely was still sufficiently isolated to encourage St Etheldreda, daughter of King Anna, who ruled East Anglia, to found there in 673 the abbey which became in time the cathedral. The power of the foundation by the 11th century was considerable, and made it a strategic target at the Conquest, especially after Hereward the Wake made it an Anglo-Saxon stronghold. William's armies, however, waited at Aldreth, where they made a causeway to Ely, and in time Ely was betrayed from within, and lost at the battle of Alrehede.

Around Ely, communication tended to be by water – along the Ouse and Roman drainage channels; what commerce there was was undertaken by boat rather than overland. It was only when Charles I backed plans for draining the Fens that the land became usable, chiefly owing to the bypassing of the Great Ouse (so liable to winter flooding because of the low-lying land surrounding it) by the Bedford rivers, named after the Earl of Bedford who partly financed the venture. A new landscape emerged, and agriculture became the principal livelihood: a high proportion of English vegetables and fruit comes from this area. Maintaining the reduced water level in the Fens became a problem of escalating proportions, particularly as the drained peat continued to shrink; one of the great steam engines devised for coping with the volume of water is to be seen at Stretham.

This part of Cambridgeshire is an area of great contrasts in landscape and human settlement. The variations in walking are equally great, and include a lot of fairly featureless (though far from uninteresting) landscape, such as the Fens. A compass and map are vital.

South-west of Cambridge

North and west of the Ashwell Cam is mainly arable country, with patches of woodland, and generally good views; meadow and rough pasture in the river valleys.

Arrington hamlet stands beside the Roman road. There are only a few agricultural cottages and a small church of St Nicholas with a fine late 13c chancel.

Barrington Enormous village green. Fine medieval hall open to the public twice a day in the form of the Royal Oak Inn (real ale). The 14c church contains some fine medieval oak benches and a wonderful chest criss-crossed with sturdy iron bands.

Bourn The oldest remains are the three Romano-British tumuli known as the Moulton Hills. Their position in the valley of the Bourn Brook shows how early settlement penetrated up the valleys in this area. The name, however, is Anglo-Saxon, and the best buildings medieval. A castle was built in the village after the Conquest, in the park of the later Elizabethan hall. Nothing of the motte is visible now, while the hall has received such alteration first in Jacobean and then Victorian times as to be rather a picturesque imitation of the Tudor style than the real thing. St Helen and St Mary's church is a large cruciform building, with a 13c tower and later leaded spire at the west end. Inside, there are: a fine hammerbeam roof in the chancel with its modern figures of angels, good arches in the nave, medieval choirstalls and benches, and the curious little tiled maze in the ground floor of the tower.

Comberton is the largest of the villages along the B1046. St Mary's is relatively unaffected by restoration: the Early English chancel and north aisle roof are the best parts, and the nave contains some medieval benches with fine carvings.

Coton A typically East Anglian street village, rarely more than a couple of houses deep at any one place. There are two excellent pubs, and a delightful little church.

Croydon The country to the north and west of Croydon is remarkable; there is a wealth of old bridleways and footpaths connecting medieval moated sites and old villages that are now no more than names. It is intensely arable, generally poor walking except along farm tracks and roads, and now more deserted than it has been for at least 2000 years. In Roman times, the proximity of Ermine and Ashwell Streets ensured an early occupation, which was maintained through Anglo-Saxon and medieval periods. 16c enclosure began the decline of the area.

Croydon Wilds on one of our routes is, however, famous for its rare butterflies and birdlife, and well worth a visit.

Great Eversden Orchards greet the walker descending from Mare Way, and the pub stands opposite the path.

Little Eversden 14c church with lovely east window and timbered porch is worth a diversion, especially as opposite it there is a magnificent thatched barn even older than the church. Abandoned clunch quarry north from the ridge into the village.

Grantchester

I only know that you may lie
Day long and watch the Cambridge sky,
And, flower-lulled in sleepy grass,
Hear the cool lapse of hours pass,
Until the centuries blend and blur,
In Grantchester, in Grantchester.

It is impossible to get away from Rupert Brooke. The path between here and the city is through meadows with cows, and the river winding between pollarded willows. There are four fine inns in the village, including the Red Lion and Green Man, a tea-garden, and a superb ashlar church. St Andrew and St Mary's church has a Saxon window and a Norman font, but the treasure is its beautiful 14c and magnificent east window. Brooke's memorial lies appropriately in a shaded part of the yard.

Hardwick Once an important place, with a Benedictine priory refounded (after being sacked) in 970 AD. Little of this remains. The parish church is in the centre of the hamlet, with a 14c tower and the rest Perpendicular. The only path here is the broad bridleway from Coton to Bourne: this is easy walking, with good views east to Cambridge. Hardwick Wood to the west is a deciduous woodland nature reserve.

Harston A long street-village, with a good pub. All Saints has embattled exterior and a medieval pulpit.

Haslingfield Its enormous views over the Cam to Cambridge and Ely include all the colleges, and 80 parish churches. Delightful path to Hauxton.

Hauxton The Mill here stands by probably the most important Iron Age settlement in the entire area, at a major crossing of the river. This ford was used by Romans and Anglo-Saxons, and numerous weapons and other reminders of 9-10c occupation have been found. Inside the Norman church of St Edmund is a medieval painting of Thomas Becket, its condition reflecting the centuries it spent in hiding after Thomas Cromwell's campaign against Becket at the Reformation.

Kingston In the middle ages Kingston was important enough to have not merely its own market but also an annual fair. Inside the church are some of the finest medieval wall-paintings in East Anglia. On the north wall is a 13c painting showing the battle of the virtues and the vices, with two knights in chain mail confronting a thicket of spears. Over the chancel arch is a wheel of the seven works of mercy and the seven deadly sins. The two paths south-west up the hills from Kingston are both unusually broad and good. **Mare Way** is a true, prehistoric ridge-path through woods and along field boundaries south of Kingston and

Great Eversden. The original path would have continued from here to the crossing of the Cam at Hauxton Mill – a route now regrettably lost. The existing short section commands magnificent views north over Barton radio telescope and Cambridge; Ely cathedral is sometimes just visible.

Longstowe The village has shrunk during the last 200 years, and is now only a single street of old cottages capped at the north end by the hall and church.

Orwell The village clings to the foot of the ridge above the easily flooded lands of the valley bottom, and a strategic half mile from the Roman road of Akeman Street (A603). St Andrew's clunch-built tower is 13c, the nave Decorated. The chancel has a tall east window and excellent 19c roof. Bust of Jeremiah Radcliffe, one of the scholars responsible for James I's Authorised Version of the Bible; also a rare medieval Calvary in the south chapel, hidden at the Reformation and rediscovered during 19c restoration.

Toft The name suggests a settlement during the brief period of Danish occupation in the late 9c. Victorian mock-Tudor manor house, church rebuilt in the 19c, having lost most of its fine stone sculpture to Dowsing in the Civil War. One of the few figures still identifiable is St Hubert with hart, key and hound cured of rabies beside his headless trunk.

Wimpole 'The most spectacular country mansion of Cambridgeshire' is Pevsner's verdict, and it is certainly the best in the old county. The farmland between the road and Mare Way is beautiful, soft and wooded with some excellent little views. Our route passes through the grounds of Wimpole and across its enormous 17c facade: pediments, wings, a host of chimneys, parapets and a series of rectangular windows give this precisely the air of aristocratic grandeur for which it was designed. It was started by a mere knight, Sir Thomas Chicheley, but quickly passed to a succession of nobles including the Earl of Oxford and that harsh judge of the 1745 Rebellion, the Earl of Hardwicke. It was the latter who replaced the medieval church east of the house with the current yellow-brick chapel, with its wealth of monuments. He too ordered the landscaping of the grounds. This involved the removal of the elaborate formal gardens laid out by Chicheley, and still visible as bumps, hollows and banks in the lawns about the house. Some of those bumps, however, remain not from the gardens but from the little hamlet of Wimpole that once stood here, and which Sir Thomas demolished to build his mansion. The reconstructed Wimpole village to the south was demolished again in the 18c to lay out the grand avenue of elms for which Wimpole was so famous. Ironically, the elms themselves have now vanished, through Dutch elm disease. The landscaping of the 18c also involved the construction of an artificial ruin on a wooded hill north of the mansion, visible from the road. Rudyard Kipling's daughter, Mrs Bambridge, was the last person to live here, and it was she who gave it to the National Trust, who have restored house and garden – and the sunken bath. Open: every afternoon except Friday and Monday, from April to mid-October.

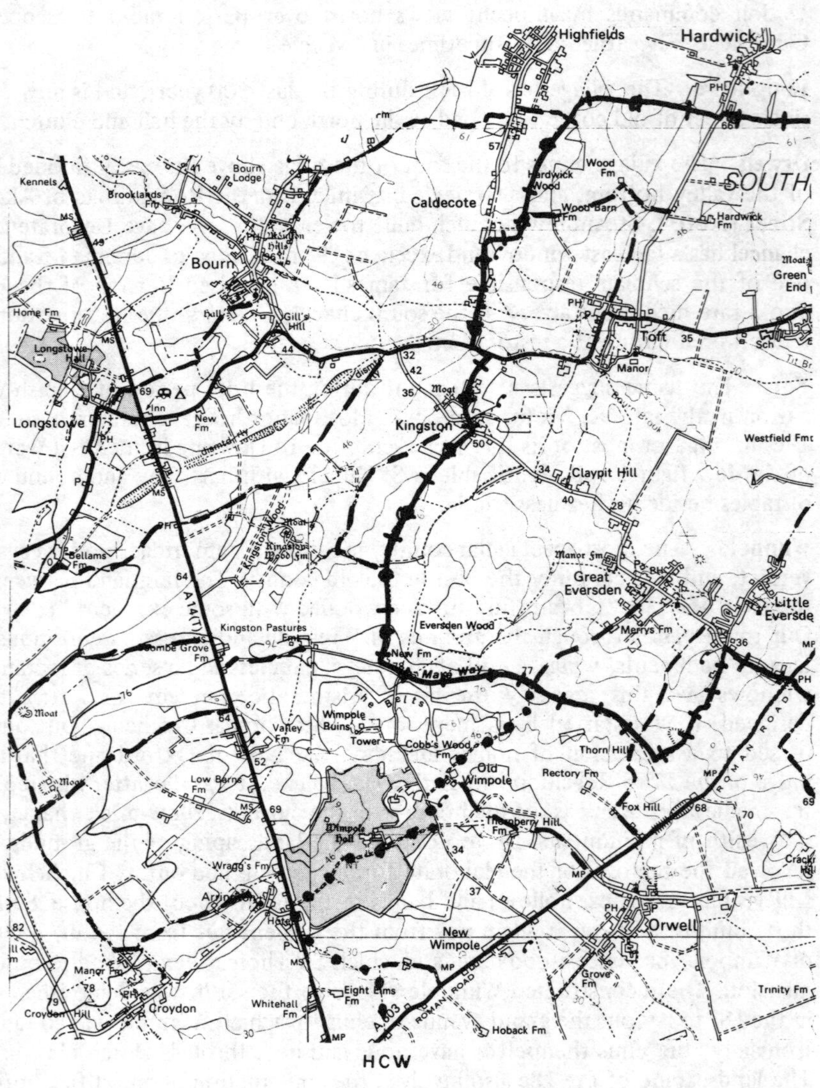
Highfields
Hardwick
SOUTH
Kennels
Bourn Lodge
Brooklands Fm
Caldecote
Hardwick Wood
Wood Fm
Wood Barn Fm
Hardwick Fm
Bourn
Green End
Home Fm
Gill's Hill
Toft
Manor
Sch
Longstowe Hall
Longstowe
Inn
New Fm
Moat
Kingston
Westfield Fm
Claypit Hill
Manor Fm
Great Eversden
Little Eversde
Bellams Fm
Kingston Wood
Kingston Wood Fm
A14(T)
Kingston Pastures Fm
Coombe Grove Fm
Eversden Wood
Merrys Fm
New Fm
Mare Way
The Belts
Wimpole Ruins
Tower
Cobb's Wood Fm
Old Wimpole
Valley Fm
Thorn Hill
Rectory Fm
Low Barns Fm
Fox Hill
ROMAN ROAD
Wimpole Hall
Thornberry Hill
Wragg's Fm
Arrington
Hotel
Orwell
New Wimpole
Grove Fm
Manor Fm
Croydon Hill
Croydon
Whitehall Fm
Eight Elms Fm
Hoback Fm
Trinity Fm
A 603
HCW

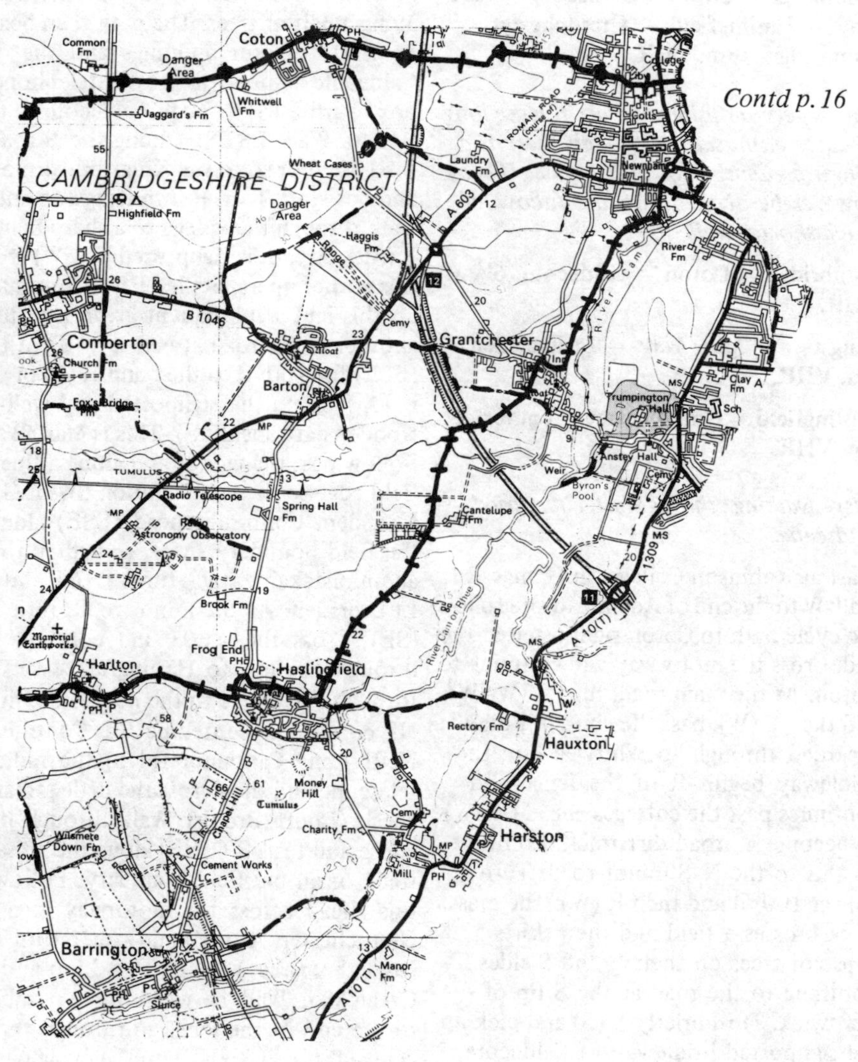

Common Fm
Coton
Danger Area
Colleges
Whitwell Fm
Jaggard's Fm
ROMAN ROAD (course of)
Wheat Cases
Laundry Fm
Newnham
CAMBRIDGESHIRE DISTRICT
A 603
Highfield Fm
Danger Area
Haggis Fm
Range
River Fm
River Cam
B 1046
Comberton
Cemy
Grantchester
Church Fm
Barton
Clay Fm
Fox's Bridge
Trumpington Hall
Sch
Anstey Hall
Weir
Byron's Pool
TUMULUS
Radio Telescope
Spring Hall Fm
Cantelupe Fm
Radio Astronomy Observatory
A 1309
Brook Fm
A 10(T)
Manorial Earthworks
Frog End
Harlton
Haslingfield
River Cam or Rhee
Rectory Fm
Hauxton
Money Hill
Tumulus
Chapel Hill
Charity Fm
Harston
Wilsmere Down Fm
Cement Works
Mill
Barrington
Sluice
Manor Fm

Contd p. 16

RECOMMENDED WALK

Cambridge – Coton – Caldecote – Mare Way – Haslingfield – Grantchester – Cambridge. 18m. VHR.

This is very definitely a walk for the long-distance enthusiast, although there is a Kingston-Cambridge bus service. It may however be divided into the following much shorter walks:

Cambridge – Coton – Caldecote. 6¼m. VHR.

Kingston – Mare Way – Lt Eversden. 5m. VHR.

Haslingfield – Grantchester – Cambridge. 4m. VHR.

Easy walking throughout, in varied landscape.

Start at Robinson College, in Grange Rd. Walk W to the end of Adams Rd and follow the cycle path to Coton signposted at the end. Cross the motorway and continue to Coton. At the main road, turn R (WNW) and then L (W), past the church. Follow the road through to Whitwell Fm; the bridleway begins R of the fence and continues past the cottages ahead (WSW) to become a broad dirt track. Continue on this to the N-S minor road. Turn L (S) for 100yd and then R (W). The grass track crosses a field and then skirts a copse of trees on their E and S sides. Continue to the road at the S tip of Hardwick. Turn briefly L (S) and pick up the signposted bridleway to Caldecote. After 1m, the broad track turns abruptly L (SW) towards Hardwick Wood. Continue down the W side of the wood on a narrower track past the SW corner and along a belt of trees. The path then bears R (SW) to farm buildings and the Caldecote minor road, by a telephone box. Turn L (S) through Caldecote to the B1046. Walk L (ESE) along the B road for 100yd or so to the Kingston turn-off and bus stop. Turn R into Kingston and walk through the village to a sharp bend L (SE). A path is signposted R (SW) from this corner up a metalled lane. Continue up this and a subsequent green lane to another minor road at New Fm. Turn L (ESE) for 100yd to the bend R (S) in the road. Pick up the signposted and well-trodden path ahead (E). This is Mare Way. Follow past the woods and along a fine field edge to the water station SW of Gt Eversden. Continue ahead (ESE) along the field boundary. After a further 1m, an unmistakable track turns L (NE) into Lt Eversden. At the minor road, turn R (SE). Cross the A603 and continue through Harlton to Haslingfield. Walk through the village to the new estate in its NE corner, on Cantelupe Rd. Continue NNE along Cantelupe Rd to the radio telescope and then cross the little stream ahead (Bourn Brook). Walk through the copse and turn R (ENE) along the grassy track of an old field boundary. Follow this ahead across the motorway into Grantchester. At the main street, turn R (past the garage) to the Red Lion and Green Man. Walk between the two pubs to the end of the lane, go through the gate and turn L (NNE) up the cycle path into Cambridge. Turn L and then R to regain Grange Rd.

OTHER SUGGESTED ROUTES

Day Walk

Bourn – Hardwick Wood – Caldecote – Kingston – Mare Way – Wimpole – Arrington – Croydon Wilds – Longstowe – Bourn. 15m.

This may be reduced to 13m by omitting Bourn and using the Longstowe-Kingston RUPP as the first stage.

Medium Walks

1. Bourn – Hardwick Wood – Caldecote – Kingston – Kingston Wood – Longstowe – Bourn. 9m.
Mostly easy tracks.

2. Longstowe – Kingston Wood – Kingston – New Fm – Croydon Wilds – Longstowe. 9m.
The return journey can be fairly heavy.

3. Croydon – Croydon Wilds – New Fm – Mare Way – Wimpole – Arrington – Croydon. 8m.
Variable, with broad tracks and arable walking.

4. Comberton – Toft – Caldecote – Hardwick – Highfield Fm – Comberton. 7m.
The return is easier than the first part.

Short Walks

1. Haslingfield – Harston Mill – Barrington – Chapel Hill – Haslingfield. 5m.
The long return journey road is worth it for the grand views from Chapel Hill.

2. Cambridge – Grantchester – Cambridge. 3m.
The most famous walk in the area.

3. Hauxton – Haslingfield – Grantchester – Cambridge. 5m.
An easy and pleasant walk.

4. Gt Eversden – Mare Way – Lt Eversden – Gt Eversden. 3½m.
Likewise.

5. Longstowe – Bourn – B1046 – Kingston Wood – Longstowe. 5m.
A lot of roadwork.

Fen Drayton to Ely

Generally the best walking conditions are along the floodbanks of the Ouse and Bedford rivers. There are also some cart tracks and green lanes; many of the old Fen roads were concreted during the Second World War – public roads where the small population could not justify metalling. In the Isle, riverbank walking is interspersed with muddy paths beside smaller streams; rights of way often exist along the edge of streams and drainage ditches, and can be treated as headland; signposting non-existent, bridging unreliable.

Great Ouse The river in the section between Earith and Ely is in fact narrower than the Cam to the south-east – mainly because the bulk of the water has been drawn off down the Bedford rivers created in the 17c by Vermuyden's drainage. Ouse and Cam alike are bordered by tall floodbanks, covered in grass and cow parsley, which make up some of the best walking in the area. The rivers are slow, with splendid birdlife and huge flat views. At Smithey Fen Farm is a steam pumphouse; irregularities in the ground probably indicate Roman occupation.

Aldreth The High Bridge was of particular importance in prehistory and the middle ages. The village is presumably also the site of the Battle of Alrehede, when William the Conqueror finally stormed the Isle of Ely and defeated the Saxons led by Hereward the Wake. Now, Aldreth is the tiniest of hamlets, and the Bridge suitable only for the lightest traffic.

Bluntisham Surrounded by orchards. Two Jacobean inns stand by the village green to the north – the Rose and Crown and the George.

Boxworth A fine inn, the Golden Ball, and the neat little pebble-rubble church of St Peter standing among fields and woods with an old farmhouse and some thatched outbuildings to keep it company.

Childerley A village that has vanished: Little Childerley's population suffered badly from the Black Death and the village was wiped out by 15c. Great Childerley was demolished by Sir John Cutts just before the Civil War, to enlarge his deer park and provide a fine position for the hall he was then constructing, which in 1647 played host to an unwilling Charles I, after his kidnap by Cornet Joyce and the soldiers of the Eastern Association.

Cottenham On the very edge of the Fens; the church lies to the north, with remarkable gargoyles, carved stone seats in the chancel, and Victorian oak benches. **Car Dyke** (1½m north-west), today only a low bank and ditch running SSE-NNW, was a major Roman canal, part of a network of commercial and drainage waterways in the southern Fens.

Earith The name means Muddy Harbour, again indicating its commercial ancestry. The most interesting feature lies east of the village at Earith Lock. Ahead to the north-east stretch two broad and parallel rivers raised above the surrounding fenland by high banks, and separated from each other by a strip of ground known as The Wash. Apart from a brief bend around the western edge of the Isle of Ely, at Mepal, the Bedford rivers run die-straight for 19 miles to Denver Sluice, cutting off a gigantic bend in the Great Ouse. The Bedfords were the lynchpin for Vermuyden's drainage of the Cambridgeshire fens in the 17c, and owe their name to the prominent position in the drainage scheme taken by the Earl of Bedford. The intention was to provide a short cut by which the great rivers of the interior could escape quickly to the sea. The Wash between the cuts was designed as a reservoir to contain extra water during floods – a function made more necessary by the unforeseen shrinkage of the peat fen around the rivers in the later 17c. Between the two rivers at the lock stands the Bulwark, a large and rectangular earthwork erected by the Parliamentarians during the Civil War. The atmosphere at the Lock is incredible, especially on a winter's morning before other people stir. The black earth, silently flowing channels and immense views from the bridge leave an unforgettable impression of the Cambridgeshire fens.

Ely History of the cathedral goes back 1300 years to the foundation of Ely abbey, by Etheldreda Queen and Saint. During early Anglo-Saxon times, the Isle was the refuge of the Gyrwe, a Celtic/Saxon tribe. After Etheldreda's foundation, Ely quickly became the most important abbey in East Anglia, rivalled only by Bury St Edmunds. The abbey suffered during the early medieval period from the defeat of the two political rebels who operated from the Isle, Hereward and Geoffrey de Mandeville; but until the Dissolution, it remained dominant not only in the Isle itself but also large parts of the old county of Cambridgeshire. Ely too prospered, as the market town for the Isle and a major port on the Great Ouse. The draining of the Fens and construction of the Bedford rivers affected this commercial importance, but it remained a significant harbour until the 19c, and retains its docks. Nature trail south-east of the town in the Roswell Pits area: this contains rare wildlife as well as good views of Stuntney and an indication of the Gault clay upon which the Isle and town lie.

Fen Drayton A thatched cottage bears a Dutch motto traditionally linked with Vermuyden. If so, the motto is apt, for it translates as 'Nothing without Labour'.

Fenstanton See p.45.

Holywell Timbered cottages spread out along a previous bank of the Ouse known as The Front. The Ferry Boat Inn is recommended, but the ferry has vanished. The well was a pre-Christian shrine; tradition credits it with the power to cure sore eyes and reveal the face of a future husband.

Knapwell The walk linking Boxworth, Knapwell, Childerley and Lolworth is one of the finest in the county. The flint-and-rubble church stands alone in the fields to the north, surrounded by the bumps and hollows of demolished buildings. Knapwell was founded in the middle ages, owned by Ramsey abbey, which built a 30ft wide motte-and-ditch to protect the manor from the rebellion of Geoffrey de Mandeville, in King Stephen's reign. This earthwork, known as Red Well, now stands in the beautiful woodlands east of the village, and can be visited. The name comes from the iron in the water that bubbles to the surface here.

Mepal Typical of the villages in the Isle of Ely: small, with little brick houses opening directly onto the pavement, and the very opposite of the conventionally picturesque. The church is 19c, and so are most of the cottages.

Over Surrounded by orchards and fruit fields.

Rampton King Stephen levelled ground here to build one of a ring of fen edge castles against that later rebel in Ely, Geoffrey de Mandeville. The latter's death assaulting Burwell was to make this construction unnecessary. (Swavesey and Cottenham both had castles built by Stephen, but the sites have been ruined by subsequent quarrying of the stone.) At the east end of the village are the church and Giant's Hill. The earthworks of the latter go back to a castle built here by the de Lisle family later in the middle ages. The church has a fine Elizabethan canopied pulpit, but was in 1685 described as 'dilapidated and very nasty. The windows are all over broaken. Pidgeons as well as Owls horribly bedaub ye church.' Restoration was timely.

St Ives See p.47.

Stretham Its position on a hill commands broad views, and shows off to best advantage the windmill and church which are its main two buildings. 14c church stands in centre of village, surrounded by typical small houses of a fen town. Stretham lies on Akeman Street, the road between Ely and Cambridge now followed for long stretches by the A10, and among the traces of occupation during this period is a large 3-4c villa. This confirms that the Isle was well-drained during that period, and indeed that the many drainage works undertaken then were also successful in providing a reasonably dry surface for the laying of Akeman Street. Later, the collapse of Roman rule led to an isolation of the Isle, and to a general deterioration in the fen drainage: fen islands were always seen by the Anglo-Saxons as isolated and devil-ridden places. Ely, as the largest and closest to the mainland, was never totally de-populated, but Akeman Street with its relatively long stretch of fen-bottom, was abandoned for the old route via Aldreth High Bridge. Stretham fen engine south of the village on the banks of the Ouse is the only steam drainage engine to be found in the peat fens, and a precious survival. It was built in 1831, and successively increased in power to match the shrinking of the peat until the last waterwheel could raise 30 tons of water on each revolution, or 120 tons a minute. The engine is open to the public daily, a fascinating relic.

Sutton A large village surrounded by orchards, on a little ridge within the Isle. 14c church dominates the countryside to the south: enormous, with a wide, airy nave and chancel and a superb clerestory from the same period. North stand the remains of Mepal's Second World War airfield, where the RNZAF flew Lancasters and Stirlings as a sub-station of Waterbeach.

Swavesey The -ey ending for once comes not from island, but hythe or harbour. Swavesey had a medieval fair that rivalled Cambridge in importance. The old dock can still be seen, abandoned and overgrown at the north end of the village. St Andrew's church has carved bench-ends. North of the church stood Swavesey priory, now visible only as a few pieces of masonry in the grass. Navigation Drain a Roman canal into the Ouse.

Wilburton The village straggles along a single street, surrounded by orchards, at the south edge of the Isle. The site is strategic, and it is unsurprising that it should have produced archaeological finds, among which is the hoard of Bronze Age weapons discovered in Wilburton Fen. The position on the old course of the Ouse suggests that the river was even then used as a trade route, and that these were lost cargo.

Willingham Willingham Fen has produced a remarkable find of Roman objects, while more finds, including an important hoard of coins, have also been made in the village itself. Willingham church has everything: a grand tower with flying buttresses and spire, three original wooded screens, a fine double-hammerbeam roof and fragments of medieval wall-painting. There is also a curious sacristy or north chapel originally used by bishops on their way between Ely and Cambridge. **Belsar's Fort** is east of Willingham. Hereward's bridleway exactly bisects the fort – an oval enclosure 750-880ft in diameter with a single bank and ditch, still visible after centuries of ploughing. The area here was occupied in Stone Age times, while in the Bronze Age a timbered causeway ran from this site across the fens to Aldreth High Bridge. The fort itself is Iron Age. Its name is traditionally linked to one Belasius, deputy-commander of William the Conqueror, who is meant to have directed the assault against Hereward in Ely from this point before the battle of Alrehede. There is, however, no evidence for the existence of Belasius.

Witcham Another small Isle village on a little rise. Inside St Martin's are a rare medieval stone pulpit and a fine 13c carved font.

Witchford East lies old RAF base, as muddy an airfield as any airman could hope to miss, and now returned almost without any remains to agricultural use. The station was used for bombing in the latter days of the war, and for supply of the Dutch population during their passive revolt of 1944-5.

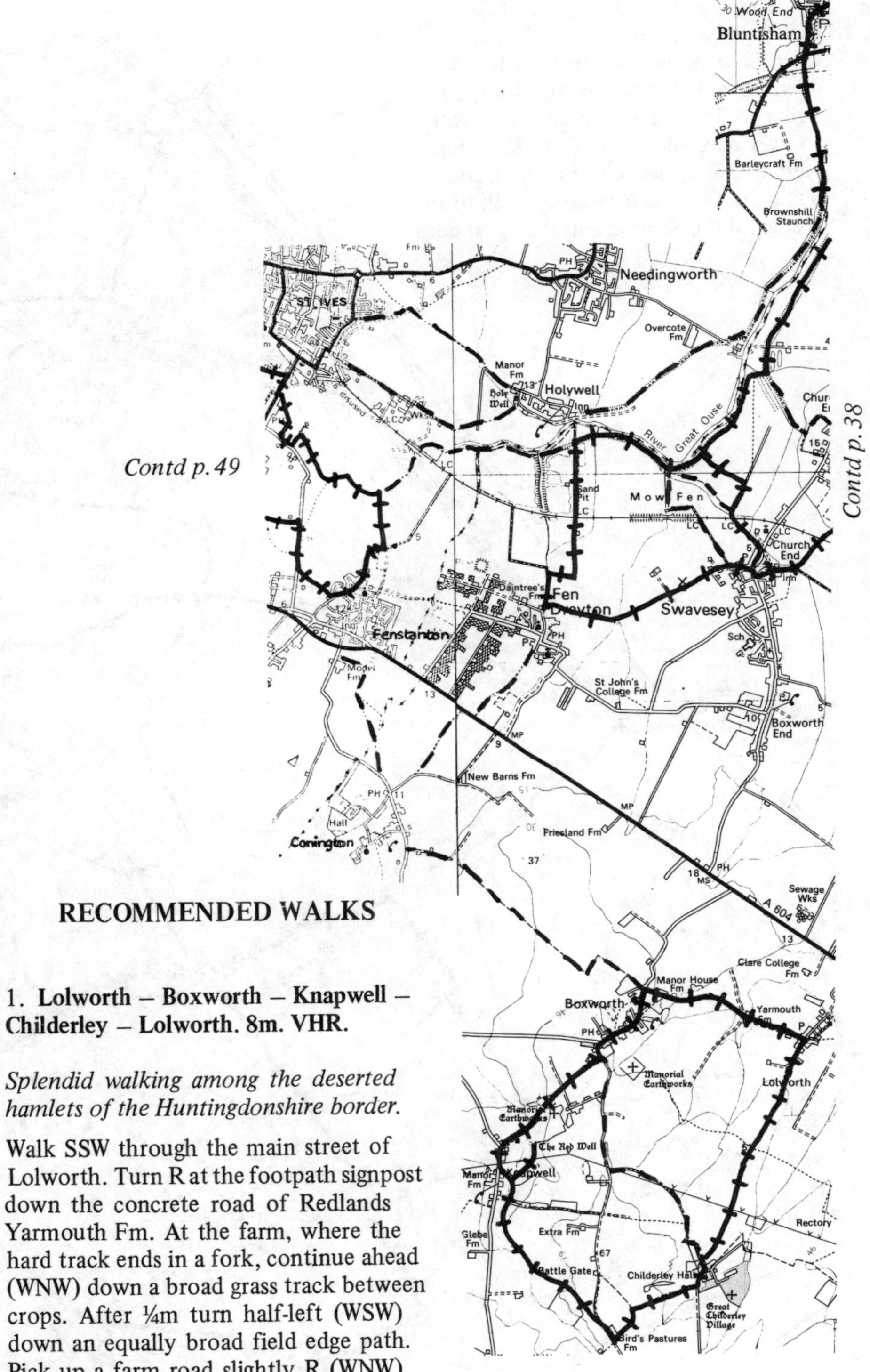

Contd p. 49

Contd p. 38

RECOMMENDED WALKS

1. Lolworth – Boxworth – Knapwell – Childerley – Lolworth. 8m. VHR.

Splendid walking among the deserted hamlets of the Huntingdonshire border.

Walk SSW through the main street of Lolworth. Turn R at the footpath signpost down the concrete road of Redlands Yarmouth Fm. At the farm, where the hard track ends in a fork, continue ahead (WNW) down a broad grass track between crops. After ¼m turn half-left (WSW) down an equally broad field edge path. Pick up a farm road slightly R (WNW) into Boxworth. Turn L (SSW) through the village. At the fork in the roads, take the L road and follow around a bend L (SE). Shortly afterwards, turn R (SW) down a hedged lane by the footpath signpost. This lane soon ends in a gate; go over and follow the good field edge path ahead to the R (N) of the farm buildings. Go over a crossing track to the N edge of the S wood and skirt that edge

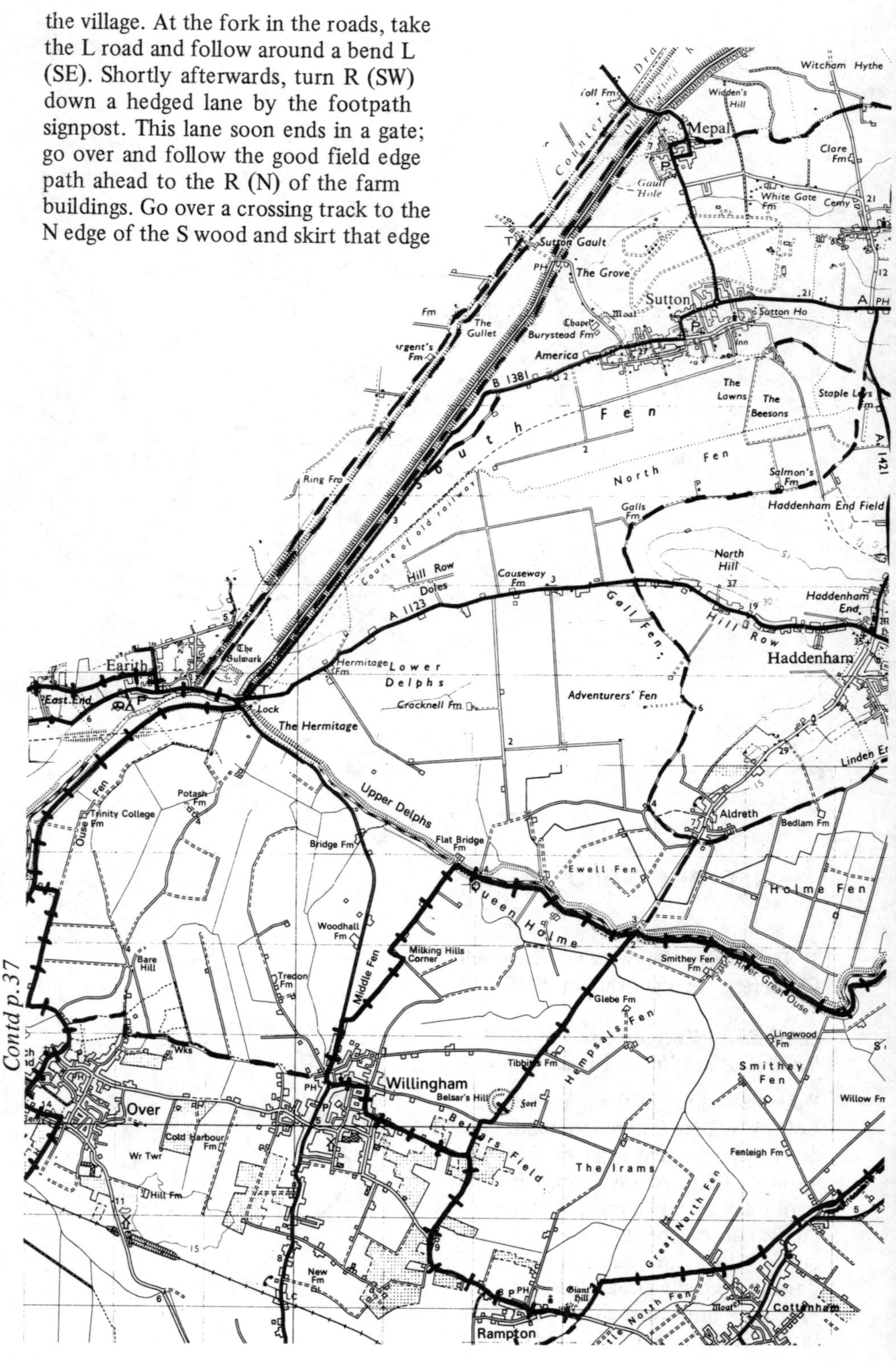

Contd p.37

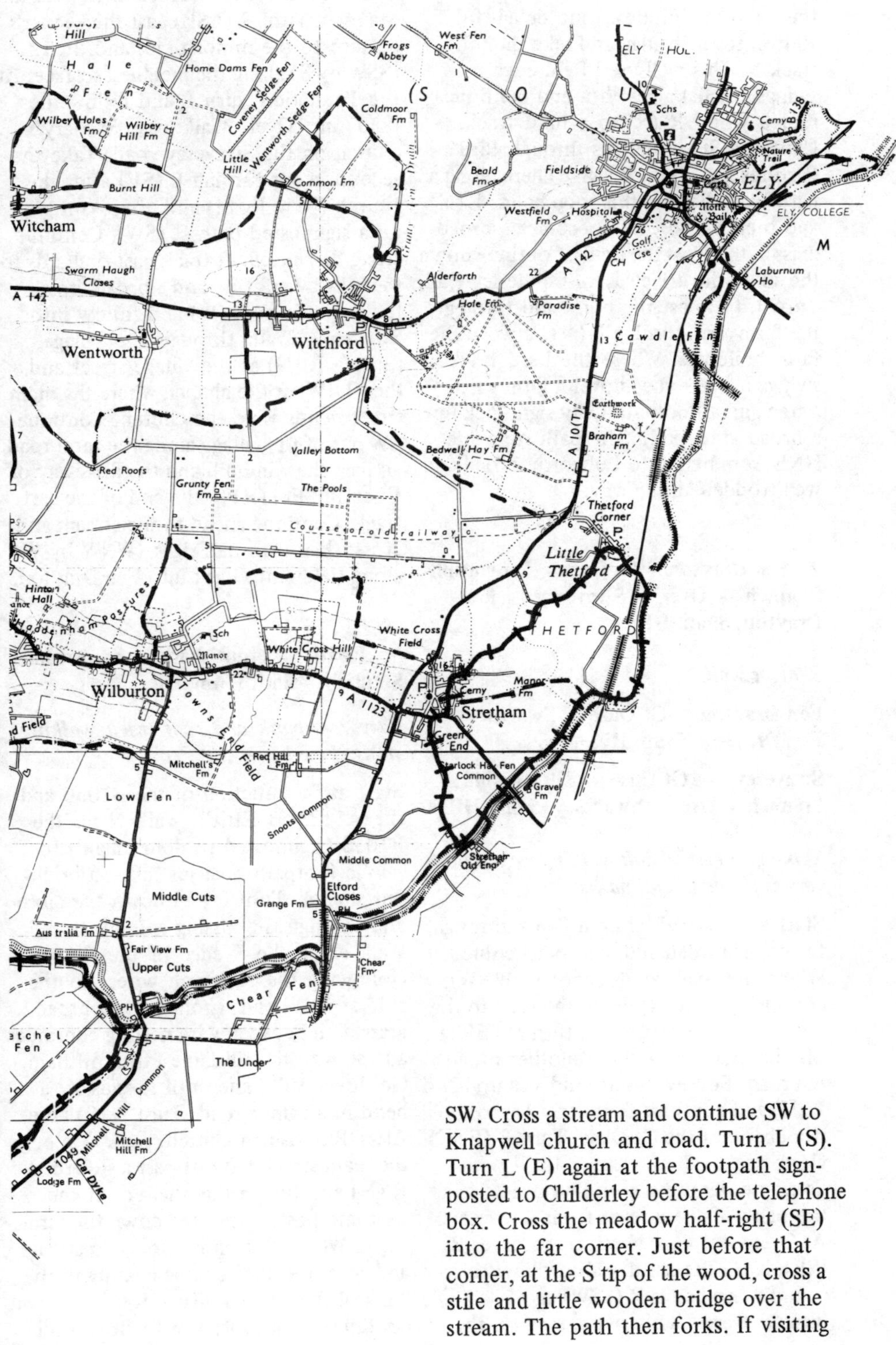

SW. Cross a stream and continue SW to Knapwell church and road. Turn L (S). Turn L (E) again at the footpath signposted to Childerley before the telephone box. Cross the meadow half-right (SE) into the far corner. Just before that corner, at the S tip of the wood, cross a stile and little wooden bridge over the stream. The path then forks. If visiting

Red Well, take the L track into the woods; this is often muddy, but delightful. Return to the bridge and take the other track S. This well-used field edge path swings L (SE) after ⅓m and continues past a wood R (S) to a hard track. Continue SE along this through Bird's Pastures Fm. Turn R (NNE) here along a narrow bridleway; this soon bends L (N) and then R (NE) and becomes a broad grass path across the fields. Continue down the hill to the driveway of Childerley Hall. Turn L (N) past the pond and through the farmyard, turning L (N) between the farm buildings. Where the hard track swings L, walk ahead over a farm gate by a tree and a Footpath Only sign. Pick up a broad grass path. The path runs due NNE from here into Lolworth, broad and well trodden all the way.

2. **Fen Drayton – Gt Ouse – Brownshill Staunch – Over – Swavesey – Fen Drayton. 8¾m. HR.**

Shorter walks:

Fen Drayton – Gt Ouse – Swavesey – Fen Drayton. 5½m. HR.

Swavesey – Gt Ouse – Brownshill Staunch – Over – Swavesey. 5½m. HR.

Some good riverbank walking mixed with very variable inland paths.

Start at St Mary's church. Walk through to the main road and Methodist church. Where the road bends sharp L (WNW), continue ahead (N) down the road to the quarry. Where this forks, turn R (ESE) off the main track onto another broad fen road. Follow this around a sharp bend L (N) and continue for nearly 1m to the floodbank of the Gt Ouse. Turn R (ENE) along the bank. Continue for 1m to Overcote, ignoring a bridleway R along the bank of the stream from Swavesey. At Overcote, a broad fen track leaves R (SE); if on the short walk, follow this round sharp bends R (SSW) and L (SSE) into Swavesey. Otherwise, stay on the Ouse floodbank to the lock at Brownshill Staunch. Turn R (ESE) past the keeper's cottage to the minor road, and then L (SSW by S) along the metalled surface. At the T-junction, turn L and follow the road into Over. Walk past St Mary's church on the Swavesey road. Take the second major turning L (SE) after the church (New Road) and after ⅓m pick up a signposted path R (SW). Continue along this excellent track past orchards to the railway, pasture and a broad crossing fen road. Turn R (W) and follow into Swavesey. Walk through the village, turning R (N) at the village street and then L (W) at the chapel, where the main street bends R to the church. Continue SW out of the village along the farm road; go past the windmill and the driveway of Friezland Fm (R) to the end of the cart track. Continue ahead to the stream and cross; then turn half-right (WNW by W) along field paths back into Fen Drayton.

3. **Earith – Bluntisham – Brownshill Staunch – Earith. 6m. HR.**

Easy riverbank and cart track walking along the edge of the Fens.

Start at the junction of the B1050 and the A1123 in Earith. Walk N up the B1050 (signposted to Somersham) to a public footpath post just after a brick bus shelter. Turn L (W) down the close and through the kissing gate at its end. Walk along the S edge of the field (following the telegraph wires) to the stile at its W end. From here, a broad grass path between wire netting continues all the way to Mill Lane in Bluntisham. Go down Mill Lane until it ends by a bend in a minor road. Turn L (S) here. After Bluntisham church, walk W along the main street. Go just past a side road R (N) and then a bus shelter. At the footpath post, turn L (S) down the farm track. Where this ends, cross the stream and continue on the same bearing to the bank of the Gt Ouse. Turn R (S) here and continue for a short ½m to Brownshill

Staunch. Cross the river here and turn sharp L (NNE by N) along the S bank. Follow for 2m until the bank ends in a B road at Earith Lock. Turn L to the A1123 and then L (W) again onto the trunk road above the washes of the Bedford rivers. Continue back into Earith.

4. **Willingham – Gt Ouse – Cottenham Lode – Rampton – Willingham. 14m. VHR.**

Shorter walks:

Willingham – Gt Ouse – Aldreth High Bridge – Willingham. 6m. VHR.

Rampton – Aldreth High Bridge – Cottenham Lode. 10m. VHR.

Good walking along tracks and through places with a great deal of historical and archaeological interest.

Walk out of Willingham along the B1050 (signposted to Earith). At the very N edge of the village, by the speed de-restriction sign, turn R (E) down a broad cart track. This almost immediately bends L (NNE) and becomes a green lane. Where it ends in a crossing track, turn L (NW) and follow the broad track around a sharp bend R to resume your original NNE bearing. Continue for ¾m to the river bank and there turn R (ESE) along the S floodbank of the Gt Ouse. After 1½m, a broad cart track comes in from the L (SSW) and crosses the river over an old bridge, Aldreth High Bridge. The long and short walks divide here. (If on the short walk, turn L (SSW) down the cart track. Ignore side tracks L and R after 1m, and continue ahead over Belsar's Hill fort to the minor road. Turn briefly R (W) but then L (SSW) down another broad green lane to the edge of the orchards.) If on the long walk, continue along the S bank of the Ouse for a further 3m. Eventually, a broad drainage channel flows in from the L (SSW). This is Cottenham Lode. Turn R (SSW) along a path on its W bank. Follow this for 1½m to a minor road. Those desiring a reminder of human beings can turn L here onto the B road and past Cottenham church; turn R (NW) at the minor road ½m later. Otherwise, cross the minor road and continue along the grassy floodbank. After 1m, it is joined by the second minor road; 1m later still, the straight WSW bearing ends by a wood. Turn L (SSW) here down a broad cart track to the road. Turn R (WNW) past Giant's Hill and on for 1m through Rampton. Follow the road round one sharp bend R (NNE by N), but at the next bend L (WNW) continue ahead down a broad cart track. After a long ½m, the cart track comes out of orchards and immediately becomes a grassy path ahead. At this point, turn L (WNW) down another unmade lane back into Willingham.

5. **Stretham – Lt Thetford – Gt Ouse – Stretham Fen Engine – Stretham. 5½m. VHR.**

Excellent riverbank and green lane walking, including Stretham and its unique steam engine.

Start at Stretham church. Walk through to the NE part of the village onto Wood Lane, and then turn off R (E) down Berry Green. Turn L (NNE) down a gravelled cart track, just after the last house and before the farm buildings. After 200yd, follow the track around a sharp bend R (E) by a little brick shed; after 300yd, the path continues half-left (NE) beside a little stream. Pick up a broad green track – an excellent example of an Isle of Ely green road – ahead; this runs NNE and divides. Take the R fork E and NE into Lt Thetford. At the village street, turn R (SSE) and continue through the village and over the railway line to the banks of the Ouse. Turn R (S) along the E bank. Continue S for ¾m to the division of the Cam and Gt Ouse, by the Fish & Duck Inn. At this point, the floodbank turns R (W) along the Gt Ouse and over the railway line. At the minor road, it is possible to turn R and continue to the pub; otherwise, keep on the N bank of the Ouse for a further 1½m, over the A1123 to Stretham Fen Engine. Then turn R up the minor road back into Stretham.

OTHER SUGGESTED ROUTES

Weekend Walks

1. Cambridge – River Cam – River Ouse (*see map pp. 000*) – Ely (overnight stop). Ely – Lt Thetford – Stretham – Gt Ouse – Aldreth High Bridge – Belsar's Hill – Histon (*bus to Cambridge*). Day 1: 16m. Day 2: 17m.
Energetic but easy walking along river banks and historic tracks.

2. Histon (*bus from Cambridge*) – Aldreth High Bridge – Gt Ouse – Brownshill Staunch – Holywell – St Ives (overnight stop). St Ives – Fenstanton – Conington – Boxworth – Childerley – Hardwick – Coton – Cambridge. Day 1: 15m (from Histon). Day 2: 16m.
Riverbank walking, with tracks and fen villages.

Day Walks

St Ives and Ely and Royston are linked to Cambridge by bus – Ely also by rail. It is thus possible to use any of the daily stages of the Weekend Walks.

1. St Ives – Holywell – Earith Lock – Aldreth High Bridge – Willingham – Over – Gt Ouse – St Ives. 16m.
River banks and broad inland tracks.

2. Fen Drayton – Gt Ouse – Aldreth High Bridge – Willingham – Over – Swavesey – Fen Drayton. 14m.
A slightly shorter version of 1.): it may be reduced still further (12m) by starting and finishing at Over.

3. Earith – Sutton – Wilburton (via Staple Leys Fm) – Linden End Field – Aldreth High Bridge – Earith. 15m.
River banks and fen roads for the most part. A variation on this walk of the same length is Earith – Mepal – Witcham – Gall Fen – Gt Ouse – Earith. This may be reduced to 13m by omitting Mepal and going via Sutton.

4. Stretham – Gt Ouse – Wilburton – Witchford – Stretham. 14½m.
The same Isle of Ely mixture of floodbank, riverside and (often concreted) fen road.

Medium Walks

1. Over – Gt Ouse – Earith Lock – Willingham – Over. 9m.
Excellent tracks and floodbank walking.

2. Earith – Mepal – Earith. 10m.
The ultimate floodbank walk – straight, high and atmospheric. It may be reduced to 7½m by turning round at Sutton Gault (excellent pub).

3. Witcham – Common Fm – Red Roofs – Witcham. 7½m.
A lot of hard surfaces to be walked.

4. Lt Thetford – Stretham – Grunty Fen Fm – Witchford – Lt Thetford. 8m.
Mostly along stream banks: heavy but enjoyable.

Short Walks

1. Witcham – Hale Fen – Burnt Hill – Witcham. 3½m.
Easy, unremarkable.

2. Witchford – Common Fm – Witchford. 3½m.
Likewise.

3. Ely – Gt Ouse – Lt Thetford. 3m.
A classic river walk.

3 HUNTINGDON DISTRICT

South of Huntingdon and the Ouse Valley; Kimbolton and Grafham Water; North-west of Huntingdon

Geographically and geologically, there is a great similarity between Huntingdonshire and the arable interiors of Norfolk and Suffolk, although this part of the country was never part of the ancient kingdom of East Anglia. Most of the area is clay, and is very sticky, heavy ground, totally resistant to water and not as fertile as the more loamy soil of Suffolk clay. As with all clay, the landscape before human interference would have been one of thickly forested rolling hills. Pre-Roman settlement was almost non-existent, and even the Romans generally passed this area by, except as country through which their roads, especially Ermine Street, must pass. The forests were only gradually cleared after the arrival of the Anglo-Saxons, and even then, as in the contiguous district around Boxworth and Childerley to the east, the hamlets that were established generally remained small, and often died out entirely.

The valley of the Great Ouse, which carves through the clay south of Huntingdon, is one of the major drainage systems for the middle parts of England. The Ouse enters this area as a broad, slowly-flowing river continually fuelled by a variety of tributaries. The resulting landscape is a narrow strip of water meadows, sometimes rendered into arable but often kept as pasture for sheep and cattle. The valley was never very heavily wooded, and thus attracted settlement relatively early, during the Early Iron Age, with settlements at Brampton, Buckden, Little Paxton and St Neots. The typical settlement discovered is a single farmstead within a small enclosure – huts about twenty to twenty-four feet across, with upright wattle-and-daub walls and a roof supported every six feet or so by posts. Significantly, the major Roman settlement was not along their roads across the clay but upon the edge by the valley of the Ouse: Godmanchester, at the junction of Ermine Street, Silver Street and the so-called Via Devana. It was only in Anglo-Saxon times that any real settlement took place in the Ouse valley, and St Neots developed into a market town and river port of reasonable size. It was not until the middle ages that Huntingdon and St Ives developed in importance. Today, the landscape of the river Ouse is still a pleasant combination of old towns and villages and large water meadows. Among the latter, Port Holme between Huntingdon and Brampton is the finest example, one of the largest meadows in England, soft and pastoral. All in all, the meadow walking in the Ouse valley is among the best in the area covered by this book.

Grafham Water was established under the Great Ouse Water Act of 1961, a remarkably enlightened statute for those days providing not only for the creation of the huge reservoir but also for its use as a leisure centre. The Water Authority was directed to allow public access to all parts of the lake, and to create facilities for such recreations as yachting, bird-watching and fishing.

The country north of Huntingdon has only two settlements of any size, Sawtry and Alconbury. In both cases, their development can be entirely explained by modern development capitalising on their position beside the A1. These apart, it is a district of shrinking and sometimes entirely deserted villages. The difficult farming conditions of the wet clay and the resultant emphasis upon the maximum possible mechanisation has left a landscape that is much closer to the outsider's stereotype of East Anglia than any place actually within the heartland of the region. The land is a low clay plateau, with very few features to break up the monotony of an arable countryside. The fields are enormous, and the hedges where they exist extremely small. There are a few remaining patches of woodland, particularly in the vicinity of Coppingford and Wood Walton, and surprisingly few streams. Above all, the landscape is deserted. In mid-Huntingdonshire, and to a lesser extent south of Godmanchester, it is quite possible to spend a day's energetic rambling without seeing another human being or indeed any concrete evidence of the existence of man.

The amount of fen included in this area is confined to the countryside around Ramsey. Nevertheless, it is a microcosm of the Fens as a whole, demonstrating the same landscape and historical features. The inhabited settlements like Ramsey lie upon either peninsulas jutting into the fen, or islands of clay surrounded by the peat. Settlement occurred late, and here, too, the initial impulse was religious, the foundation of an abbey free from the temptations of the outside world. Again, as at Ely, it was only a comparatively short time before Ramsey Abbey acquired wide temporal power in the form of manors and lands throughout the area. Like the other fen islands, Ramsey suffered badly from the monastic dissolution, not having any bishopric to take its place as in Ely. As a fen port, activities were always fairly muted, and the drainage of the 17th century did not revitalise the economy of the town. It remains, like most fenland towns, a market centre, overwhelmingly arable, and extremely isolated. The fen itself bears all the hallmarks which we have learned to expect: huge dark fields, laid out in geometric patterns; drainage ditches rather than hedges; enormous skies, and a featureless landscape.

This brief summary gives some idea of the difficulties and delights to be met with by the rambler. Apart from the Ouse valley and Grafham Water, it is fairly sticky underfoot. Signposting is only fairly good, and paths can be heavily ploughed. Nevertheless, any rambler who claims to know about East Anglia has at some time walked in south Huntingdonshire. It is a tribute to the dedicated efforts of groups like the Huntingdon RA that so many paths do remain open – and that the District Council is prepared to envisage extensions of the footpath map like the projected Ouse Valley Path, from Huntingdon to St Neots.

South of Huntingdon and the Ouse Valley

The small population makes little impression on the paths, which can be quite hard work in places. Broad green tracks like Silver Street make a welcome change.

Brampton Samuel Pepys was born here. Pepys was the fifth son of a London tailor, and like Cromwell attended Huntingdon Grammar School. His career in public service included the posts of Secretary to the Admiralty, MP for the pocket borough of Castle Rising, and Master of Trinity House; but it is his cypher diaries which have made him so well known. Pepys's house lies at the east end of Brampton, and is a curious mixture of 16c timber with Georgian brick.

Buckden Lying off the paths. The village has some excellent buildings including a fine coaching inn (the George) and another hotel, the Lion, once the guesthouse of Buckden Palace, built by the late Victorian brewer, Sir Arthur Marshall. Buckden Palace, of which little of the original remains, was once the palace of the bishops of Lincoln. Open: Sunday afternoon in late summer.

Caxton A Roman site has been discovered here, near to Ermine Street, close to ridges and hollows in the fields west of the road that define the Anglo-Saxon and early medieval village.

Croxton Thatched cottages, late medieval hall; village originally south-east of current position, about the church, but demolished in 19c to expand parkland of mid-Georgian redbrick hall. Spread Eagle pub on main road can be recommended (real ale).

Eltisley A neat green, several thatched cottages and two fine timbered houses. 13c church. South of village in the wood is the moated site of Eltisley's Anglo-Saxon nunnery of St Pandiana, an Irish princess who shares the dedication of the church with St John. A nearby spring is still called St Pandiana's Well. The community was transferred to Hinchingbrooke after the Conquest, the wood itself becoming a deer park later in the middle ages.

Fenstanton Inside the church lies the tomb of Capability Brown, who rose from being an ordinary gardener to become the prophet and creator of a new, natural style of landscaping to replace the old formal gardens that had been in vogue since Elizabethan times. Brown's technique was in fact highly artificial, involving the planting of trees in clumps among fine grass parkland. He became a cult figure among the aristocracy, and was given the manors of Fenstanton and Hilton by the Earl of Northampton as payment for work at Castle Ashby.

Graveley An Anglo-Saxon village, part of the Ramsey Abbey estates in 964; its church has a pre-Conquest dedication, to St Botolph. The country between here and Godmanchester is enormously open, flat and arable, with no villages.

Godmanchester Now officially one borough with Huntingdon, by a shotgun marriage of 1961 after centuries of neighbourly rivalry. Godmanchester is much older than Huntingdon, and was a thriving agricultural town even in Roman times. Three Roman roads meet here: the A604 or Via Devana to Cambridge and Colchester; Silver Street, which walkers to Graveley and Caldecote follow; and above all, Ermine Street, the A14. The main roads define the pentangular shape of the original town. In Anglo-Saxon and medieval times, it belonged to the Crown by ancient demesne – which conferred the privilege of self-government but not the right to sell property or hold a market. As a result, Godmanchester has remained a town of farmers, without high street, market place or shopping centre. It has a number of timber-framed houses, and a large 12-15c church with a mass dial on south buttress of chancel.

Great Gransden lies in a curious gridiron pattern, almost suggesting that it was a planned settlement. There is an unspoilt village pub and many timber and plaster houses. Church with original chancel screen and bench-ends carved with faces, fishes, animals and birds.

Hemingford Abbots and **Hemingford Grey** The villages offer some good meadow walking.

Hilton Village green landscaped by Capability Brown, surrounded by houses from Tudor times to our own century, and a lovely church. Hilton's most charming and unusual feature is its turf-cut maze.

Houghton Pleasant wooded country between here and St Ives, known as The Thickets. Houghton is a pretty riverside village with a fine church, village square, pub (Three Horseshoes), and watermill now owned by the Youth Hostels Association.

Huntingdon The 14c stone bridge built at the height of Huntingdon's commercial prosperity is almost the equal of St Ives. Oliver Cromwell was born here in 1599 and was Huntingdon's MP between 1628 and 1630. After a quarrel with the town council, he left to live in St Ives in 1631. This is why St Ives has the statue and Huntingdon the Cromwell Museum. The Cromwell Museum is open: daily except Monday, all year – once the grammar school, Cromwell and Pepys were both pupils here.

Offord Cluny and **Offord Darcy** Separated only by a brook. As their names imply, one village was owned in the middle ages by the Darcy (or Daney) family, the other by the great French monastery of Cluny. There is an attractive river crossing, and some lovely thatched cottages. The church is mainly 13c.

Papworth Everard At the Conquest, the village had land for seven plough-teams and about twenty peasant families. Its ownership by Sir Everard de Beche in the 12c gave Papworth its second name. The population remained steady at about eighty people right through the middle ages and 16-18c. A wagonner's inn to the north of the village still known as Kisby's Hut from the man who founded it in the 18c. Papworth's expansion began in the late Victorian period when the unscrupulous financier Ernest Hooley bought the 19c classical hall. Hooley held lavish weekend parties here, which brought money to the village, but Hooley's real contribution was in expenditure on farm improvements. After 1918, the hall came into the possession of a young Welsh doctor called Varrier-Jones, whose ambition was to found a new type of tuberculosis sanatorium. Where conventional homes prescribed complete idleness for three years and then 'released' patients to the outside world with the full rigours of work, Varrier-Jones proposed to reintroduce patients to work very gradually while in the hospital, and never to compel a patient to leave at all. The success of Papworth Village Settlement, as it became, is visible in the size of the village, the astonishing range of goods produced by its patients, and its international reputation. Now, of course, it has replaced TB with treatment of other disabilities including polio, spina bifida, multiple sclerosis.

St Ives The approach is through broad, flat meadowlands and over the wide Ouse crossed by St Ives' picturesque bridge. The causeway and bridge are 15c, built by Ramsey Abbey when the monastery owned St Ives. The little building in the centre of the bridge began life as a chapel, one of only three such in England. In the 18c it became an inn, with two extra brick storeys, which were removed in the restoration of the 1920s. The best buildings lie in the main square, with its statue of Cromwell, and in Slepe, around the spired church. Slepe is the oldest part of the town, dating back to the original small Saxon village. The early expansion of the town in Anglo-Saxon times was partially religious, partially commercial: the bones of the 7c Persian bishop St Ivo were supposedly discovered here in the early 11c, and a monastery founded. At the same time, St Ives was beginning to capitalise on its position as the highest navigable point on the Ouse. In the middle ages trade through King's Lynn to Flanders grew up, with St Ives gaining its own charter and the right to hold trade fairs at Easter and August. The Easter fair dominated the trade of the Ouse until the rise of Cambridge in the later middle ages. This, the dissolution of Ramsey Abbey in 1539, the construction of the Bedford rivers in the 17c, and a series of disastrous fires, all combined to undermine the town's position. It remained however a prosperous market town, and appears entirely as such today. The river meadows between here and Huntingdon make splendid walking.

St Neots Dates back at least to the Iron Age, although the Romans apparently did not use the site. The Saxons established a settlement bounded by the Fox Brook and a defensive ditch along Cambridge and Church Streets. A priory in honour of the Cornish St Neot was founded here in the 10c, which later died away and was re-founded as a Benedictine monastery in the 12c. At this time, the town stood not on the river crossing but on higher, agricultural land. The commercial position on the Ouse was not exploited until the growth of a market town about the monastery in the middle ages. There is a Georgian market place, and a parish church, an array of real and mythical creatures in the roof.

Southoe A good pub, the Three Horseshoes, a church with a prominent Elizabethan tower and no fewer than three moated manor-sites surviving from the middle ages. This is an area of shrinking villages; Midloe, to the west, has shrunk from agricultural hamlet to a single farmhouse.

Toseland Sarsen stone by the south wall of Norman church shows the village was once the centre of the Anglo-Saxon Hundred. In the bluebell wood north of the village lies an extensive medieval moat, and it has been suggested that the fields between were once also part of the village; today there is a single row of modest cottages.

Weald Another deserted medieval village on Roman road from Godmanchester to Sandy, now a splendid grassy cart track.

Contd p. 55

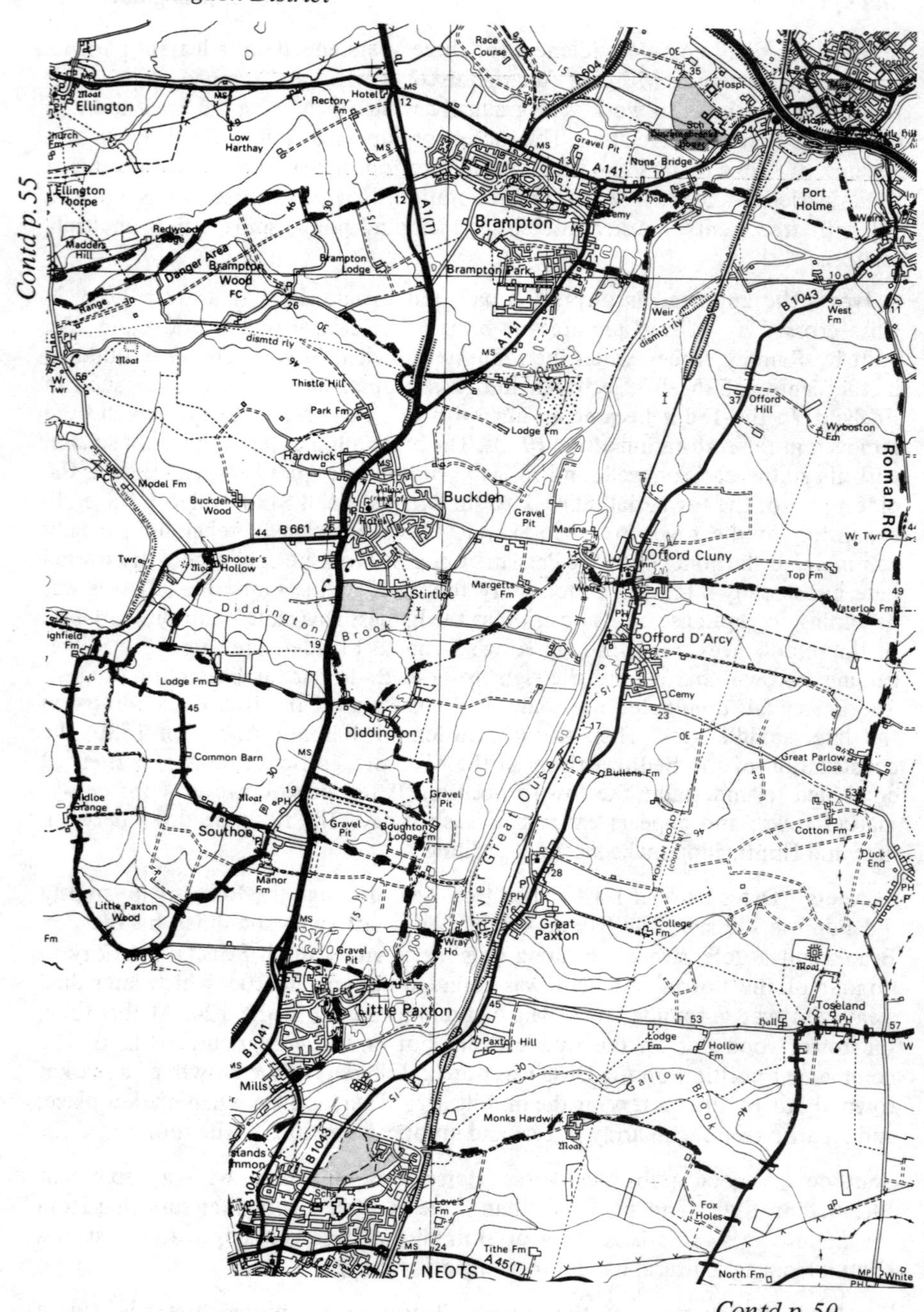

Contd p. 50

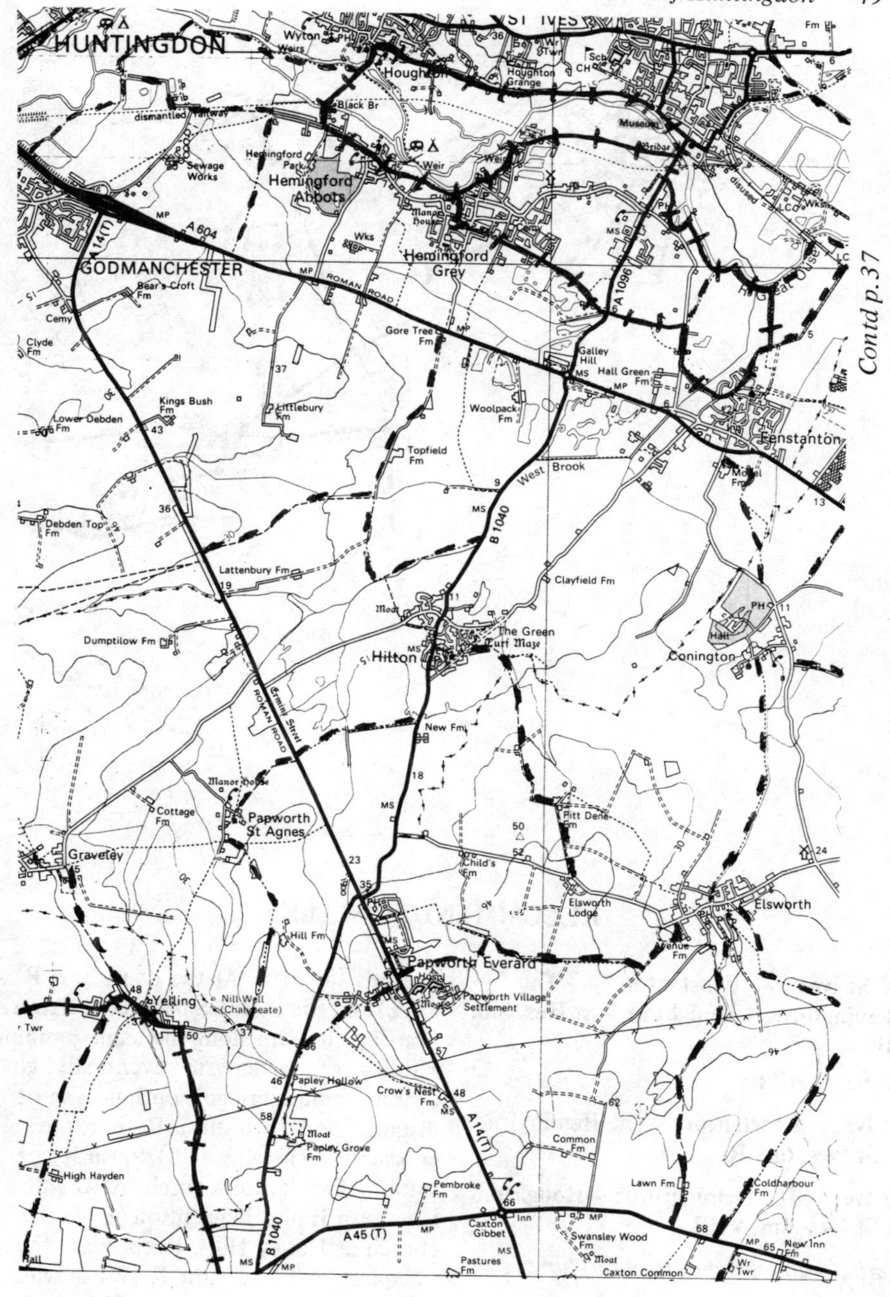

HUNTINGDON
ST IVES
Wyton
Weirs
Houghton
Houghton Grange
Wr Twr
Sch
CH
Black Br
dismantled railway
Museum
Bridge
Hemingford Park
Sewage Works
Hemingford Abbots
Weir
Manor House
disused
Wks
Hemingford Grey
MS
A 1096
GODMANCHESTER
A 14(T)
A 604
MP
ROMAN ROAD
Bear's Croft Fm
Cemy
Clyde Fm
Gore Tree Fm
Galley Hill
Hall Green Fm
Great Ouse
Kings Bush Fm
Littlebury Fm
Lower Debden Fm
Woolpack Fm
Fenstanton
Topfield Fm
West Brook
Motel Fm
B 1040
Debden Top Fm
Lattenbury Fm
Clayfield Fm
Moat
The Green
Turf Maze
Dumptilow Fm
Hilton
PH
Hall
Conington
Ermine Street
New Fm
Manor House
Cottage Fm
Papworth St Agnes
Graveley
Pitt Dene Fm
Child's Fm
Elsworth Lodge
Elsworth
Avenue Fm
Hill Fm
Papworth Everard
Hospl
Papworth Village Settlement
Yelling
Nill Well (Chalybeate)
Papley Hollow
Crow's Nest Fm
Moat
Papley Grove Fm
Common Fm
Lawn Fm
Coldharbour Fm
High Hayden
Pembroke Fm
Inn
Caxton Gibbet
A 45 (T)
Swansley Wood Fm
Moat
New Inn Fm
Wr Twr
Pastures Fm
Caxton Common
Hall

Contd p.37

Contd p. 48

RECOMMENDED WALKS

1. **St Ives – Fenstanton – The Hemingfords – Houghton – St Ives. 8m. HR.**

Shorter walks:

St Ives – Fenstanton – The Hemingfords – St Ives. 6m. R.

St Ives – The Hemingfords – Houghton – St Ives. 5m. VHR.

Varied walking: one stream to jump.

Walk SSW out of St Ives over the bridge and along the causeway to a footpath post on the L (SSE). Walk down the unmade lane until it bends R (S); then bear half-right (SSE) across the meadows to the river. Turn R (S) and skirt the Marina to the road. Turn L (ESE) round a double bend and then L (N) along a good path towards the lock. At the river, turn R (SSE) and follow the S bank of the river. Continue for ¾m along the bank, jumping a side stream after ⅓m. Eventually, go over a concrete bridge, continue a short distance and then turn R over the enormous field ahead (S) towards the spire of Fenstanton church. At the dirt lane, turn R into Fenstanton (L for the church at Honey Hill). Keep on to the Chequers pub and turn R (W) down Hall Green Lane to its end. Pick up a well-trodden path ahead (NW) from here over the stream and ahead past the cricket field to the minor road. Turn R (N) up the road for ¾m to the point where it crosses a small stream. Then turn L (W) down a signposted footpath along its N bank. Follow this to the B1040. Turn

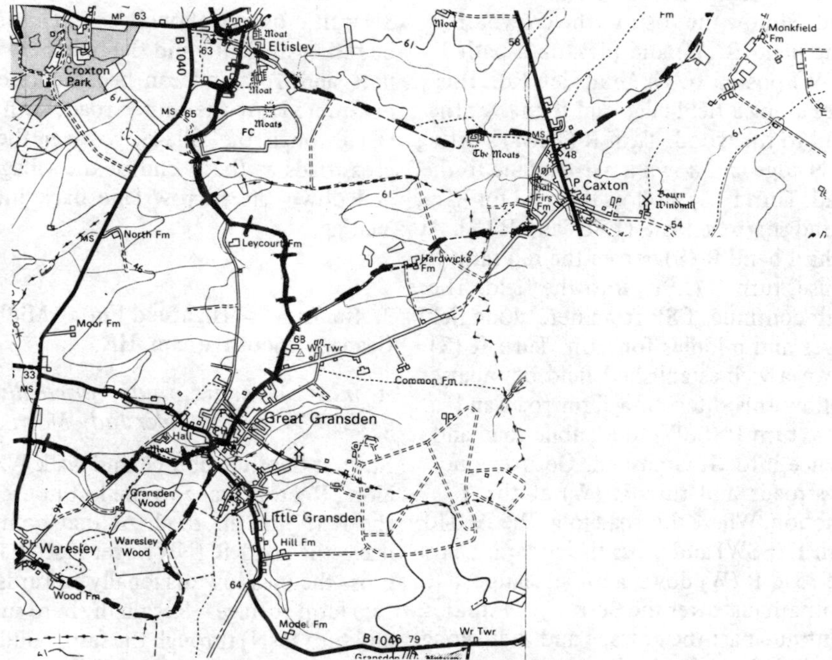

briefly R (N) but then L (WNW) down the road into Hemingford Grey. Where this turns sharp R (NNE by N), keep on ahead (WNW) down a narrow path and then a road. Go straight over the next road and down Manor Lane. After a short distance, turn R (N) at the footpath signpost down the edge of a playing field and on to the W end of a charming village street (Cleveland Gallery). The long and short walks divide here. If on the short walk, pick up a narrow metalled path NE to the church, then turn down Church St to No. 18; pick up a signposted little lane NE, continue to the gravel pits and then turn E along the well-defined meadow path back to St Ives. If on the long walk, turn L (W) beside the river. Continue along the bank for a short ¼m and then between a caravan site and a housing estate to the high street of Hemingford Abbots. Turn R (WNW) through the village and past the church. Where the main street turns sharp L (SSW), continue ahead on the road to Black Bridge. After ¼m, turn R (N) down Meadow Lane and cross the bridge. Continue down the narrow cyclepath to Houghton Mill and cross the river. Turn L at the lane and follow into the little square, then immediately R down a metalled lane. Continue along this ESE for 1m back to the bank of the river, and follow back into St Ives.

2. **Yelling – Eltisley – Gt Gransden – Abbotsley – Toseland – Yelling. 15m. HR.**

Mostly good walking, but with some field-work, the walk takes in several attractive villages.

Start at Yelling church. Walk E along the main street to a notice saying High St, by Hill Top Fm. Turn R (S) here down a semi-gravelled track. This broad track continues for 1¾m to Eltisley, variously as a green lane and unmetalled cart track. Ignore all side tracks and keep on a general S heading. At its S end, cross the A45 and go down the grass path opposite to the church. Turn L (E) to the village green and then R (SSW by S) down a road immediately to its W side. Ignore two footpath signposts, to Caxton and Caxton End. Follow the road to the crown of a long bend R (W) and pick up a path L (SSW) posted to Gt Gransden Rd. This goes along a field edge and then over the field to the wood. Turn R (WSW) skirting its N edge and down a narrow lane to the road. Turn L (S). Follow the road for ⅔m, round sharp bends L (ESE) and R (S). At a third bend R (S) before the red farmhouse, turn L (ESE) into the field. The path continues ESE from here along field edges and middles for ⅓m. Turn R (S) down a well-established field boundary. Follow this ditch to a farm road and there turn R (SSW) to a public road and thence into Gt Gransden. Go over one crossroads and turn R (W) at the T-junction. Where this road joins the B1046, turn L (SSW) and cross the stream. Leave the road R (W) down a broad signposted footpath just after the Berry Close studios. Continue past the cottage and then along a well-defined field edge path. Cross a field of pasture ahead (W) and pick up another good field edge path to the minor road. Turn L (SW) over the brow of the hill and then R (NW) at the signpost down a broad bridleway, by the shed. Continue to the B1040, cross and pick up a broad track upon the other side. This continues W to a minor road, on a bend. Keep ahead (W) here and follow this narrow lane for a long ½m to the end of a belt of trees L (S) just before a large wood. Turn R (N) here along a field boundary, and then L (W) at the first hedge, to the trees. Turn R (N) along the E edge of the wood and thence into Abbotsley. Walk through the village to the church and the small triangular green. Pick up Hardwick Lane W at the green's S tip. Enter the field and follow the telegraph lines ahead (W) along field boundaries. After 1m, with the W edge of a large wood away to your L (S), turn R (NNE) down a much broader track. This is the old Roman road from Sandy to Godmanchester (see area description). Follow this for 4m. After ¾m, it crosses the B1046; after 2½m, by the site of the deserted medieval village of Weald, it goes over the A45; after 3½m, it crosses Gallow Brook. This may be rather difficult, and the mile between here and Toseland can become rather obstructed. At the minor road, turn R (E) through the village; go over the crossroads at the E end of the village and down the narrow lane back into Yelling.

3. Southoe – Highfield Fm – Midloe Grange – Southoe. 5m. HR.

A most attractive route, originally devised by local rambler Judy Morris.

Start at Southoe church and walk WNW along Rectory Lane to the last house on the R (N) of the road. At that point, leave the road R (NW) over a stile and cross the meadow diagonally towards the two farm cottages. Regain the hard surface and turn R (N) through the farm buildings; continue ahead (N) down a broad cart track under telegraph lines. After ½m, the track turns L (WNW) and continues past pylon lines to the S tip of Diddington Wood. Follow the grassy path WNW to the L (S) of the farmhouse visible ahead. Turn R (N) by the old corrugated iron shed if visiting Grafham Water; otherwise, take the cart track L (S). After ½m, it vanishes entirely in the middle of a single enormous field. The right of way lies across this – though walkers, doubtless inspired by Judy Morris's excellent booklet, seem to follow the field edges to the W of the true course. Both routes lead to Midloe Grange. Walk through the ancient farmyard, and cross the tarmac farm road bearing half-left to a gate. A fine track leads from here S to the NW tip of Lt Paxton Wood, and then skirts the wood on its W and SW sides to the minor road. (There is an attractive ford just S of here, for those willing to make a brief diversion.) Walk E along the road for 300yd and then pick up a path L (N) back to Lt Paxton Wood. The track then turns R (E) and crosses the stream, before turning L (NNE by N) once more. Go past a side track L. After a short distance, the right of way leaves the track and continues along field paths to the bushy clump and thence to the farm road. Most walkers however continue along the track until it ends in a crossing track, and then turn R (ESE). Again, the right of way lies W of the farmhouse among the fields (ENE); but most walkers continue ESE to the farmyard and turn L (N) down the tarmac drive to the road. Continue N past the Three Horseshoes to the church.

OTHER SUGGESTED ROUTES

***Weekend Walk**

Huntingdon – Gt Ouse Path – St Neots (overnight stop). St Neots – Wintringham – Roman Rd – Toseland – Graveley – Roman Rd – Godmanchester – Port Holme – Huntingdon. Day 1: 12m. Day 2: 12½m.
Riverside walking and broad upland tracks. This walk must await completion of the river path between Huntingdon and St Neots before becoming usable.

Day Walks

Kimbolton and St Neots are well connected to Huntingdon by public transport. It is thus possible to use any of the daily stages above as Day Walks.

1. St Ives – Fenstanton – Conington – Elsworth – Pitt Dene Fm – Hilton – Topfield Fm – Hemingford Grey – St Ives. 13m.
Quite a long walk in this heavy soil.

2. Papworth Everard – Eltisley (via Yelling) – Hardwicke – Caxton – Lawn Fm – Elsworth – Papworth Everard. 14m.
Can be reduced to 12m by taking the Eltisley-Caxton short cut.

* **3.** St Neots – Wintringham – Roman Rd – Gravely – Waterloo Fm – Offord Cluny – Gt Ouse Path – St Neots. 15m.
The heaviest going lies in the first few miles.

* **4.** Huntingdon – Brampton – Brampton Wood – Grafham – Grafham Water – Southoe – Gt Ouse Path – Huntingdon. 15m.
Mostly broad tracks and meadow paths.

* **5.** Huntingdon – Gt Ouse Path – Offord Cluny – Waterloo Fm – Roman Rd – Godmanchester – Port Holme – Huntingdon. 10¼m.
Easy and good.

Medium Walks

1. St Neots – Wintringham – Roman Rd – Monk's Hardwicke – St Neots. 6½m.
Variable.

2. St Neots – Hen Brook – Roman Rd – Wintringham – St Neots. 6m.
Mostly arable.

3. Eltisley – Caxton – Hardwicke – Eltisley. 6½m.
Mostly broad tracks but some field-work.

4. Toseland – Weald – Croxton – Yelling – Toseland. 7m.
One of the many good walks devised by Judy Morris for her excellent local booklet.

Short Walks

1. Gt Gransden – Lily Hill – Waresley – Gt Gransden. 4½m.
Good farm tracks.

2. Abbotsley – Eynesbury Hardwicke – Caldecote Manor Fm – Abbotsley. 4m.
Headlands, unmetalled lane and farm road.

3. Huntingdon – Port Holme – Brampton – Port Holme – Huntingdon. 5m.
Excellent meadow walking.

* These walks must await completion of the river path before becoming usable. Contact Huntingdon District Council for details.

Kimbolton and Grafham Water

Excellent walking along grassy banks around Grafham Water. North of Kimbolton Park is a return to open, clayey agricultural land.

Catworth A scattering of fine old cottages and farmhouses in the twisting lanes about the church. The latter has another fine, tall spire typical of the district, useful for bearings.

Easton Secluded village of high street, thatched cottages, village church.

Grafham has sprung from a remote agricultural village into a weekend resort. Rights of way exist round most of the reservoir, and have been amplified by permissive paths so that one only need have recourse to the road in the East and West Perry area. The wooded banks at the west end of the reservoir are particularly attractive.

Kimbolton At the bottom of a wooded valley, spread out along a single main road. The only kink, at Market Place, was created deliberately in the middle ages by the burgesses of Kimbolton, determined to collect tolls on market days. Inside the church is a handsome north chapel, and a series of medieval portraits, mainly of saints and kings, at the west end. Kimbolton's castle has the facade of a grand 18c building in the classical style, with a porch designed by Vanbrugh. It is now part of Kimbolton School, with magnificent grounds and a Robert Adam gatehouse. Behind the classical exterior of the castle lies Tudor fabric. The original building on this site was built for Sir Robert Wingfield in the 1520s, and acted as a prison to Catharine of Aragon in 1534. Open: Sunday afternoons in August, some Bank Holidays out of term time. The medieval castle was a mile south-west, by Park Farm: very little of the original motte and bailey can now be seen.

Spaldwick The centre of a medieval estate that included most of the adjoining villages, with a small triangular green where markets were held. There are several fine old buildings, including the late 15c George Inn and the church, 'the cathedral of the valley'.

Stonely Views across the Kym valley from the moat by Pertenhall Hoo Farm.

Stow Longa A pleasant, almost deserted village.

Tilbrook Church has a magnificent canopied rood-screen containing painted panels of a bishop, a deacon, and a female saint (probably Helen) holding a cross.

Contd p. 60

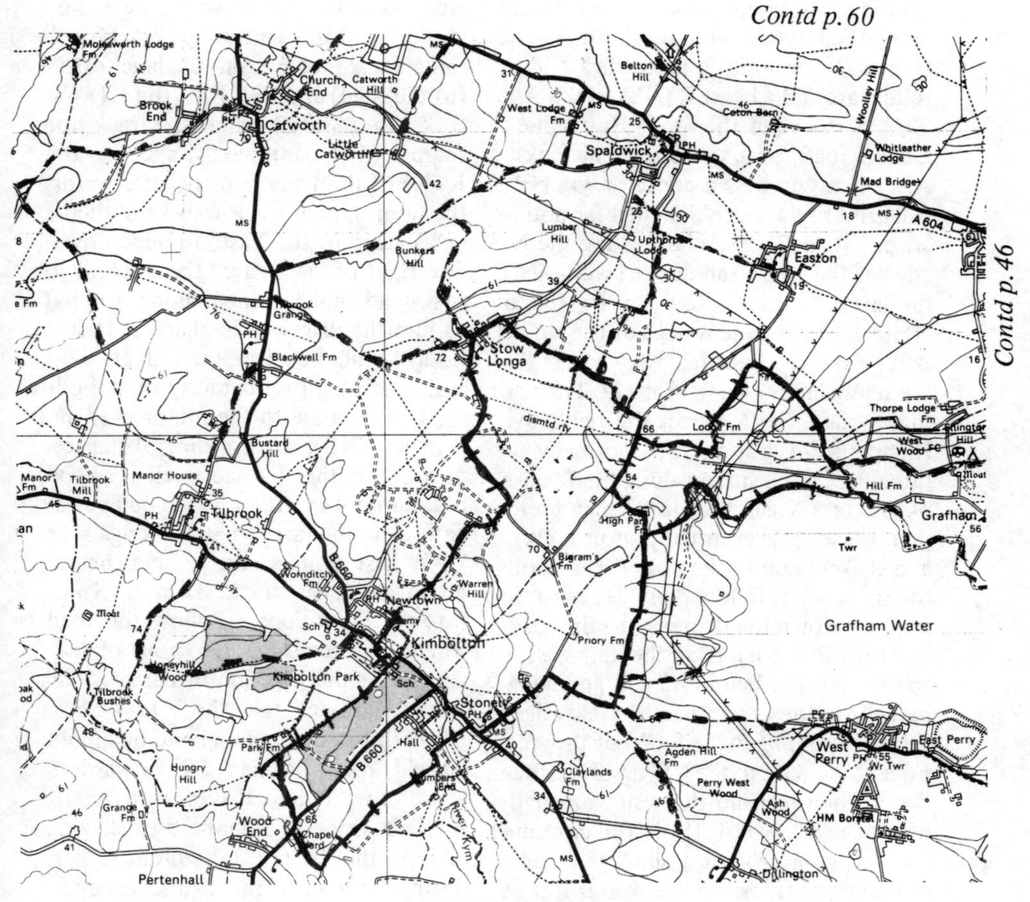

Contd p. 46

RECOMMENDED WALK

Kimbolton – Wood End – Stonely – Calpher Wood – Stow Longa – Kimbolton. 12½m. HR.

Shorter walks:

Kimbolton – Wood End – Stonely – Kimbolton. 4m. R.

Highpark Fm – Calpher Wood – Easton Lodge – Calpher Wood. 4m. HR.

Kimbolton – Stonely – Stow Longa – Kimbolton. 7m (or 10m if combined with either of the other shorter walks). HR.

Many attractions including open views of Grafham Water; there is, however, a great deal of roadwork and some fieldwork to be done en route.

Start in Kimbolton High St at the entrance to the castle park. Walk WSW through the gate, and continue WSW through the trees and along a fence to and through the old buildings at Park Fm. Cross the meadow ahead diagonally and turn L (SSE by S) along a field edge to the B660. Turn R (SW) down the road into Bedfordshire and then L (SSE) down a stony cart track signposted to Gunnersbury Cottage. Where this bends R, turn L (NE) down the zig-zagging cart track. At the second R-hand bend, continue half-right over the field to the three trees ahead. This then becomes a field edge path ahead (ENE). Continue ahead and pick up a good track down the hill to a building ahead. There, turn L (NNW) onto a hard track and follow around a bend R (NE) to the A45. Turn R (SE) and then L (NE) up the Easton road, past the telephone box. After ½m you pass a copse on your R (SE) and spy a white thatched farmhouse ahead. Turn R (ESE) here along the N edge of the copse and down a well-used bridleway to the woods. Turn L (NNE by N) here, skirting the W edge of the woods. After ⅔m, the trees fall away to the R, leaving an enormous field ahead. The right of way here lies N across the fields to Highpark Fm; but there is normally a broad track continuing along the W edge of the trees which the farmer may prefer you to use. This eventually turns L (W) and R (W) again to the farm drive. If on the short walk, follow these bends to the farm, go down the driveway to the road and turn R (NNE). If on the long walk, ignore the first bend (W) and go ahead past the pylon onto a narrow field edge path, continuing to the L (W) of the trees. Follow this path to the NW tip of Grafham Water, then pick up the well-worn path beside the reservoir R (SE). This continues for 1m, going round a small wooded promontory (most of the woods shown on the map have disappeared) and then curving ESE towards Hill Fm. Turn sharp L (NW) before the farm down a broad lane under the old railway bridge and ahead for nearly 1m. Before reaching the minor road into Easton, the lane forks N (to the road) and SW. Take the L (SW) fork. After 300yd, where the track turns sharp L (SE), continue SW ahead to the R (N) of the trees. Shortly afterwards, the farm track turns R (NW) and then L (SW) again to the Easton Lodge drive. The right of way leaves the track at its first bend, and continues along field paths to join the driveway actually at Easton Lodge. I did, however, see walkers on the farm track, so it is obviously used. Follow the tarmac drive to the minor road and turn R (NNE). After a short distance, pick up another tarmac track L (WNW) to a farmhouse with a tall chimney. The path from the farm to Stow Longa runs WNW first along a narrow, and then a broad and easy, track. Turn L (SW) through Stow Longa. Follow the road where it bends sharp L (S) out of the village. At the junction of narrow roads a long ½m later, take the L fork SE. Leave this at the second bend on an old airfield road heading SW towards Kimbolton. The road soon turns sharp R (NW). Later, another hard track comes in from the SW (L), by buildings. Turn down this road to the T-junction and then continue straight ahead along well-used field edges SW into Kimbolton.

OTHER SUGGESTED ROUTES

Weekend Walk

Huntingdon – Port Holme – Brampton – Brampton Wood – Grafham – Grafham Water – Highpark Fm – Warren Hill – Kimbolton (overnight stop). Kimbolton – Stonely – West Perry – East Perry – Lodge Fm – Southoe – Gt Ouse – Huntingdon. Day 1: 12m. Day 2: 13m.
Some excellent riverside and lakeside walking. This walk must await completion of the river path between Huntingdon and St Neots before becoming usable.

Day Walks

Kimbolton is well connected to Huntingdon by public transport. It is thus possible to use either of the daily stages above as a Day Walk.

1. Kimbolton – Stonely – The Perrys – Grafham Water – Stow Longa – Kimbolton. 13m.
Extensive lakeside walking and good tracks.

2. Catworth – Stow Longa – Easton – Spaldwick – Catworth. 9m.

Good walking in a difficult part of the area.

Medium Walks

1. Kimbolton – Stow Longa – Tilbrook Grange – Tilbrook – Honeyhill Wood – Kimbolton. 7½m.

2. Catworth – Stow Longa – Tilbrook Grange – Brook End – Catworth. 7½m.

3. Spaldwick – Grafham Water – Stow Longa – Spaldwick. 9m.

4. Easton – Grafham Water – Highpark Fm – Upthorpe Lodge – Easton. 6½m.
An enjoyable walk taking in some heavy arable work.

5. Grafham – Highpark Fm – West Perry – East Perry – Grafham Water – Grafham. 9m.
The ultimate lakeside ramble.

Short Walks

1. Highpark Fm – Grafham Water – Calpher Wood – Easton Lodge – Highpark Fm. 4m.
Generally fine walking with good lakeside views.

2. Easton – Easton Lodge – Upthorpe Lodge – Easton. 4m.
Rather heavy going.

3. Spaldwick – Stow Longa – Upthorpe Lodge – Spaldwick. 5m.
Likewise.

4. Stow Longa – Tilbrook Grange – Bunkers Hill – Stow Longa. 3¼m.
Generally good walking.

North-west of Huntingdon

The walking is very energetic; depopulation has reduced the number of rights of way, and the amount of usage each footpath receives. Some broad agricultural tracks, otherwise field middle and headlands.

Abbots Ripton The centre of the Ramsey estate, and as neat as any estate village. North-west is Monk's Wood, the nature reserve housing the famous research station where scientists study the flora and fauna of the country.

Broughton In the church two books in a glass case over the font are all that remain of a rare and valuable collection since transferred to Cambridge University library. East of the church are more mounds and banks, the only remains of the medieval Ramsey Abbey estate office.

Buckworth A tiny hamlet with an outstanding church. The walker certainly has the opportunity to admire it, for it stands on a ridge of the wolds visible for miles in every direction. The spire is one of the finest of its type in a county renowned for good examples. It is a broach spire, octagonal in shape but standing on a square tower with little half-pyramids of wood and masonry where they meet to effect a neat transition; also a moulded west doorway and wheel window.

Coppingford On Bullock Road; the drove road, with two or three cottages, a farm or two, extensive moats and trees from the demolished hall, a pond that must once have stood by the village green, and some splendid views north-east over the Fens and south-east along the valley of the Alconbury Brook.

The Giddings Classic examples of shrinking villages. Great Gidding remains the largest, but is small enough. Little and Steeple Gidding are each reduced to a mere handful of cottages. In each, the site of the old manor house and village can be identified from irregularities in the fields. Steeple Gidding stood in the field opposite the church, while Little Gidding Hall is a moated site on the lane to Bottom Farm. It was at Little Gidding that the 17c businessman and merchant Nicholas Ferrar turned his back upon the world to build a religious community of friends and relatives, the inspiration of T. S. Eliot's fourth Quartet. The community became known as the Protestant Nunnery, and combined contemplation with a range of crafts including drawing, bookbinding and printing. They eventually produced some of the finest Old Testaments, Acts and Gospels ever made, as much treasured today as any illuminated medieval bible. The death of Ferrar effectively ended the community. The house itself briefly sheltered Charles I on his flight to the Scots at Newark. In retaliation, the Roundheads sacked Little Gidding, in 1647.

Ramsey A fen town, one of the smallest towns in England to have its own mayor. Like so many of the fen islands, it attained early importance with the foundation of the abbey in 969. The abbey survived right through to the general dissolution of the monasteries in the 1530s; little now remains except for one gatehouse in the east of the town, the property of the National Trust. Open: daily. There is talk of reopening the rights of way across the wartime RAF base to Ramsey Heights, but these will presumably be concrete paths of relatively little merit. The best paths lie in Bury Fen (old drove roads) or through the golf course to Bury, another fen island with good views.

Sawtry is a large and expanding village on the A1. The old abbey of St Mary lies south-east of the village, in Sawtry Fen, like most Cistercian houses situated in as isolated a position as could be wished for. Banks and ditches encircled the monastery, still visible today, and more excavations to the north mark the medieval quays and docks of Monk's Lode. This was a key harbour for Sawtry Abbey; in an agreement of 1192 with Ramsey Abbey, the Cistercians agreed to close all their channels between Whittlesey and Ugg Meres 'except that great channel which runs from Whittlesey Mere to Sawtry, which shall remain open, for by it the monks of Sawtry bring stones and such necessaries for the building of their monastery'. The rectangular enclosures of saltpens and fishponds can also be seen.

Upton Large, spired church, two former manor houses, Manor Farm and Christ's College Farm. The village stands on an important drove road, still known as the Bullock Road and a splendid green lane.

Upwood The path between here and Great Raveley commands some fine views across to Wood Walton Fen.

Wood Walton is divided into two parts. To the north is Castle End – the castle being a motte-and-bailey used by Geoffrey de Mandeville prior to his assault on Ramsey. Beyond this and the few houses lies Wood Walton Fen, including the permit-only nature reserve where fen is being allowed to 'grow out' into true woodland. To the south lies Green End, a small village with a pub and some pleasing cottages. The large church stands in the fields between the two, now closed.

RECOMMENDED WALKS

1. **Sawtry – Wood Walton – Upton – Sawtry. 11m. HR.**

Mostly good; the Bullock Rd is excellent.

Start by parking your car in the minor road just E of the A1, S of the stream E of Sawtry. Walk ESE down the broad track here. Where this forks, take the L-hand track ENE into Sawtry Fen. After 1¾m, this turns sharp R (SE). Continue down the black dirt track until it is joined by a ı twin from the R (SW). Climb onto the stream bank there, walk L (SSE) to the bridge and cross. Continue under the railway bridge E and pick up a metalled road ahead. This bends R (SSE) and then L again (E). A right of way leaves the road at this second bend and continues S to the church across the fields; more field walking SSE by S will take the walker across the minor road and ahead into Wood Walton. The road, however, is narrow and quiet, and in my view the preferred track. At the T-junction in Wood Walton, turn L (WSW) under the railway line. The bridleway SSE leaves this road up a field edge opposite the entrance to Abbey Fm. Walk uphill to the wood ahead and then down ahead to the B road. Continue SE down the road and around a bend half-right (S) by a little wood. Pick up a broad track R (W) where the road bends back again; this track continues round several bends but generally SSW to the NE corner of Hill Wood. Turn R (W) here and skirt the N edge of the wood. Continue W briefly along the S side of Bevill's Wood. Then turn half-left (SW). The route goes along a field path but soon picks up a pebbled track to the farm buildings. The official right of way passes L (S) of the farmhouse through an orchard: but the farmer told me that he prefers walkers to turn R (NW) through the yard and then L (SW) down another pebbled drive. Where this bends sharp L (SE) to the wood, the right of way continues across the field under the telegraph poles to the minor road. Most walkers use the field edges. Turn L at the road and go over the A1; at the junction, turn R (NE) and pick up the L (W) verge of the trunk road. Walk N to the parking place, and go through a gate into the field. The right of way goes WNW across the fields to the church; most walkers follow the E and NE hedges of the field to the minor road, and turn L. Visit the church in Upton and pick up Coppingford Lane, immediately to the E of the yard. This becomes a broad unmetalled track WNW and then NNW to the minor road at Coppingford. Turn R (NE) for a long ¼m. Pick up the Bullock Road L (WNW) just before Hill Top Fm and continue along it to the S tip of Aversley Wood, after 1m. Skirt the wood on its SE side and then pick up a hedgeside path ahead (NNE) into the new Sawtry estates. Be sure to take especial care when crossing the trunk road back to your car.

2. **Abbots Ripton – Wennington – King's Ripton Lodge – Abbots Ripton. 6m. HR.**

Easy walking around the attractive country and village of Abbots Ripton.

Start at Abbots Ripton church. Walk briefly up the B1090 NW and then turn off R (NNW) up the Wennington road. Turn R (ESE) in Wennington and follow the road until the edge of Wennington Wood on the R (SE). At this point, turn R (S) down a track skirting the wood on its W side. After ¾m, a broad track leaves the wood to the R (SW); but our route continues to skirt the wood on the S and SE sides, for a further ½m. Where the trees fall away sharply to the L (NW), turn R and pick up a broad track E. Cross the stream and then turn L (ENE) along its S bank to the road. At the minor road, turn R (S). The road soon bends L (E) and then runs on to a crossroads. At that point, turn R (SSW) down the King's Ripton road for nearly 1m. Walk down

Moonshine Gap
Lower Glebe Fm
Inn
B 660
High Haden Fm
Top Lodge
Upper Glebe Fm
Manor Fm
Glatton
Conington
Hemington Ho
Glatton Lodge
Flittermere Lodge
Moat
Beaulieu Hall
Rectory Fm
Glatton Folly
Middlemarsh Fm
Bruce's Castle Fm
Moat
Luddington in the Brook
Lodge Fm
Sawtry
Rectory Fm
Mill
Great Gidding
W T Sta
Top Fm
Green End
LUDDINGTON
Chapel End
Woodfield Fm
Wood End Fm
High Holborn Hill
Manor Farm
Bufflock Rd
Bottom Fm
Cold Harbour Fm
Toll Bar Cottages
Luddington Lodge
Gidding Grove
B 660
Little Gidding
Moat
Averley Wood
Whitehall
Manor Fm
Grange Fm
B 1090
Ermine Street
ROMAN ROAD
Steeple Gidding
Moat
Archer's Wood
Moat
Manor Lodge Fm
Winwick
Hill Top Fm
Coppingford
Coppingford Wood
Lodge
Hamerton Grove
Hamerton
Upton Wood
Mile Brook Br
Grove Fm
Upton Lodge
UPTON AND COPPINGFORD
Cottage Fm
Lodge Fm
Holly Lodge
B 662
B 660
Grange Fm
Upton
Howson's Lodge
High Street
Salome Fm
ROMAN ROAD
Salome Wood
Vinegar Hill
Old Weston
Salome Lodge
Black Lodge
Brook Lodge
Alconbury Weston
B 660
Buckworth
North Lodge Fm
Corner Fm
Top Farm
Fuller's Lodge
LEIGHTON
Park Lodge
Alconbury
East Lodge
Leighton Bromswold
Moat
Barham
Brooklands Fm
Stounch Hill
BARHAM AND WOOLLEY
Woolley Leys Fm
Manor Farm
Woolley
Glebe Fm
Woolley Lodge

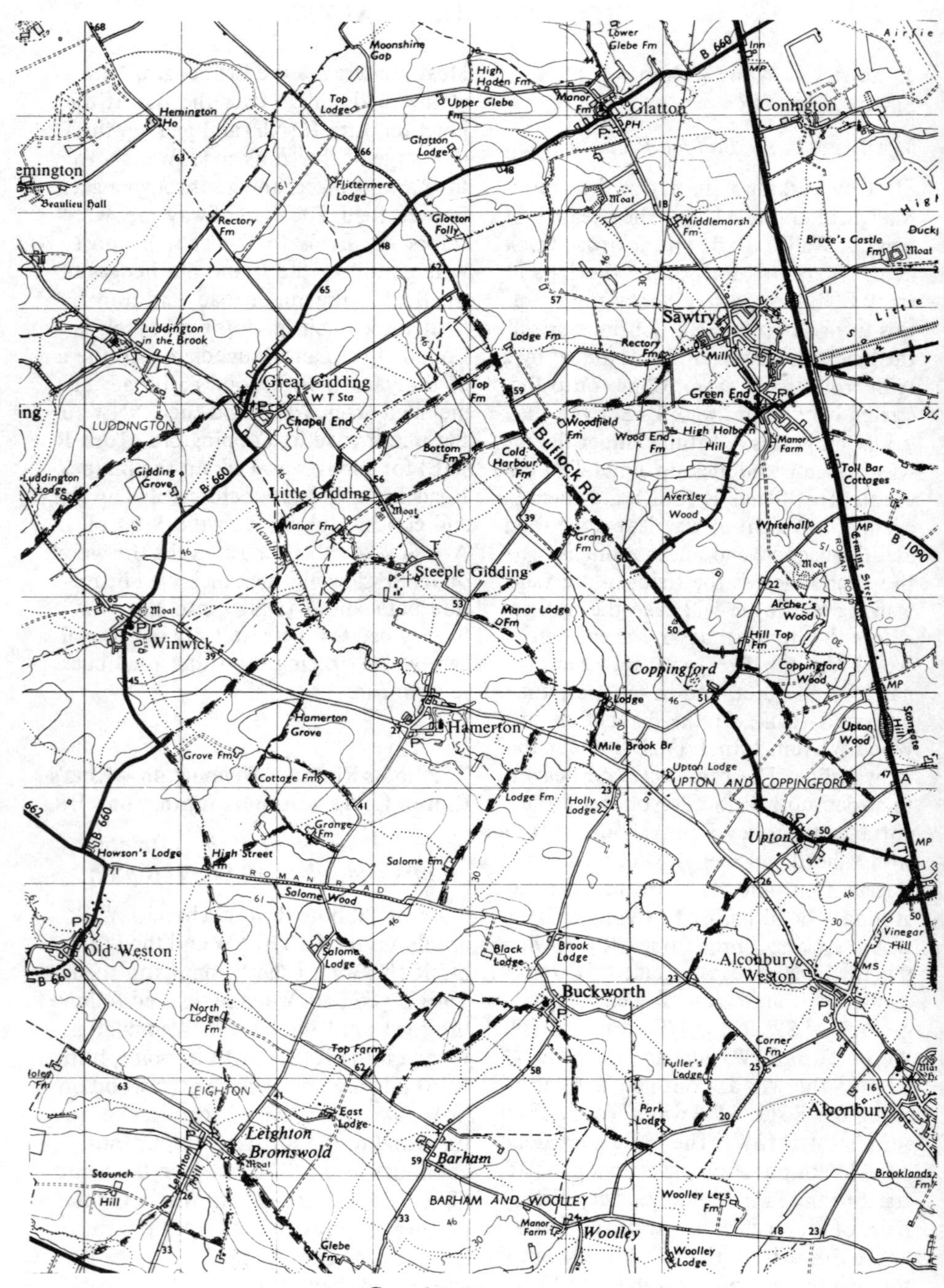

Contd p.55

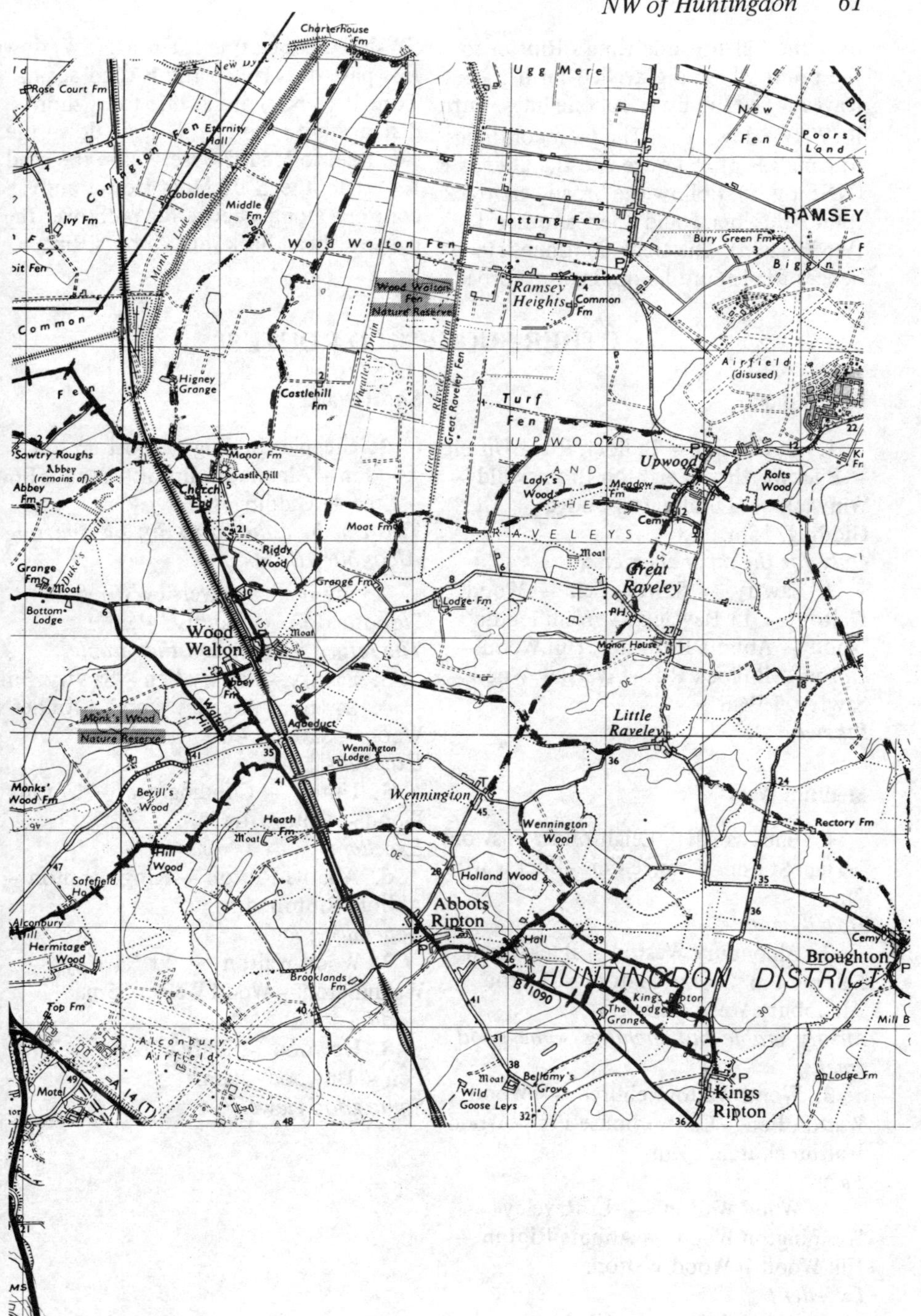
Charterhouse Fm
New Dyke
Ugg Mere
New Fen
Poors Land
Rose Court Fm
Conington Fen
Eternity Hall
Cobalder
Middle Fm
Monk's Lode
Ivy Fm
Lotting Fen
RAMSEY
Wood Walton Fen
Bury Green Fm
Biggin
Ramsey Heights
Common Fm
Wood Walton Fen Nature Reserve
Common
Airfield (disused)
Higney Grange
Castlehill Fm
Wheatley's Drain
Great Raveley Drain
Great Raveley Fen
Turf Fen
UPWOOD AND THE RAVELEYS
Sawtry Roughs
Abbey (remains of)
Abbey Fm
Manor Fm
Castle Hill
Church End
Upwood
Lady's Wood
Meadow Fm
Rolts Wood
Cemy
Moat Fm
Duke's Drain
Riddy Wood
Moat
Great Raveley
Grange Fm
Grange Fm
Lodge Fm
PH
Bottom Lodge
Wood Walton
Manor House
Abbey Fm
Little Raveley
Monk's Wood Nature Reserve
Aqueduct
Wennington Lodge
Monks' Wood Fm
Bevill's Wood
Wennington
Rectory Fm
Heath Fm
Wennington Wood
Hill Wood
Safefield Ho
Holland Wood
Alconbury Hill
Abbots Ripton
Hall
Hermitage Wood
Cemy
Broughton
HUNTINGDON DISTRICT
Brooklands Fm
B 1090
Kings Ripton Lodge
The Grange
Top Fm
Mill B
Alconbury Airfield
Moat
Bellamy's Grove
Lodge Fm
Motel
Wild Goose Leys
Kings Ripton
A 14 (T)

over the hill towards King's Ripton to the point where a gravelled farm track leaves R (WNW) by telephone lines. Turn R (WNW) down this. The path continues to King's Ripton Lodge and then bends R (NNE by N). Follow the broad cart track round this bend and then another L (WNW again). The track continues along hedges for 1m until stopping by a broad SW-NE crossing track. Turn L (SW) down this past the Hall to the B road again. Turn R (WNW) along this for a short distance but then turn R again down the side road to Moat House. Leave the road L (W) to the S of Moat House and continue along a hedgeside path over the pasture ahead back into Abbots Ripton.

OTHER SUGGESTED ROUTES

Day Walks

1. Gt Gidding – Bullock Rd – Upton – Buckworth – Leighton Bromswold – Winwick – Luddington Lodge – Gt Gidding. 15m.
Only for the most energetic.

2. Sawtry – Sawtry Fen – Wood Walton – Lt Raveley – Wennington Wood – Abbots Ripton – Hill Wood – Upton – Bullock Rd – Aversley Wood – Sawtry. 15½m.
Likewise.

Medium Walks

1. Buckworth – Leighton Bromswold – High St Fm – Grange Fm – Buckworth. 7m.
Heavily arable.

2. Alconbury Weston – Buckworth – Salome Fm – Coppingford – Upton – Alconbury Weston. 8m.
Mostly arable but includes some good tracks.

3. Wood Walton church – Wood Walton Fen – Charterhouse Fm – Wood Walton church. 6½m.
Easy.

4. Wood Walton – Lt Raveley – Wennington Wood – Abbots Ripton – Hill Wood – Wood Walton.
Excellent.

5. Wood Walton – Gt Raveley – Moat Fm – Church End – Wood Walton. 7m.
Tracks and headlands.

Short Walks

1. Steeple Gidding – Bottom Fm – Top Fm – Alconbury Brook – Manor Fm – Steeple Gidding. 5m.
This can be reduced to 3m by omitting Alconbury Brook.

2. Sawtry – Aversley Wood – Woodfield Fm – Sawtry. 4½m.
The return journey is rather arable.

3. Sawtry – Sawtry Fen – Sawtry. 3m.

4. Sawtry – Aversley Wood – Archer's Wood – Sawtry. 4m.
Excellent.

5. Upton – Coppingford – Upton Wood – Upton. 4m.
Excellent.

6. Abbots Ripton – King's Ripton – Abbots Ripton. 4m.
Generally good.

7. Wood Walton – Lt Raveley – Wennington – Wood Walton. 5m.
Good.

8. Upwood – Lady's Wood – Turf Fen – Upwood. 3¼m.
Some good views.

4 THE SOKE OF PETERBOROUGH

Peterborough to Stamford; South-west of Peterborough; King's Cliffe District

In addition to the Soke, this chapter also includes a fragment of northern Huntingdonshire, and a few miles outside the boundaries of the county, in Lincolnshire and Northamptonshire. A soke was an Anglo-Saxon district independent of royal justice and administration. Judicial powers were instead granted to a local magnate or major landowner, in this case the great abbey at Medeshamstede (Peterborough). The Soke therefore had a tradition of administrative independence and religious government, but the reasons for this are obscure. It is possible that after the Viking invasion in 870AD, that part of Halfdan's army which made its centre at Stamford defined the area now called the Soke as the limit of their power.

After the dissolution of Peterborough abbey at the Reformation, the Soke came into the possession of the newly created bishopric and then by transfer to the great Cecil family of Burghley. After a period of being counted as part of Northamptonshire, the Soke was established as a separate Victorian county. It was always one of the smallest shires in England. Only as recently as in 1965 was it merged with Huntingdonshire, now part of modern Cambridgeshire.

As a walking area, the Soke and the outlying districts joined with it in this chapter are similar to south of Huntingdon, but the intensively farmed clay stands upon the end of a ridge of limestone extending south-west into Northamptonshire. It is therefore higher above sea level, and there are some considerable hills particularly around King's Cliffe.

Settlement away from the river valleys was almost unknown during the prehistoric period, and the Romans ignored the then forest except to drive their roads through it: Ermine Street, King Street and the road from King's Cliffe to Wansford. Clearance of the forests began in Anglo-Saxon times, and was not completed until the middle ages. Throughout the district clearance was never really completed: the cluster of woods around Castor Hanglands and the forested area around King's Cliffe speak for themselves and south of Peterborough there are still a few corners of original woodland. There are a number of sizeable and prosperous villages between Peterborough and Stamford. For the most part, these are situated on the edge of the hills, overlooking either the Fens or the valley of the Nene. The interior is not merely still very wooded, but almost entirely depopulated. Ufford, Southorpe and Wittering are the exceptions to this rule, but Southorpe lies on the old route of Ermine Street while Wittering has mostly grown up about the air-base. In the south, there are relatively few villages of any size, and some deserted village sites, like Papley and Washingley.

There is only a very short stretch of fen walking, between Helpston and Market Deeping in the valley of the Welland and Maxey Cut. It is very unfortunate that the floodbanks of the river and cut have not been generally opened as public rights of way. The little walking that does exist is mainly good, either in rough fenny meadow or along the headlands of arable fields.

Walking in the valley of the Nene is very reminiscent of the Ouse south of Huntingdon. There are the same broad water meadows and low slopes of pasture, the best rambling to be found in the area. The first evidence of settlement along the river valley visible today is the pair of Bronze Age monoliths east of Castor. This area has also thrown up the earliest finds, some Neolithic axeheads in Orton Longueville. Generally, settlement remained very light until the coming of the Romans. Their impact was major but geographically limited. Castor and Water Newton (Durobrivae) were important both as a junction of Roman roads and the place where the united road crossed the Nene. The wealth of finds from this vicinity includes the Water Newton treasure. During the middle ages, the Nene was fairly important as a trade route, and it is not surprising to find a number of villages upon its banks. These villages are generally the prettiest in the area. Many are built in the creamy-grey stone that is such a feature of the Soke, and comes from the quarries at Barnack and Ketton. There are several magnificent watermills, and stone churches that are grander and much later in date than the simple, often Saxon buildings of the upland settlements. Spires, useful landmarks, are a speciality.

Much of the area is now threatened by the expansion of Peterborough as a new city. The walker around its edges must expect changes in the condition of the routes, and indeed their closure or diversion from year to year. The Development Corporation is however to be commended for its efforts to create a medium-distance continuous path from Peterborough to Wansford, up the Nene valley. This will be by far the best walk in the area, if and when it is completed. The Nene Park in the bend of the river north of Orton Longueville is also a noble undertaking – when not under water.

Peterborough to Stamford

The clay makes for sticky arable walking, often along headlands, but also with a number of ploughed field middles to be negotiated. Signposting is relatively poor, though the waymarking of routes by the active Peterborough RA group has to an extent relieved the problem. In the Nene valley there are broad water meadows and low slopes of pasture – the best rambling in the area.

Ailsworth and **Castor** are now one large village, threatened by possible future development. There are some good stone and timber houses especially in Ailsworth, an excellent pub and a large 12-13c cruciform church at the Castor end, dedicated to St Cynaburge, a 7c Mercian princess who founded a nunnery in Castor. Even in the 7c, however, Castor and Ailsworth were centuries old: they stand on the junction of the two main Roman roads in the district, Ermine Street and King's Street. Excavations in Castor during the 19c uncovered Roman buildings and such a wealth of characteristic pottery that it has given its name to the style. The name, too, deriving from *castra* is one traditionally given to Roman settlements by the early Anglo-Saxon invaders. **Castor Hanglands** and **Ailsworth Heath** make the most delightful upland walking in the district, splendidly wooded and now protected from the bulldozer by its designation as a nature reserve. Hanglands has no gory implications – the name comes from an Old English word meaning hilly wood. The Heath was originally called Emmonsailes, and was then owned by Helpston; the story goes that Ailsworth took it over when Helpston refused to bury a dead man found upon the grass here. The two main tracks in this area are interesting; aligned almost due N-S, they run parallel to and on either side of the line of King Street. The Street is now preserved as the die-straight C road from the north-west corner of the Heath past Helpston and West Deeping. It was definitely used as a drove road in medieval and early modern times, and has been linked by some with the Bullock Road north-west of Huntingdon. The tracks through the Hanglands could therefore be alternative extensions of King Street after the original line had been destroyed.

Ashton With Bainton and Helpston, once part of the huge medieval manor of the Torpel family. Extensive ruins of a large Norman castle with a central keep 20yd across and still partially moated were discovered recently during the deforestation of Lady Wood.

Barnack Barnack has a wealth of cottages built in the local creamy-grey stone, which was actually quarried in the village, the bumpy grassed-in remains of the workings being preserved at Hills and Holes. Barnack stone was widely used throughout the area, and can be found as far afield as Ely cathedral. Barnack was a Saxon village, its name coming from Bernake or Fighter's Oak – a place where justice would have been dispensed in the early days of the Anglo-Saxon occupation. The fine church preserves a great deal of Saxon work. Note particularly the long and short work (cornerstones placed with the longer sides upright and horizontally in alternation). The archaic round arch into the nave and the unusual panels and window openings in the exterior of the tower also betray its early origin. The nave, aisles and chancel date from the 12-13c, the chancel containing one of the most beautiful six-light east windows in England, and leading into the Walcot chapel.

Burghley Burghley House was originally owned by Peterborough abbey, and came into the hands of the Cecil family in 1526; the grand house now standing was built much later in the same century by Lord Burghley, Queen Elizabeth's treasurer. Verrio painted the murals in the Heaven Room, there are silver fire-places, richly decorated state apartments – a great air of affluence. In September the Burghley Horse Trials are held in the park. Open: afternoons in summer, except Mondays and Fridays.

Helpston John Clare was born here in 1793, and his cottage still stands, south of the church. He achieved a surprising and instant success with his first book of poems at the age of 27. The success was never to be repeated. From that time, despite desperate efforts to make a living by a number of unlucky expedients, the poet's life went downhill. The last 23 years of his life were spent in an asylum at Northampton. Clare was a poet of the countryside and violently opposed the Enclosure Acts that were taking away the freedom of the people to roam over the commons as they chose. In our own time, he would doubtless have been a pillar of the local Ramblers' Association. The village lies on the edge of the Fens, the best part of Helpston about the old crossroads, with several old cottages, an early 14c village cross, and a memorial to Clare. There are two pubs: the Blue Bell (Clare's local) and the Exeter Arms, the latter being the old court-house in days when Helpston was a market town. This market was held at the heart-shaped foot of the buttercross, and sellers would be required to swear by the heart of the cross concerning the quality and value of their wares. The countryside around Helpston is mainly arable, but has some pleasant little woods. To the south of Hilly Wood stands Swaddy Well, where stone was quarried for Ermine Street; a villa uncovered at nearby Oxey Wood was also built in stone from this quarry. Daniel Crowson's *Rambles with John Clare* explores the poet's connections with the surrounding countryside in more detail.

Longthorpe This old village is becoming absorbed by the expansion of the city. Longthorpe Tower, a fortified medieval manor house, in the care of the Department of the Environment, contains the most comprehensive series of 14c murals in this country. The subjects are both religious and lay, including the five senses, the work of the seasons, the apostles and the ages of man. Open: daily except Monday all day and Tuesday morning.

Market Deeping A large market town on the Welland beside the Fens. There is an excellent inn, the Bull, and some fine stone cottages and houses about the Market Place and Church Street. The church is dedicated to St Guthlac, the Saxon saint who established the abbey across the fens on Crowland Island.

Maxey A fen village with a 14c fortified manor house at the north end of Pound Lane. The church, a mile west of the main village, has arcaded Norman tower and Lady Chapel with window tracery. Lolham Bridges are 17c, but their predecessors on the same site can be dated back to the Romans. There is also a fine mill in Maxey, restored to working order.

Milton Park A right of way cutting through the golf course, south of the hall, home of the earls of Fitzwilliam, hidden behind trees.

Peterborough Greater Peterborough is now swallowing up large areas of the surrounding countryside, particularly towards Milton Park. I personally found the design of its new estates quite interesting, with their walkways and enclosed courtyards, but it is clearly not a place to incorporate on a country walk. The old city has a cathedral with painted roof, but is remarkable for the ease with which a walker can head for the country: footpaths follow the bank of the Nene almost from the very centre of the town.

Sibson Stone hamlet surrounded by the river on three sides with some attractive water meadows.

Southorpe At the point where the footpath to Thornhaugh leaves Ermine Street, look across the road; one of the fields contains banks, ditches and a fish-pond remaining from a hospital of Peterborough abbey established here in the 13c.

Stamford Like a small cathedral town, with numerous excellent buildings, mostly in the same grey stone as the lovely bridge over the Welland. A morning's walk in the surrounding countryside followed by an afternoon in the town make a splendid day. Paths cross two pleasant parks: Uffington, north-east of Stamford, and Burghley Park to the south-east, landscaped by Capability Brown. See Burghley above.

Stibbington Home of the Nene Valley Railway, with many interesting old steam engines and miles of track. Steam train trips most weekends April to December, some weekdays in summer.

Sutton Some stone cottages typical of the area, as well as an estate of modern houses that has won praise from architectural experts. At one end of the estate stands Manor Farm, a beautiful 17c house. The medieval church is separated from the main part of the village by the deep cutting of the old Wansford – Barnack railway line.

Thornhaugh At the foot of a steep little valley, the main street going up the west slope of the hill, to the large 18c manor house at the top.

Ufford The church is 14c, and commands some good views over the Welland valley. There is also an excellent pub.

Wansford A large and pleasant village, almost entirely constructed in Barnack or Ketton stone on a steep little hill in the Nene valley with the woodland of Old Sulehay Forest to the south-west. At the foot of the hill, beside the Nene, is the 13c church, and nearby an attractive row of thatched stone cottages, an unusual combination of materials. South of the river across the old bridge stands Wansford-in-England, with a famous coaching inn, the Haycock.

West Deeping A pleasant stone village similar to those in the Stamford district. 18c houses include the Red Lion pub.

Wittering Terribly affected with noise from the nearby RAF base. The church has a Saxon nave and chancel, with much long-and-short work and a characteristically massive chancel arch. It is one of the best preserved pre-Norman churches in the country.

Woodcroft The castle is really a fortified manor house, with a forbidding round tower from which a royalist chaplain fell to his death trying to escape the Roundheads during the Civil War.

Yarwell A number of thatched and stone cottages, church on the bend of the road. The 13c chancel has both north and south chapels.

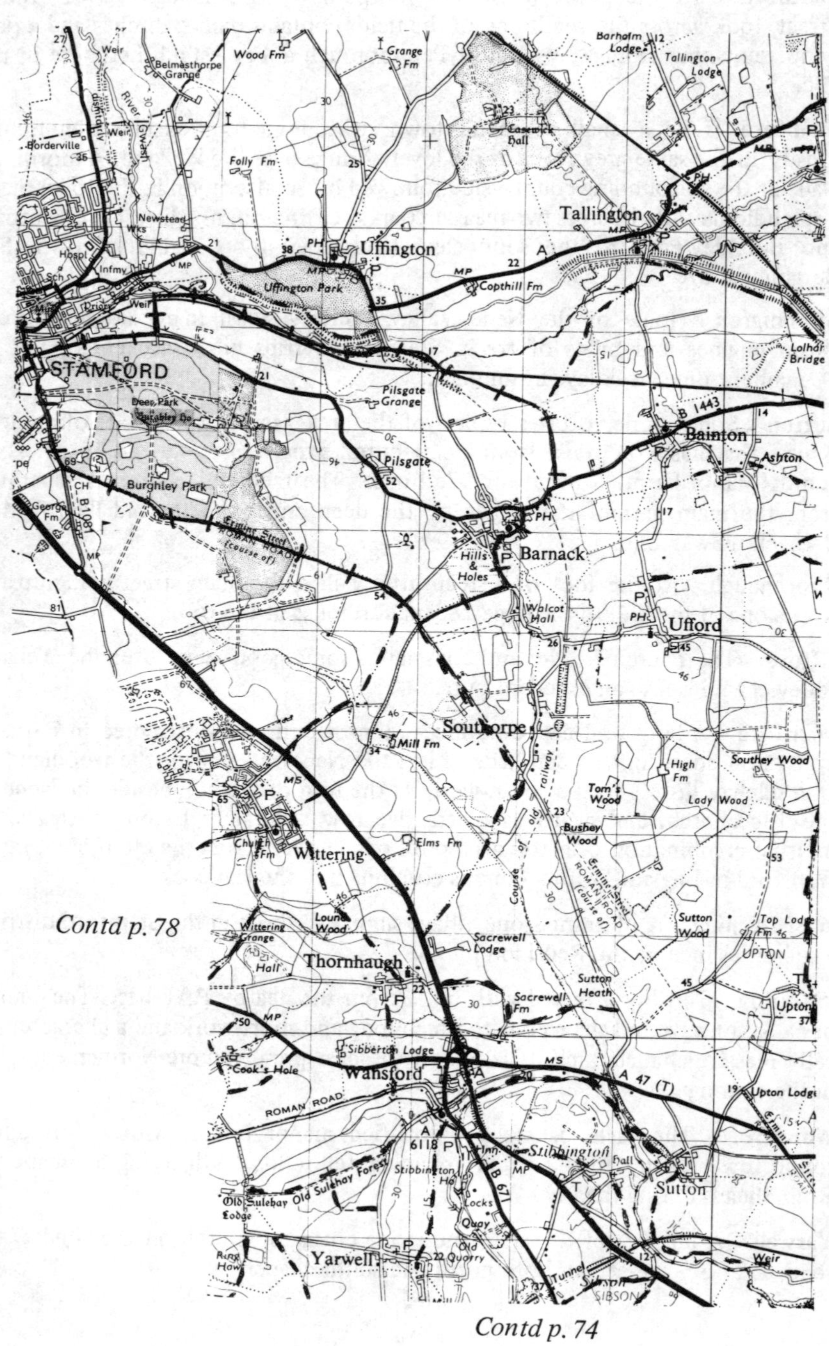

Contd p. 78

Contd p. 74

RECOMMENDED WALKS

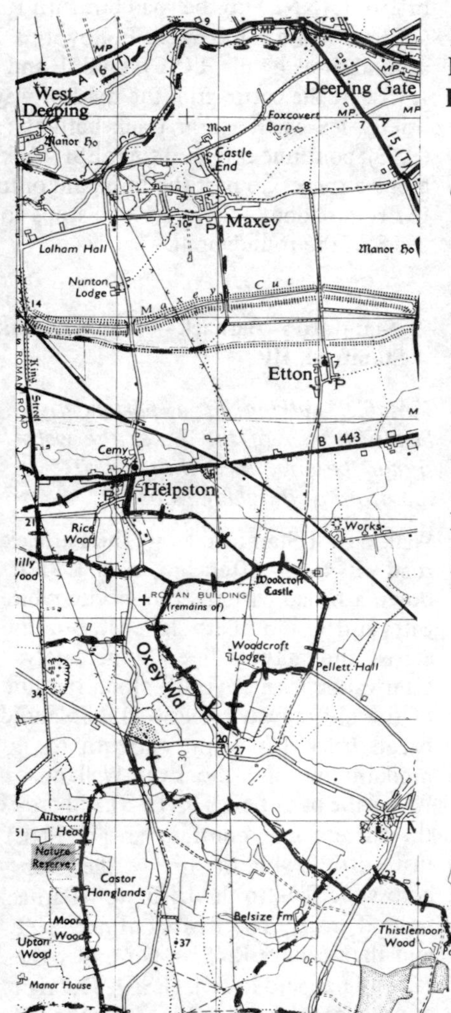

1. **Peterborough – River Nene – Castor Hanglands – Park Fm – Bretton. 12½m. R.**

Only for the energetic rambler and the able map reader.

Start in Bridge St and pick up a lane opposite the Scout Shop. This almost immediately bends L (S) and continues to the river just E of the first railway bridge. Pick up the towpath along the N bank of the Nene here and walk W along it. Go under the railway bridges and on for 1½m to Orton lock. Continue under the road bridge here and on along the riverbank. After a further ½m, cross a little inlet over the footbridge thoughtfully provided and continue ahead. The river here swings increasingly to the R (NNW), with excellent views over Nene Park (when not under water). Go past the footbridge into the park however and continue along the bank to the edge of Bluebell Wood. Pick up the gravel track NE and then L (NW) around the woods: this is not a right of way, but has been opened to the public on a permissive basis by the Development Corporation. Turn L (W) along the A47 for ½m to the W edge of Milton Park at Milton Ferry. Turn R (N) here up the edge of the trees for ½m until they turn away half-right (NNE). At that point, turn L (WNW) along a track to the minor road. Cross the road and continue ahead under pylons and across a crossing SW-NE footpath ½m later. Just after the second crossing of pylon lines, the track turns L and continues W and SW to the Ailsworth-Helpston road. Turn R (N) for ¼m and then L (W) along a broad cart track. At the crossing track, turn R (N) into the nature reserve of Castor Hanglands and Ailsworth Heath. This path can be very muddy in wet weather. Continue for over 1m to the N edge of the nature reserve. From here, the path swings R (E) around a quarry to the minor road. Turn L (N) down the road and then R (ESE) at the crossroads. Leave the road R (S) after a short distance down an overgrown field edge; this broad 'path' continues to the field edge running E from the tip of the wood. At its end, enter the next field and bear very slightly L (SSE) across it to an old gatepost and hedge. Look diagonally across this field E to the left-hand of the two woods. This is where you want to get to. Follow the field edges on the S and E sides and continue to the trees. Skirt the trees on their N edge (SE). At their SE edge, look ahead to the next wood and continue to its right-hand (S) edge. The right of way lies through the wood ESE, but I could not find it; it is perfectly possible however to skirt the wood on its SW side and then walk slightly L (NE) up its SE edge. From here, continue down the gentle slope and over the stream to the minor road. Walk briefly L (NNE) up the road but turn R (ESE) down a farm track. Follow this around three bends R (SE), L (ESE and R (S). At the cattle-grid, the right of way briefly leaves the farm track half-left (SSE); continue SSE and then ESE back along a track. Go past the farm and onto the roundabout. There are bus stops to the S of the roundabout.

2. Stamford – Barnack – Burghley Park – Stamford. HR.

Variable walking in a particularly beautiful part of the Soke: the walk should be combined with a visit to Stamford or Burghley House.

Walk out of Stamford along the Barnack road (B1443). After ¾m, turn L (N) down a broad cart track opposite white gates and by a footpath signpost. Continue across the railway line. Immediately afterwards, turn R (ESE) along the line of the old railway. Follow this splendid broad track for 1¼m, between the modern line and the river Welland. Where the bank bends R (ESE) and crosses the current line, continue ahead (ENE) instead following the line of the river across the field to the Uffington-Barnack road. Turn R. The road continues ESE and then swings R (SE). Go under the railway line and look L (ESE). The right of way lies on that bearing across the field for over ½m. Most walkers instead skirt the field edge by the railway line E. Eventually, turn R (SSW by S) down a good field edge track and follow for nearly ¾m to the B1443. Turn R (WSW) into Barnack. Leave Barnack on the minor road to Ufford. After ¾m, turn R (WSW) down a broad track skirting the ancient wall and woods of Walcot Hall park. Follow this for over ½m to the minor road. Turn R (NNW). Go past one side road R (NNE) to the point where the road forks. The official right of way continues ahead over the field WNW to the left-hand telegraph pole; most walkers walk L (WSW) along the road to the field edge and then R (ENE) along the wall to the pole. There, turn L (WNW) under the poles to the edge of Burghley Park. Go through the gate, down the grass track and over a crossing track. Continue under trees to a huge wheatfield with two telegraph poles in it. It is easy to mistake the right of way here: a good grass path runs W from the left-hand pole to a pebbled track by buildings; turning R there will even bring the walker to the same park gate that is our aim. This is not however the footpath, despite appearances. The right of way instead continues WNW past the right-hand telegraph pole and diagonally over two ploughed fields to the edge of the grassed parkland. Continue ahead there down a line of trees, through another belt of woodland and along the sunken wall by the lodge. Walk round the back of the lodge to the park gate and go left to the junction of tracks just outside it. Turn R (WNW) along the broad track between the wall and the golf course to the B1081. Turn R (NNW) and follow back into Stamford.

3. **Helpston – Woodcroft Castle – Oxey Wood – Hilly Wood – Helpston. 5¾m. R.**

Shorter walks:

Helpston – Woodcroft Castle – Hilly Wood – Helpston. 3m. HR.

Woodcroft Castle – Oxey Wood – Maxham's Green Lane – Woodcroft Castle. 4m. HR.

A lot of fieldwork, but normally well trodden: the publicity given to this walk by Daniel Crowson's booklet and Country Walks *seems to have had a beneficial result.*

Start at Helpston church and walk down the Ailsworth road S past John Clare's cottage. Go past a side road joining from the R (WSW) and enter the field to your L (E) shortly afterwards, over a stile. The route crosses the field E, goes down a short fenced track ahead and then E again over the rest of the field to the W edge of a hedge. Continue E along the S edge of that hedge until it bends sharply R (S). Push through here into the next field and cross the field half-right (SE) to the barn and farm track ahead. Continue on this bearing past the farm buildings and over two small fields, towards the trees. At the broad crossing track, the long and short routes divide. If on the short walk, turn R (WSW) and follow Maxham's Green Lane round two slight right-hand bends (W and WNW) to the minor road. Otherwise, turn L (ENE) to the minor road W of Woodcroft castle. Turn R and follow the road for a long ½m, round a bend R (SSW by S) after ¼m. Where the road bends sharply L (SE), turn R (W) down the pebbled driveway of the redbrick farm buildings (Pellett Hall). (The right of way in fact parallels the driveway to the S, but every-body uses the drive.) After ¼m, turn L (S) through a gate by the ditch. The path continues SSW from here round the N and W edges of Hayes Wood to the ditch at its SW corner. Turn very sharply R (NW) here over three fields to the E edge of the woodland. Skirt Oxey Wood to its NE corner and pick up a track NNE by N to Maxham's Green Lane. Turn L (WNW) along this to the minor road and turn L (SW). At the next bend L (S), pick up a signposted footpath R (W). Follow this W beside a ditch for a long ½m, to the next minor road. Turn R (N) here up King Street. Go past a side road R (E) and then turn R (E) into the second field. Cross this ahead E, then turn half-left and continue ENE across more fields back into Helpston.

OTHER SUGGESTED ROUTES

Weekend Walk

Peterborough – River Nene Path – Wansford – Thornhaugh – Southorpe – Ermine St – Burghley Park – Stamford (overnight stop). Stamford – Uffington Park – Barnack – Ufford – Hilly Wood – Oxey Wood – Marholm – Bretton. Day 1: 16m. Day 2: 12m.
Fairly heavy going in this soil. A reduced walk to Wansford is an alternative. Both depend on the completion of the riverside path, scheduled for 1982-3.

Day Walks

1. Wansford – Sacrewell Fm – Upton – Milton Pk – River Nene Path – Wansford. 11½m.
This may be reduced to 10m by substituting Castor for Milton Park.

2. Wansford – Sutton – Sibson – Elton – Park Spinney – Nassington – Old Sulehay Forest – Wansford. 12m.
This can be reduced to 10½m by taking a direct line from Elton to Nassington.

3. Barnack – Ufford – Hilly Wood – Maxham's Green Lane – Woodcroft Castle – Helpston – Ashton – Barnack. 10m.
Generally arable.

4. Helpston – Maxey – West Deeping – Tallington – Barnack – Ufford – Hilly Wood – Helpston. 10m.
Likewise.

Medium Walks

1. Castor – River Nene Path – Longthorpe Tower – Milton Pk – Castor. 9m.
Mostly good paths with some excellent meadow walking.

2. Ailsworth – Upton – Sutton – Ailsworth. 6¼m.
Enjoyable and varied: depends however on the completion of the Nene Path.

3. Ailsworth – Castor Hanglands – Belsize Fm – Ailsworth. 6½m.
Quite a lot of fieldwork.

4. Sutton – Stibbington – Wansford – Yarwell – Sibson (see maps p.00) – Sutton. 6m.
A good walk.

5. Barnack – Ufford – Helpston – Ashton – Barnack. 6¼m.
Mainly arable.

6. Market Deeping – Maxey – Lolham Bridges – West Deeping – Market Deeping. 7m.
Some good riverbank walking and Maxey's beautiful bridges.

7. Wansford – Thornhaugh – Wittering – Wittering Grange – Cook's Hole – Old Sulehay Forest – Wansford. 6m.
Surprisingly good conditions underfoot.

Short Walks

1. Nene Path – Milton Pk – Longthorpe Tower – Nene Path. 5m.
Well trodden paths.

2. Castor – Milton Pk – Nene Path – Castor. 3½-4½m.
Likewise.

3. Ailsworth – Castor Hanglands – 37 – Ailsworth. 4¾m.
Variable.

4. Wansford – Old Sulehay Forest – Yarwell – Wansford. 3m.
Good and easy.

5. Wansford – Thornhaugh – Sutton Heath – Nene Path – Wansford. 4¾m.
Variable.

6. Barnack – Southorpe – Hills & Holes – Barnack. 3¼m.
A well-used walk.

7. Bainton – Ufford – Helpston – Ashton – Bainton. 4½m.
Mostly arable.

8. Maxey – Lolham Bridges – King Street – Maxey. 4¾m.
Fen walking, mostly on raised banks.

9. Market Deeping – West Deeping – Market Deeping. 5m.
Excellent meadow and riverside ramble.

10. Stamford – Uffington Pk – Old Railway Line – Stamford. 5m.
Another old favourite.

South-west of Peterborough

Clayey soil means heavy walking conditions in mainly arable country. In the southern part of the area there are very few villages – many with declining populations – and fewer walkable footpaths.

Alwalton Still relatively free of development. 12c church and 18c hall with mullioned and transomed windows.

Elton The Black Horse inn stands with the church at the Over End part of Elton, along the A605 towards Warmington. The village is almost totally built in the local stone, with the best of the cottages being in Duck St near the green, and a grassy area next to the watermill.

Fotheringay 19c estate cottages mix with several medieval houses, including the Old and New inns. The church began life as a college attached to Fotheringay's castle, now only a grass-covered mound and ditches beside the footpath from Warmington. It was here that Mary Queen of Scots was kept for the year preceding her execution in 1597. The site now is incredibly peaceful, and difficult to associate with that tempestuous and unfortunate queen.

Morborne A small village, but the largest in this part of the district, with 12-13c church.

Nassington Octagonal church tower and spire guarded by host of gargoyles. Remnants of 14c wall-paintings between the windows of the north aisle. A cemetery of 50 early Saxon skeletons was discovered near the church. In the middle ages, it was large enough to have two manor houses, both visible today. One is a 15c building, the other a farm originally built for the Prebendary of the Nassington stall in Lincoln cathedral. The farm has a remarkable dovecote over 24ft high accommodating over a thousand birds. The pub is the Black Horse.

Stilton This fairly large village stands on the line of the A1, but has now been bypassed, leaving it quiet but with an air of abandon. This is where the cheese known as Stilton, but really a Leicestershire cheese, came to be put on the coach for London.

Warmington Pretty watermill in the meadows by Eaglethorpe, 13c church, fine stone cottages and a pub.

Water Newton Now tiny, a little to the east stood the great Roman town of Durobrivae, on the junction of Ermine and King Streets. Little of this town remains visible, but look out for archaeological diggings on the path between here and Castor, and for ambitious amateurs everywhere with metal detectors. It was in these fields that just such an amateur discovered the famous Water Newton treasure, a remarkable hoard of late Roman silverware currently in the British Museum.

Contd p. 68

Contd p. 78

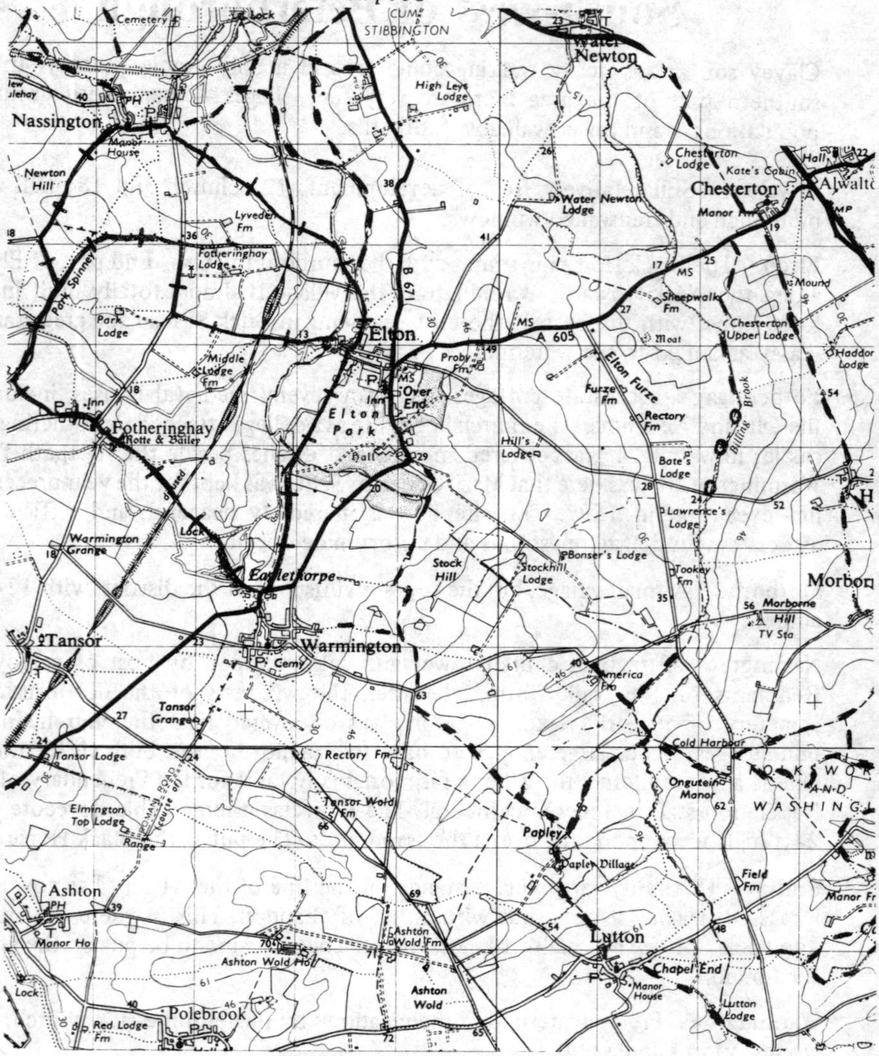

RECOMMENDED WALK

Nassington – Elton – Warmington – Fotheringay – Nassington. 8m. VHR.

Shorter walks:

Elton – Park Spinney – Nassington – Elton. 5½m. HR.

Elton – Warmington – Fotheringay – Elton. 7m. VHR.

Some good walking taking in the beauty of Elton and the historical interest of Fotheringay.

Start at the Black Horse in Nassington, just S of the T-junction at the E edge of the village. Walk S along the road past the first footpath signpost. At the second, turn L into the field. The path lies ESE across fields to Elton. Cross the first field diagonally, then ahead to a wooden gate,

then along a field edge. When this turns abruptly L (N), continue ahead to and over the railway line. Look ahead to the stand of trees ESE. Go diagonally over the next field towards their R-hand (S) edge and ahead to the black bridge. Cross the Nene here. Turn R (SSE) across the field and through the trees L (E) of the farmhouse to the driveway. Turn L along this and then R (S) at the crossing path to the road. Continue S here into Elton. Walk through the village and down Chapel Lane. A well-trodden track continues from its SSW end along the edge of the park and then through it ahead to the trees at its S edge. Cross a broad track before the trees and continue half-left through them to pick up a path between the E edge of a N-S belt of trees and the open fields. At the end of the trees, continue along a low wire fence to the road. Walk briefly R (WSW) down the A605. Where it bends sharp L (S), continue ahead under the trees and down the little street called Eaglethorpe. Pick up the signposted footpath at its end to the mill. Cross the bridge and go over a stile into the meadows. Bear half-right from the river (WNW) across the meadow to the second bridge, and then ahead to the green lock gates L (W) of the wood. Cross. Look half-left over the meadow to Fotheringay church. Cross the meadow slightly L of this to a gate. Pick up a cart track ahead over the railway line and down pasture into Fotheringay. Where this joins a more definite track from the R, turn L (WNW) past the castle mound and farm. Continue W down the village street past the post office to the last house in the village. Pick up the track R (NW) before the copse and follow for ⅓m to the L of another belt of trees. Turn R (NNE) here down a broad track. This continues for ¾m before turning half-left (NNW) away from the trees to the road. Turn R and follow the road back into Nassington. If on the short walk, however, you should ignore the bend in the track and continue ahead along the belt of trees to its N tip. At that point, turn R (E) down a good track to the minor road and turn R (S). After about ½m, turn L (E) down a broad cart track. Follow this for over ½m until it goes over the railway line and into a huge arable field. Keep on the cart track as it bends L (N) into the field and pick up a path R (E) along the S bank of a ditch. At its end, continue ahead over the field to a large isolated tree and then follow the river L (NE) to the first of the bridges. Go past the mill into Elton.

OTHER SUGGESTED ROUTES

Day Walk

Water Newton – Elton – Stock Hill – Papley – Billing Brook – Chesterton – Water Newton. 14m.
A great variety of paths.

Medium Walks

1. Elton – Over End – Warmington – Eaglethorpe – Elton Pk – Elton. 6m.
Fair.

2. Haddon – Morborne – Cold Harbour – Billing Brook – Haddon. 6m.
Mostly arable and with a long stretch of country lane to finish.

3. Stilton – Folksworth – Caldecote – Denton – Stilton. 6m.
A good walk in an area of deserted villages.

Short Walks

1. Stilton – Folksworth – Washingley – Caldecote – Denton – Stilton. 5m.
Good.

2. Morborne – Folksworth – Morborne. 3¼m.
Variable. Quite a lot of road.

King's Cliffe District

Good varied walking, with forest, farmland and waterside.

Apethorpe The hall now a school, and not open. A Roman villa was discovered in the grounds of the hall. The valley of the Willow Brook between here and King's Cliffe is very pretty.

Duddington At the N end of the forests, on the river Welland. Most houses built in stone from the nearby Ketton quarries. By the river is a 17c watermill and a medieval bridge.

King's Cliffe The largest village for some miles, situated in a valley with woods rising quite steeply to either side and surrounded by the splendid woodlands of Cliffe Forest. There is a fine inn.

Southwick Deep in a little valley among wooded hills, with some extremely good walking on either side. There are many good stone cottages. Southwick also has a splendid pub, the Shuckburgh Arms.

Woodnewton Dominated by 12-13c church with Tudor tower and 15c clerestory.

RECOMMENDED WALK

King's Cliffe – Cliffe Forest – Fineshade – Blatherwycke – King's Cliffe. 7m. HR.

Some magnificent brookside and forest walking interspersed with overgrown and arable paths.

Start at the church by Hall Yard. Take the L track out of Hall Yard ESE past buildings and over the stream (Willow Brook). Cross the meadow ahead to the stiles and the green lane. Turn R (W) here for ½m to farm buildings and then R (NNW) down a broad unmade road towards houses. Cross the brook again and continue over the road into the lane. This soon becomes a broad, rough track ahead (NNW) up the hill. The lane bears L (W) through a forestry yard and then for a long mile through Cliffe Forest on the same bearing. The track then bends R (NNW) and goes through two similar turns to the road at Top Lodge. Turn R (W) down the hill and over the old railway cutting. Turn immediately L here over the signposted stile and cross into the field on your R. (Do not follow the path beside the cutting.) The path is difficult at times to follow. Clearances and planting have altered the shape of the wood ahead from that on the map. Adopt a SSW bearing with the hedge on your L. Follow that bearing to the wood, go over the fence and pick up a path ahead. This narrow grass track itself alters direction, but eventually leads to a clearing and a broader cart track leading off to the R (SSE). Take this to the road and turn R (W) past Blatherwycke Lake to the village. Walk through the village SSE. Where the road bends sharp R (SW), turn L past stone buildings onto a broad track bearing NE. Follow this past the church and round a copse. Where the track divides, continue ahead (NNE) with trees on your L and a field R. Continue along field paths past the lake and fields S of the brook to Alders Fm. Go past the farmhouse into the first field and then cross R (E) into

Bonemills Fm
Collyweston Great Wood
Collyweston Cross Roads
Duddington
Hall
Sluice
Tixover
Cemy
Inn
Wittering Lodge
Home Fm
Easton Horstocks
Wittering Coppice
Westhay Fm
Cross Leys Fm
North Spinney
Bedford Purlieus
FC
Wakerley Oaks
Westhay Lodge
St John's Wood Fm
Burton Wood
Law's Lawn
Sand Pit
Top Lodge
Great Wood
Westhay Wood
Huskisson's Lodge
Great Byards Sale
Dams Wood
Lynn Wood
King's Cliffe
Sch
Inn
dismantled railway
Great Morton Sale
Quarry (dis)
Alders Fm
Clay Pit
Bluefield
Shortwood Fm
Park
Blatherwycke Lake
Blatherwycke
Apethorpe
Hall
Spa Fm
Newton Spinney
Hostage Wood
Cadge Wood
Tomlin Wood
Lodge Fm
Woodnewton
PH
Bulwick
Willow Brook
Morehay Lawn
A43(T)
A47(T)
Blackmore Thick Fm
Boar's Head Fm
Halefield Lodge
Bulwick Lodge
Shire Hill Lodge
Stone Hill
Southwick Grange
Perio Mill
Fern Hill Wood
Crossway Hand Fm
Southwick
Forest Lodge
Southwick Wood
Weir
River Nene
Burn Coppice
Wymond Hill
Short Wood
Wr Twr
Cotterstock Lodge
Provost Lodge
Glapthorn Cow Pasture
Cotterstock
ROMAN
FOREST

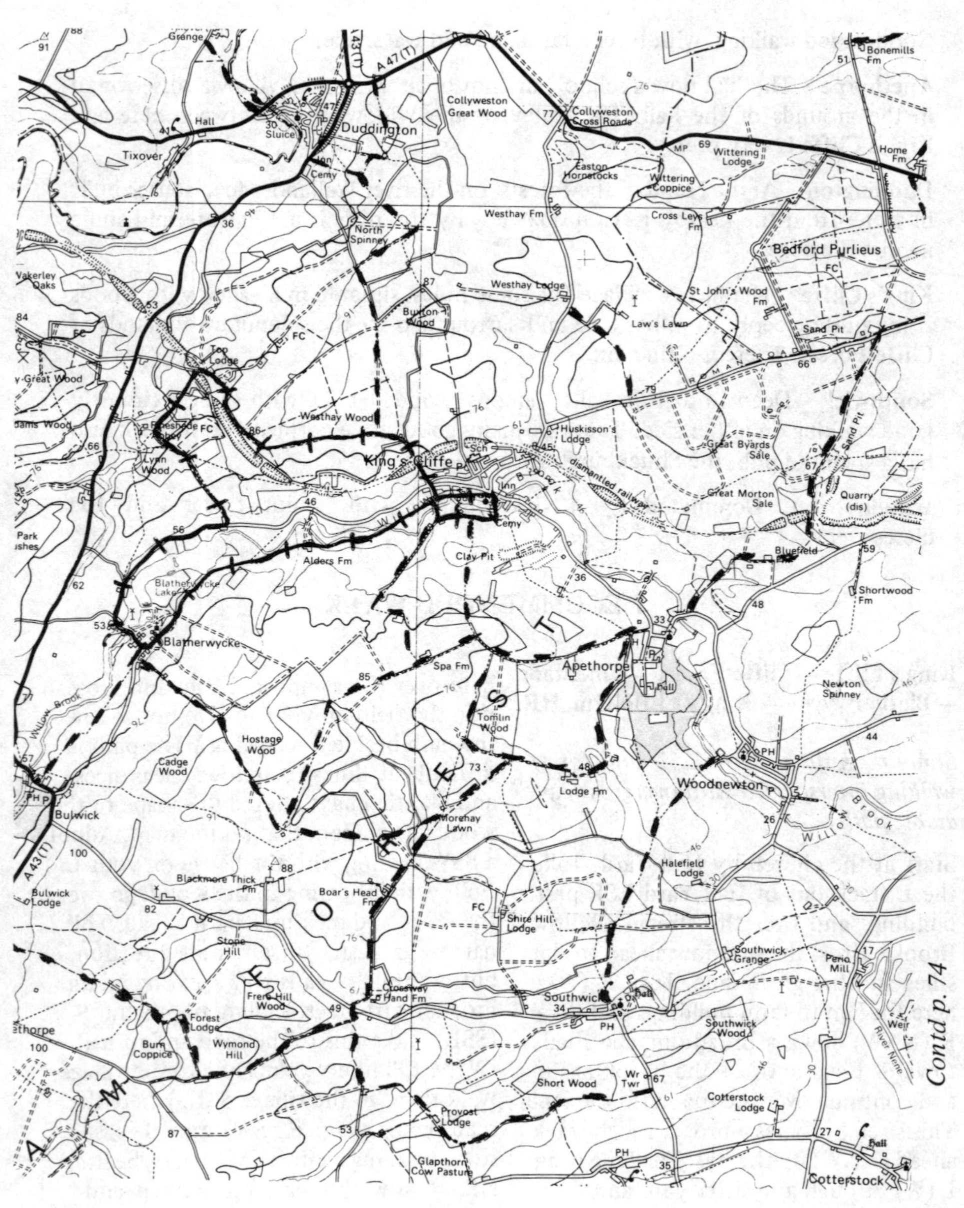

Contd p. 74

the second meadow. Cross to the brook. Continue along the S bank of the charming Willow Brook past arable and pasture to an excellent white bridge over the stream onto its N side. Continue ENE through pastures on the N bank to exit onto Orchard Lane over a gate. Cross, go down Church Walk to Maltings Lane, turn R and follow back to the church.

OTHER SUGGESTED ROUTES

Day Walk

King's Cliffe – Apethorpe – Woodnewton – Southwick – Provost Lodge – Hostage Wood – Blatherwycke – Westhay Wood – King's Cliffe. 14m.
This good walk can be reduced to 12m by taking the Willow Brook route between Blatherwycke and King's Cliffe.

Medium Walks

1. King's Cliffe – Alder's Fm – Blatherwycke – Cliffe Forest – King's Cliffe. 6½m.
Enjoyable walking with a river, lake and forest.

2. Apethorpe – Woodnewton – Southwick – Boar's Head Fm – Cheesman's Fm – Apethorpe. 9m.
Some good tracks and a few difficult patches.

Short Walks

1. King's Cliffe – Lynn Wood – Cliffe Forest – King's Cliffe. 4½m.
Not as easy as it looks.

2. Apethorpe – King's Cliffe – Spa Fm – Apethorpe. 4m.
Arable and farm tracks.

5 SOUTH-EAST ESSEX

Rochford Hundred; Dengie Hundred

Dengie and Rochford Hundreds, between Maldon and Southend, are less walked than any other part of Essex in spite of the proximity of the spreading suburbs of Southend. Many ramblers would dismiss south-east Essex entirely but there are excellent walks if you only know where to look, walks that can stand comparison with any other area.

At first sight, this would seem improbable. The landscape of south-east Essex is either urban and suburban sprawl (the particular problem of Rochford Hundred) or modern arable farming, which can be found in both districts but is especially predominant in Dengie. The urban sprawl is associated with the growth of Southend-on-Sea and its satellites during the last hundred years under the triple pressures of holidays, manufacturing and commuting. A glance at the map of Rochford Hundred shows how development has swallowed up the original, backward area of farming and fishing interests, and outside the towns the country is now mainly given over to intensive cultivation of corn and root vegetables, with few hedges or even field boundaries along which to make a decent path. This arable factory reaches its zenith in the Dengie Hundred. There are no woods here, and very few copses. Footpaths too are at a premium in both districts, and are few in number. Signposting is up to the very high Essex standard, but this almost makes matters worse; all to often, the post points the walker across the middle of an enormous ploughed field.

If this were the entire truth, there would be few reasons to walk here. Although many walkers find themselves fascinated by this strange, flat land, nowhere more than three hundred feet above sea level and usually under one hundred, this would not itself be sufficient attraction to be able to recommend other walkers to use the area. The real reason lies in the third type of landscape for which the area is famous: the marshes and coastal estuaries along the banks of the Roach, Crouch and Blackwater rivers. The marshes are as wild and desolate as anywhere in England. In area, they exceed the famous marshes of the north Norfolk coast, and here, as in the Fens or the Norfolk saltmarshes, the flatness of the land distorts all sense of time and distance. Large areas of the marshes are now drained and used for arable, but even more remain as rough pasture occasionally cropped by herds of the more sturdy breeds of cattle. Closer to the sea, pasture disappears and only marshland remains. The marshes are criss-crossed by drainage channels rather than fences or hedges. To navigate in such a landscape, a map and compass are essential; to survive and enjoy the experience, take the strongest boots. These marshes and the land beyond them were grazed by sheep in the middle ages, but now even this has become uneconomic. In the face of total absence of any modern intrusions, the slightest feature of the landscape assumes a disproportionate significance.

Dengie Hundred was originally forested clay in the interior, so that the oldest settlements cling to the point where the inlands and marshes met. Iron Age remains have been found along the line from Burnham to Bradwell, while most of the churches in the Hundred incorporate some Roman material from either the road or the great fort at Othona, east of Bradwell-juxta-Mare. Here too is England's oldest church, the little 7c chapel of St Cedd, between Bradwell Marshes and the sea. The marshes themselves have changed relatively little since the days when Cedd sailed round here from Northumbria; there are still Roman saltings, red mounds where brine was evaporated in clay containers. The duck decoy ponds, once found all over the land, may have gone, but most of the birdlife remains.

The marshes differ widely from the coastal estuaries. These have their own atmosphere, although the elements that make up their character are similar to those of the marshes: rough grasses, ungrazed wastelands, drainage channels and a mass of birdlife. The river estuaries, however, have more: white-sailed yachts and the occasional bigger craft; fishermen and fishing villages; Thames barges and yachts; broad views across the rivers to the banks and hills on the other side; and above all, the continual flow of the tides, exposing and covering mudflats, flooding and draining the little channels, lapping against the base of the sea wall. Estuary walking is usually along these sea walls, and, the paths through the marshes being few and difficult, it is often from them that the walker enjoys the rough marsh landscape, as well as the water on the seaward side. The sea wall is above all the reason why south-east Essex is such a good walking area. In by far the majority of cases these banks are public rights of way – and they always provide a magnificent walking surface. They are usually between five and ten feet above the land to either side, and covered in rough grasses and brine-loving plants. Only in rare cases is the seaward side concreted. The path along the top is narrow, but well trodden. There is a perpetual breeze even on the stillest day, and magnificent views both inland over the marshes and out over the water.

In addition to the marshes and estuaries there are two pockets in the area where ramblers can find different country. These are at Hadleigh and Hockley. Hadleigh Marshes are very similar to those of the Dengie peninsula, although the evidence of human life is always more pressing, but the hills above the marshes west of the castle are very different: steep and wooded, with large expanses of grazing. Two or three miles to the north is the leaf-shaped valley of land bounded by Hockley, Rayleigh, Eastwood and Rochford. This is farming land, but the contours of the ground have prevented the wholesale ripping out of hedgerows that has taken place elsewhere. The walking is generally very good, with good views and even that rarity in south-east Essex, woodland. Hockley Woods in particular are delightful walking. The survival of these two pockets is very near to miraculous. In both cases they are close to some major building developments; in both cases, the houses hide conveniently behind trees or the brow of a hill. Each is threatened by creeping urbanisation. Hadleigh's hills belong to the Salvation Army while Hockley's little pocket of open land is a Conservation Area, but nevertheless, the development of the surrounding land, especially in the Rochford Hundred, must be a long-term threat to their survival and indeed to the countryside of the area as a whole. It is important that this overdeveloped area should be allowed to keep its remaining environmental heritage. For this reason, too, the Rochford Hundred should be walked, as well as the deserted lands of Dengie.

Rochford Hundred

Hadleigh and Hockley offer unexpectedly fine walking in a heavily built-up area. Ploughed field paths in the interior tail off into marshland and sea-wall walking. Take a compass.

Ashingdon Chiefly famous as the possible site of the battle of Assandun, fought in 1016 between Canute of Denmark and the English levies of Edmund Ironside. As so often, the claim is disputed, in this case by Ashdon on the Essex-Cambridgeshire border. The evidence is debatable, but Ashingdon is generally considered the more likely site, if only because the Danes were retreating to their fleet on the Crouch estuary at the time of the battle. Assandun was the sixth battle fought between the two nations in that year, and the first Danish victory. As a result, the Anglo-Danish monarchy of Canute and his successors became established in England.

Barling The church is at the east end of the little weatherboarded village, with a chequer-boarded frieze on the tower and a boarded spire. The interior fittings are 15c. Barling's churchwardens used to meet here in the 18c, to discuss parish business. The cost to the parish of their refreshments during meetings in 1725 was an imposing £40. To the north of the village lie the Barling Marshes and river Roach, with some of the best sea-wall walking in the entire district.

Benfleet Now quite urban, but once a smugglers' village. The Hoy and Helmet has a secret smugglers' passage allegedly leading to St Mary's church. Alfred the Great and the Danish raider Haesten fought a pitched battle here on the site of the Anchor Inn.

Canewdon Old white-painted weatherboarded cottages, and the Ship Inn. On a ridge, it dominates the Crouch estuary, and looks in this flat landscape like a veritable mountain if walking on the Burnham side of the river. St Nicholas's church is the finest in the region, and has been identified as the minster constructed by Canute to celebrate his victory. If so, the Danish army will have camped here before the battle.

Great Wakering Once a village where seaman and peasant met in the Exhibition Inn to discuss turnips, now with several modern housing estates and ominous ribbon development reaching toward Shoebury. The main street runs up to the church, which has a beam roof. East of the village lie marshes, sea wall, tidal creeks and the islands of Foulness and Potton, now housing MOD research establishments. Do *not* take binoculars.

Hadleigh Hadleigh has some splendid walking countryside to the south. Wooded heathland with broad views descends steeply to the Hadleigh Marshes, the sea wall and Two Tree Island with its little nature trail. It also has the ruined Hadleigh Castle, on a high hill overlooking the marshes, painted by Constable, who was taken with its 'melancholy grandeur'. The first castle was built by Hubert de Burgh, the man who defended Dover for King John. The castle later passed into the hands of Henry III and his successors. It was habitually used to reward royal favourites like Edward de Vere and Edward Plantagenet, Duke of York. The current remains are of a 14c reconstruction of the original castle. At a much later date, when already in ruins, it was a signalling point for the smugglers of Leigh and Benfleet, to tell their comrades off the coast that it was safe to bring in the goods. It was also the setting for Arthur Morrison's *Cunning Murrell*, a study surely drawn from first-hand experience of one of the last 'cunning', or wise, men in Essex. The little Norman church is kept locked between services to prevent vandalism.

Hockley A large and modern town, not at first sight the kind of place which might rival Bath, yet this is precisely what it tried to do. Mrs Letitia Clay lost a persistent cough upon moving here and drinking the water of Hockley springs, and an enterprising London solicitor called Fawcett had the water analysed, pronounced that it would cure rickets and dyspepsia, and built a hotel and pump-room. The venture failed, but both buildings survive – the Spa Hotel as a pub, and the pump-room as the Baptist chapel. Hockley's 13c church and Plumberow Mount both lie off the paths. The Mount has disclosed large quantities of Roman and early Saxon pottery. Hockley was the largest Saxon settlement in the district, according to Domesday Book. Today, its most interesting feature to the walker is Hockley Woods, a square mile of oak, ash, hornbeam and silver birch trees with all the charm and beauty of a well-established English deciduous wood. Take your compass: I found a couple walking south through Hockley Woods under the distinct impression that they were going back (north) to Hockley car park.

Leigh-on-Sea 16c Leigh was 'a very proper town, well-furnished with good mariners, where commonly tall ships do ride'. Lady Arabella Stuart and William Seymour tried to flee the country from here in 1611, after being imprisoned in the Tower for a marriage that skilfully united the two families with claims to the throne of James I. By the 18c the port had declined, but Leigh had achieved new fame as a smuggling centre. The best parts of Leigh are the High Street, with its old sailing pubs like the Crooked Billet; St Clement's church, a splendid building high above the street up steps; and Ivy Osborne's celebrated Number Three cockle shed and its neighbours.

Paglesham Its story is summed up by the name of East End's inn – the Plough and Sail. The village is surrounded by fields, but these very quickly give way to marshes and the sea wall of the Roach and Paglesham Pool. The walking here is particularly good, with broad views and magnificent air. The creeks and marshes were the working place of Paglesham smugglers, none of whom was as daring as Hard Apple Blyth. As village grocer and churchwarden, Hard Apple combined his interests by wrapping butter and cheese in pages torn out of the parish register. He was a noted cricketer – but kept a pistol and cutlass about his body, even when batting. His favourite inn was the Punch Bowl at Church End, a beautiful weatherboarded pub. Captured twice by revenue men, he escaped on both occasions. The first time, he escaped by plying the men with the smuggled brandy until they became incapable. On the second occasion, the revenue cutter grounded on the Goodwin Sands and the captain was forced to enlist Hard Apple's seamanship at the cost of letting him go afterwards. His favourite spots for concealing the merchandise were some hollow pollarded elms near East Hall, and the little pond to the east of St Peter's church. Often £200 of silk could be found here at any one time, while the annual import of geneva and brandy smuggled into the area during the late 18c was estimated at a staggering 73,000 gallons.

Rochford Another historic town which has become suburbanised from Southend. The centre of Rochford does however still have some of the weather-boarded cottages typical of this area, and a number of old inns including the King's Head, Marlborough Head and Old Ship. Anglo-Saxon Rochford was the leading port in the district, and the head of the Hundred that bears its name. The trade up the Roach has mainly ceased, although the enormous modern mill east of the town remains to show how great this traffic must once have been. In spite of the growth of Leigh and Benfleet in the middle ages, Rochford remained the market town of the district. Its mainly reconstructed hall is now the clubhouse on the golf course. It is a great place for bell-ringing; all eight bells can often be heard in action.

Southend Until 1850, Southend had the reputation of a quiet, dull bathing place where nothing ever happened. Since then it has changed somewhat and it is now a favourite resort of day-trippers. Old Leigh, east of Hadleigh Marsh, gives a faint idea of what it was like before it all began. At Prittlewell, also swallowed up by the expanding town, the 12c priory is now a museum. Open: afternoons except Wednesday and Sunday.

South Fambridge There is an excellent white-boarded yachting inn behind the 'harbour'. The old ferry across the Crouch has vanished.

Stroud Green The route passes The Lawn, a square and very Georgian country house with a pinky-grey exterior and tall windows. The little agricultural valley to the south and west of Stroud Green makes marvellous walking; as at Hadleigh, the estates that surround it on all sides lie miraculously behind woods or low hills, leaving the walker in a completely rural landscape.

RECOMMENDED WALKS

1. **Leigh – Hadleigh Castle – Benfleet – Leigh. 7½m. VHR.**

Shorter walk:

Leigh – Hadleigh Castle – Benfleet – Two Tree Island – Leigh. 6¼m. VHR.

A marvellous mixture of paths and country, in the middle of a built-up area.

Start at Leigh station. Turn L (WNW) for 100yd to Castle Drive and then along to its far (W) end. Cross the stile and bear due W towards the castle ahead. Go WNW up the grassy slope to the castle and skirt on its R (N) side. At the castle entrance, turn L (SSW by S): the path is signposted here to the base of the hill. Turn R (W) at the signposts here. The path skirts the bottom of the hill. After 1m, at the third signpost, paths continue W along the marsh edge or immediately to the N among bushes. Continue to the railway line and beside the track until you arrive at a gap in the bushes R (N) leading into a grassy park. The long and short walks divide here. If on the short walk, continue along the railway line to a white gate and cross the tracks: turn L (SE) down the path behind the bushes and walk on past the boats to the sea wall and follow back to Leigh station. If on the long walk, turn R (N) into the park. Walk up to the NE corner of the grassy slope. Take the northern of two grass paths between bushes. Follow through woods to a broad N-S path used by horses. Turn L (N) uphill; the path then turns slightly R (NE), leaving the park and going downhill into a dip. Turn R (E) in the dip along pasture and field edges. The route is signposted from here to the E edge of Round Hill at frequent intervals. Circle NE through scrub to a sloping pasture field. Look for signpost in the SE corner of the same field. There is no direct official path to this signpost: the right of way lies up the hill to a junction of paths and then sharp R (S) to the signpost. At the signpost, cross into the next field and walk half-left (NE) to and through the woods to the B road. Turn R (ENE) past the school and take the first R (St John's Rd). At its end, turn R (SW) down Chapel Lane to the farmhouse at its end. Cross gate by Strictly Private notice and walk S to the R of the concrete building ahead. (When reservoir is built, the path will skirt it on the N and E side to the building.) Walk to the signpost and from there S down a valley between hills to the signpost at the marsh edge. Turn L (E) along the edge back to Leigh station.

2. **Gt Wakering – Lt Wakering – Fleet Head – Gt Wakering. 5¼m. HR.**

A short walk mainly along river bank or easy inland paths. This can be linked with the next walk to make a route of 10½m. **HR.**

Start at the church. Walk W through the village for ¼m and then turn R (N) down a gravelled lane called North St. Continue N until the path ends in a broad E-W track after ½m. Turn L (W) here towards Lt Wakering Hall. Ignore a grass path R (N) to the hall. At the junction of paths by farm cottages, turn R and then L before the redbrick barn. Skirt the arable field on its E side and then turn L (W) along its N side toward the church ahead. At the farm road to Lt Wakering Wick, turn L (W) to the church. Turn R (NW) along the road past Castle Inn. Cross the stream and turn R (E) along it by the footpath signpost. At the creek wall, turn R (E). Follow the creek bank for a long mile to Fleet Head, where the sea wall turns sharp L (NW). Pick up the track ahead (NNE) across the promontory and pick up the sea wall opposite Potton Island. Turn R (SSE) along it for ¾m. Opposite the S tip of Potton Island, the sea wall bends sharp R (W) around an

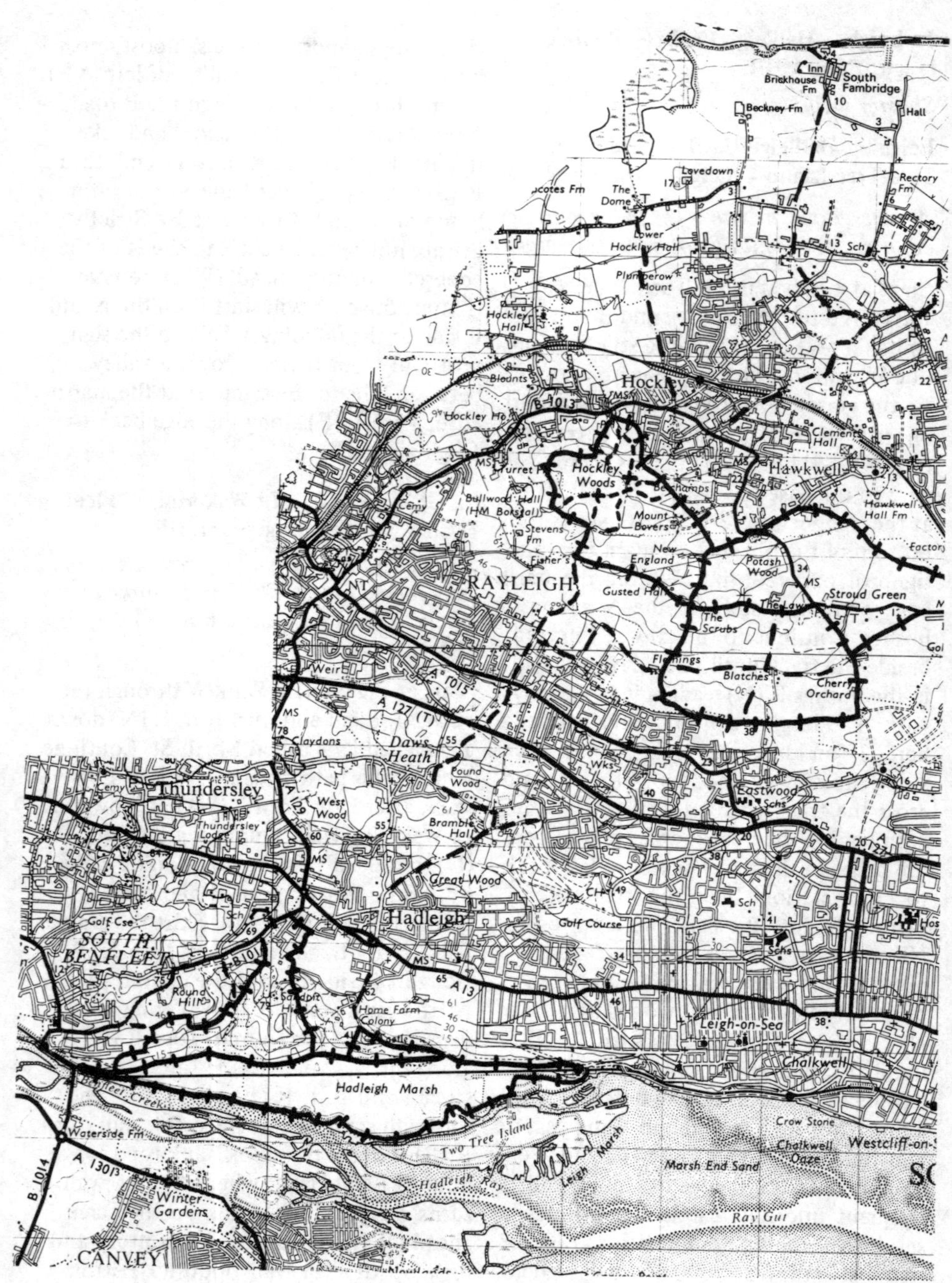

South Fambridge
Brickhouse Fm
Inn
Beckney Fm
Hall
Lovedown
Rectory Fm
The Dome
Lower Hockley Hall
Plumberow Mount
Hockley Hall
Blounts
Hockley
Hockley Ho
B 1013
Clements Hall
Hawkwell
Hawkwell Hall Fm
Turret
Hockley Woods
Belchamps
Bullwood Hall (HM Borstal)
Cemy
Stevens Fm
Mount Bovers
New England
Potash Wood
Factory
Fisher's
RAYLEIGH
Gusted Hall
Stroud Green
The Scrubs
Flemings
Blatches
Cherry Orchard
Weir
A 1015
A 127 (T)
Claydons
Daws Heath
Pound Wood
Eastwood
Thundersley
Thundersley Lodge
West Wood
Bramble Hall
Great Wood
Hadleigh
Golf Course
Golf Cse
SOUTH BENFLEET
Round Hill
Home Farm Colony
A 13
Leigh-on-Sea
Chalkwell
Hadleigh Marsh
Two Tree Island
Crow Stone
Chalkwell Oaze
Marsh End Sand
Hadleigh Ray
Leigh Marsh
Ray Gut
Waterside Fm
A 130
B 1014
Winter Gardens
CANVEY

Contd pp. 94-5

Canewdon
Great Stambridge
STAMBRIDGE
Rochford
Paglesham
Ballards Gore
Barling
Barling Marsh
Little Wakering
Great Wakering
SUTTON
Southend Municipal Airport
Ashingdon
Prittlewell
Southchurch
Thorpe Bay
Bournes Green
North Shoebury
Shoeburyness
SOUTHEND-ON-SEA
Southend Flat
SHOEBURY NESS
Potton Island
Wallasea

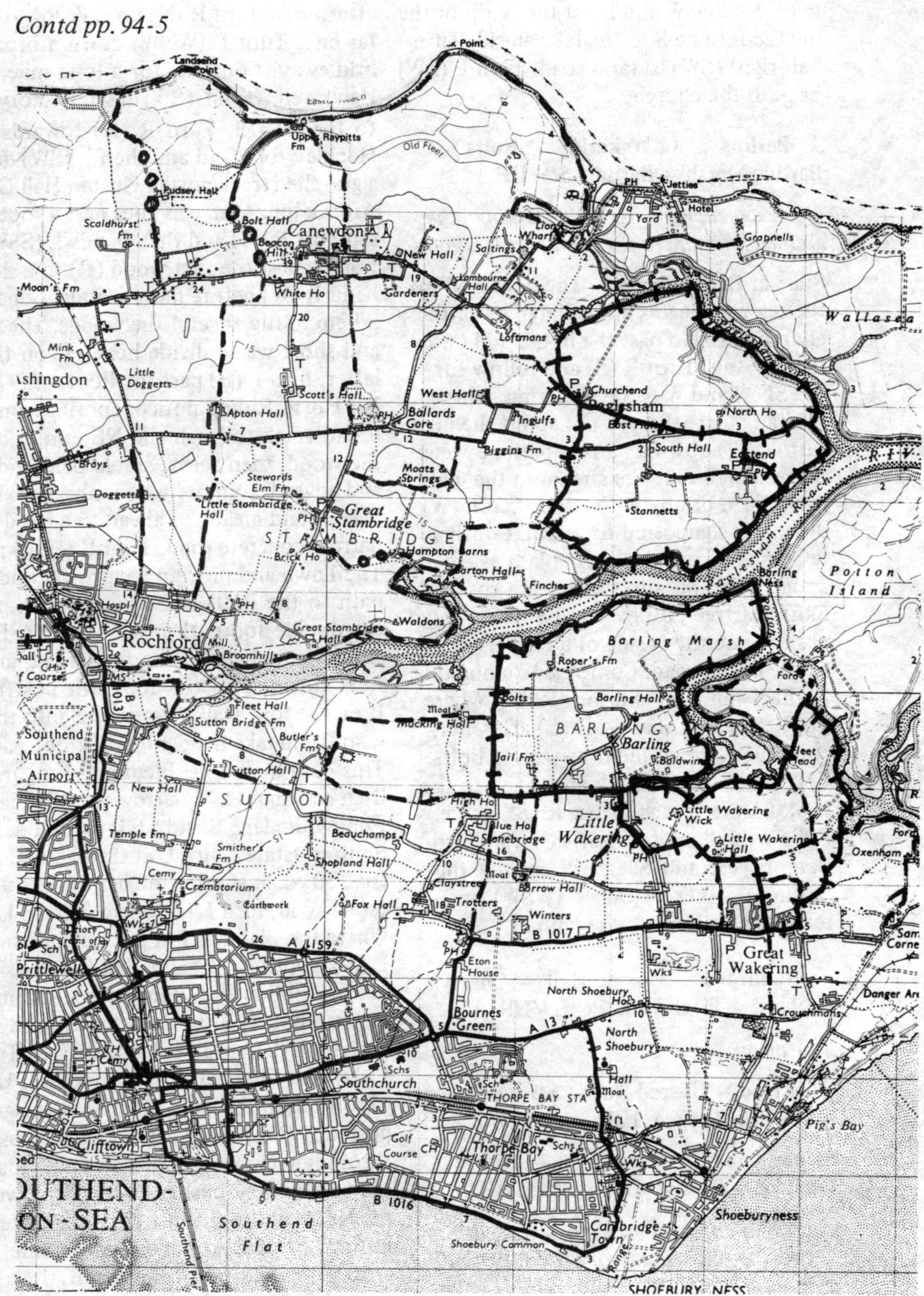

inlet. Follow W and S. At the W tip of the inlet, continue S to the lake ahead. Turn half-right (SW) to farm road. Turn L (SW) back to the church.

3. **Barling – Lt Wakering – Bolts – Barling Marsh – Barling. 5¾. HR.**

More excellent river wall walking; the arable paths and roads inland are less good.

Start at Barling church. The path ENE to the sea wall begins immediately N of the churchyard. Go past the house and onto the sea wall. Turn R (S) and follow for 1m SE, S and W to Lt Wakering. Where the bank turns sharp L (E) about the inlet, turn R (W) down a narrow path between fences and beside the stream to the main road. Turn briefly R (N) and then L (W) down the signposted footpath. Continue W along line of telegraph poles past the arable field and into the derelict rosery. Skirt Peartree Cottage on its S side through pasture and the N side of a cabbage field to the minor road. Continue W along this to the T-junction and turn R (N). Where this bends very sharply R (E) after ¾m, continue N down the driveway of Bolts. Follow this broad track ahead (N) to the bank of the Roach. Turn R (SE) here. Follow the bank for nearly 3m, ENE to Barling Ness and S and W around the Barling Marshes. Turn R (WSW) and retrace your steps to the church.

4. **Rochford – Gusted Hall – Cherry Orchard – Rochford. 5¾m. VHR.**

Shorter walks:

Rochford – Gusted Hall – Stroud Green – Rochford. 4¾m. HR.

Stroud Green – Flemings – Cherry Orchard – Stroud Green. 3¾m. HR.

Excellent inland walking with only occasional intrusion from the surrounding estates.

Start at Rochford station. Walk W along the B1013 under the railway line. Shortly afterwards, turn R (N) up Oak Rd to its far end. Turn L (WNW) down a broad bridleway. Continue for a long mile to Hawkwell. Turn L (SW) down Rectory Rd to the B1013. Turn R (N) towards Hockley for 40yd and then L (SW) down a gravelled track posted Gusted Hall Only. After a long ¼m, this goes past a footpath signpost R (N) and then bends L (SSW). Follow past the first wood (R) to a sharp bend R (W) before more woods. Continue S here to the edge of the woods. The long and short walks divide here. (If on the latter, turn L (E) past the Footpath Only. No Horse Riding notice; continue on a broad track through the NE corner of the wood, then across arable field middle and edges E to more woods ahead: skirt N edge and meadows ahead to a bend in a narrow concrete road. Turn R (ESE) past The Lawn and pick up a narrow wooded path to the B1013 at Stroud Green; at the double footpath post, turn R (SE) along field edges to the farm road, and walk down it to the footpath post.)
If on the long walk, continue S into the woods and take the central of three paths. This continues S to Fleming's Fm, and then continues as a narrow metalled lane. Follow the lane S and SE into a modern housing estate. Turn L at the T-junction for 250yd. Just after the bend S in the estate road, turn L (E) down a green lane. Where the Blatches Fm private road turns L (N), continue straight ahead (E) beside hedges. Follow between fields and some modern houses until the track ends in a grass path (S) and a pebbled lane (N). Turn L (N) past Cherry Orchard to Milton Hall. The footpath back to Rochford is signposted R (NE) along a good path across the middle of the field. At its end, cross the stile among bushes and walk down the N side of the line of trees immediately in front of you. At the end of the line, cross gate and turn half-left (NE) down a second field middle path, a grass strip. Cross to B1013 and turn R (E) back to the station.

5. **Hockley Woods – Gusted Hall – Hockley Woods. 3¾m. HR.**

A short walk mainly in Hockley Woods. Take a compass.

Start at the car park by the main entrance to Hockley Woods. Take the most easterly of the paths into the woods, following their N side. Continue on a generally SE line. After ½m, where the track forks, take the R (SE) path to the edge of the woods. The path out of Hockley Woods is a timbered causeway past a large pool (L) to a white bungalow. Turn R (W) for 30yd to Hawksmead field, then L (S) through scrub and pasture to the end of the unadopted road. Turn L (E) down the road. Halfway down, a footpath is posted R (SE) across an arable field under telegraph lines. Follow to woods. Turn L and R to skirt woods on their N and E side. Cross field to the signpost on the Gusted Hall road. Turn R (SW and S) down the road. Follow around a sharp bend R (W) and down a signposted track. Follow through the farmyard and along the S edge of the woods. The right of way from here to Hockley Woods may soon be altered. For the present, continue WNW from the corner of the woods across the field to the pylon lines and then along a field edge ahead. After 300yd, turn R (N) up a field edge track to the S edge of the woods. (This is not on the definitive map, but is almost certainly a right of way.) Enter the woods and immediately turn L (WNW). After ¼m, this goes over a crossing track and almost immediately turns R (NNE). Follow this winding track around further bends L (NW) and R (NNE). Ignore a side track L (N) out of the woods and continue E for a further ¼m. Take the next side track L (N) back to the car park.

6. **Paglesham Church End – Paglesham Pool – Paglesham East End – Paglesham Reach – Paglesham Church End. 6½m. VHR.**

Shorter walks:

Church End – Paglesham Pool – East End – Church End. 4m. VHR.

East End – Paglesham Reach – Church End – East End. 4m. HR.

The best of the sea wall walks in the district.

Start at Paglesham church. Walk NW down the minor road and pick up a field edge path in the same direction signposted by the last cottage N of the road. At the stream, turn R (NNE by N) on the path following it to the creek. At the sea wall, turn R (NE). Follow the sea wall NE and SE for the next 2m, with views over Paglesham Pool and Wallasea Island. Where the sea wall divides W and SE, the walker has two options. Walking W will bring you via field paths to East End, and thence back to Church End or past the Plough & Sail back onto the sea wall. Walking along the main bank SE will bring you to the river Roach: turn R (SW). The path from the Plough & Sail rejoins after ½m. Continue SW and W alongside the Roach. Eventually, the sea wall is broken by a major inlet to the NW. Turn half-right (WNW) to follow the bank to the point where it crosses the inlet. (This section is not on the definitive map, but is walked by everybody.) Turn R (NNE) at this point along the bank heading inland – not NE along the grassy dry ditch. At the end of the bank, continue along field edges with a little stream on your L (W). General direction is indicated by the church tower ahead (NNE by N). Cross a dry ditch and field to a red brick house and footpath signpost upon the road. Turn R (E) to the bus stop and then L (N) up a posted footpath to the church ahead. (If on the second short walk, the footpath back to East End is signposted to the E of the church past a modern house. It follows a grass path and then a cockle-shell track to farm buildings ahead. There, it joins the concrete farm road L (E) to East End.)

OTHER SUGGESTED ROUTES

Day Walk

Rochford – Sea Wall – Paglesham – Canewdon – Apton Hall – Lt Stambridge Hall – Rochford. 14m.
An excellent walk with great beauty and interest.

Medium Walks

1. Rochford – Sea Wall – Paglesham Church End – Canewdon – Lt Stambridge Hall – Rochford. 9¾m.
Inland walking is fairly heavy.

2. Canewdon – Lion Wharf – Upper Raypits – Pudsey Hall – Canewdon. 8m.
Rather a lot of road walking at the start.

Short Walks

1. Benfleet – Round Hill – Sandpit Hill – Hadleigh Marsh – Benfleet. 4½m.
An excellent part of the Recommended Walk.

2. Rayleigh – Flemings – Gusted Hall – Rayleigh. 3m.
Becoming developed.

3. Hockley – Lower Hockley Hall – Ashingdon – Hockley. 5m.
Finishes among allotments.

4. Gt Stambridge – Waldons – Rochford Mill – Gt Stambridge. 4½m.
Mainly good.

5. Canewdon – Upper Raypits – Pudsey Hall – Canewdon. 4½m.
Excellent views.

Dengie Hundred

Map and compass and stout boots are essential in the marshland. Narrow but well-trodden sea wall paths; in arable areas there are few hedges or field boundaries to make decent paths.

Althorne Mostly modern, but with two good pubs, the Three Horseshoes and the thatched Huntsman and Hounds (north of the village).

Asheldham The church, pond and hall stand within a large ditched enclosure of 16 acres whose history is obscure.

Bradwell-juxta-Mare The village comes in three main parts. To the NW stands Bradwell Waterside, with several timber cottages, a yacht club and the excellent Green Man inn. Inside the tap room is a huge fireplace and an enormous collection of objects hanging from every available inch of roof space. Behind the houses stands the square, modern bulk of Bradwell's nuclear power station, such a landmark for those walking along the sea walls of the Blackwater. A mile to the SE of Bradwell Waterside lies the main village, clustered about the church and lodge. The third part of the village lies down the Roman road running NE from the church. **Othona** and **St Peter's** lie at the end of this road. St Peter's chapel is a tall, square building, of rough-cut masonry mixed with some obviously Roman bricks and tiles. It looks much like a barn, and was used as such until the 1920s. It was a casual visitor who recognised the building for what it was – the oldest intact church in the country. It was built about 654 AD, by St Cedd. At that time, Essex was uncompromisingly pagan, the last Wodenist stronghold in England. Eventually, the other nations like Northumbria forced Essex to admit a Christian mission, led by the brightest of Aidan's graduates from Lindisfarne,

St Cedd. Cedd carried out his task for ten years from this deserted spot, before dying from plague. Thirty yards south of the chapel is an overgrown rectangular hollow with some pieces of masonry visible at the sides. This is all that remains of an institution even older that St Peter's – Othona, the Roman fort of the Saxon Shore, founded here during the 3c. The fort is about five hundred feet long in its present state, but an equal length or more may have been washed away at the east end by the sea. Little is known of its history, except that it was garrisoned with North African auxiliaries.

Burnham-on-Crouch Above all, a yachting centre, with five clubs including the Royal Corinthian. In summer, the Crouch is alive with small boats, and the quay bustles with yachtsmen and visitors. The tangle of boats and pretty terrace of timbered cottages here make up quite the best part of this little town. It was from here that they shipped grain for London during the Black Death, when only Burnham and Bradwell of all the capital's outports would trade into the city. In the middle ages, when large flocks grazed around Southminster and Tillingham, Burnham was a wool port.

Dengie The name comes from the Saxon Denningaes, meaning forest-dwellers. The forests have entirely vanished; the country around this tiny hamlet is now typical of the peninsula as a whole, flat arable land shading gradually into the tussocky grassland of the marshes to the east.

Maldon The battle of Maldon – part of the long struggle of the East Anglians against Danish invasion in Saxon times – is known only because of the chance survival of a single manuscript. But for this, the battle would be known only as another defeat that ended in the payment of Danegeld. Instead, the heroism of Byrhtnoth and his men have been preserved in some of the finest poetry in Old English. Byrhtnoth was a Cambridgeshire noble, earl of East Anglia during the difficult days at the end of the 10c. A Viking raiding party came by sea to the Blackwater and established a base on Northey Island, east of Maldon. From there they demanded gold as the price of their departure:

you must quickly send
Riches for ransom; better for you
That you buy off with tribute a battle of spears
Than that we should wage hard war against you.

The earl replied by besieging the causeway and offering his spear only as tribute. The two armies faced each other across an ebb tide, neither side willing to cross, until Byrhtnoth disdainfully – and with half an eye to tactical advantage – retired upslope to allow the Danes onto the mainland. In the ensuing fight, Byrhtnoth was killed but the remnants of his household fought on, defending the body to the last and encouraging each other with memories of the hospitality and generosity of their dead lord. Archaeologists single out as the site of the battle a spot just south of South House Farm, conveniently on a right of way. Maldon is a large and bustling town, a great centre for sailing barges and smacks, and it is the quayside with its boats, ropes and cobblestones that has most appeal. In the middle ages, it was Essex's leading seaport and oldest borough, with two MPs until 1834. The High Street is handsome, with several timber and brick houses and a 15c moot hall. All Saints, overlooking the river, has an unusual triangular tower; St Mary's was used as a lighthouse in the 16c.

Mundon An excellent pub, the Round Bush.

North Fambridge Another mainly modern village on the branch line to Burnham. The best of North Fambridge lies down by the river, around the Ferry Boat inn and boatyards. The inn and the cottages are weatherboarded.

Purleigh It lies on what is for the area very high and agricultural land, with some magnificent views north-east over the estuary of the Blackwater. George Washington's great-great-grandfather, the last English Washington before the family left for Virginia, was curate here. The inn is the Bell (real ale).

Southminster Large, modern and completely agricultural. The railway station and large number of footpaths make it a good place to start an exploration of the Dengie peninsula's arable interior.

Steeple The village lies on the Roman road from Woodham Ferrers to Othona, and its Victorian church incorporates Roman brickwork. The best walking lies along the sea wall, past Stansgate Abbey. This medieval priory was dissolved in 1529 to pay for Cardinal Wolsey's university endowments, and is now the property of Tony Benn.

Tillingham Around the green stand the Cap and Feathers pub, its sign looking like a technicoloured snail, and to east and west more weatherboarded houses so typical of the village. The churchyard of the unusually grand church, with its oaks and well-kept lawns, is an attractive point on St Peter's Way.

RECOMMENDED WALKS

1. **North Fambridge – Althorne – Burnham-on-Crouch. 8m. HR.**

Entirely sea wall; ends in the attractive little town of Burnham. This may be divided into two 4m walks by beginning or ending the walk at Althorne station.

Start at North Fambridge station. Walk S down the road past modern houses. At the second bend, continue down the main road signposted to the river and the Ferry Boat inn. Keep on to the inn car park and pick up the sea wall here. Follow past the boatyards to the river. Turn L (E). The path follows the river wall all the way into Althorne. Walk along the bank until you come to a large boat anchorage and white bungalow with a Bridgemarsh Marine notice-board. If on the first short walk, turn L (N) here up the rough lane to Althorne station. Otherwise, continue along the sea wall for 1¾m until it is crossed by a fence with a Private notice upon it. At this point, turn L over a stile and then R (SE) along the meadow hedge. This ends in a minor road. Turn R (S) and continue past the car park and along the river front to its end in a private driveway. Ignore a signposted path to Ostend; go over a stile and along the river wall into Burnham.

2. **Tillingham – St Peter's Chapel – Bradwell Waterside – Bradwell-juxta-Mare – Tillingham. 13m. VHR.**

An atmospheric walk taking in St Peter's Way, the chapel, a great deal of sea wall and Tillingham village.

Start at Tillingham church. Go over a stile in the SE corner of the churchyard and between two fences to a small field. Cross this diagonally under telegraph poles to a low hedge. Turn half-right (E) along this and then ahead beside a ditch ENE. Continue to the R (S) of the clump of trees ahead and then on along the field edge to the road. Keep on ENE through the farm and pick up a rough lane ahead. At a totally featureless point in the landscape, a grass track forks L (NE) off the main track. Follow this and then an indicated path between crops to concrete barns visible in the distance. Look E (compass needed) to the most R-hand clump of trees, by a building. This is your aiming point. Follow a broad ditch and then a fence to the trees and Sandbeach Fm. Continue ahead (ESE by E) to the sea wall down the farm road. At the bank, turn L (NNE) along it. Follow the main bank NNE, E, NNE, WNW and N for 2¼m to a copse on your L. You may either turn L here skirting the woods to St Peter's chapel or continue down between the wooden buildings of the bird observatory. The second path then crosses the rectangular hollow of the old Roman fort on wooden planks. Visit the chapel. Walk to the stilted building and then up steps back onto the sea wall. Follow for 3¾m, past the end of the Blackwater estuary and Bradwell nuclear power station. Follow the bank to a minor road by the yacht club office. Turn L (E) here up the road and past the Green Man to the bend R (S) and telephone box. Pick up the signposted path here L (SE). Where this enters the field and forks, turn R (SE) down an excellent path between crops. Continue to the minor road. Turn L and follow the road S past Bradwell church and round a sharp bend R (WSW). Go round a further bend half-right (W) and a side road coming in from the N. Eventually, turn L (SSE) at a dilapidated footpath sign shortly after the side road. Go down the L (E) side of a meadow to a gap between trees and then continue ahead (SSE) to the pylon and L (E) side of the wood. Go downhill along an old field edge to the L (E) edge of the next wood. Pick up a path ahead just inside the trees to a concrete slab bridge over Bradwell Brook. Go over the stile and into the field on your L. Turn R and pick up a broad cart track past the farmhouse to a metalled road. Turn R (W) down this and then L (S) down a signposted hard track to Mark Fm. Go down a dirt track (this may be concreted soon) to a clump of trees and then retrace your steps to Tillingham church.

OTHER SUGGESTED ROUTES

Weekend Walk

Althorne Station – Burnham-on-Crouch – Holiwell Point – Tillingham Marshes – St Peter's Chapel – Bradwell-on-Sea (overnight stop). Bradwell-on-Sea – Tillingham – Steeple – Maylandsea – Lawling Hall – Althorne Station. Day 1: 16m. Day 2: 14m.

An energetic and atmospheric walk through Dengie following the sea bank and St Peter's Way.

Day Walks

1. Chelmsford – River Chelmer – Maldon. 12m.

Although our maps do not show the path in its entirety, walk 1 is among the finest in the district.

2. North Fambridge – Sea Wall – Althorne – Lawling Hall – St Peter's Way – Cold Norton – North Fambridge. 14½m.

Fairly heavy inland.

3. Steeple – St Peter's Way – Tillingham – Bradwell Waterside – Sea Wall – Steeple. 14½m.

The general walking conditions are good.

Medium Walks

1. White House Fm – Mundon Hall – St Peter's Way – Sea Wall – Battle of Maldon – White House Fm.

Generally arable interior.

2. Steeple – St Peter's Way – Mott's Fm – Ramsey Island – Sea Wall – Steeple.

The section after Ramsey Island is the most interesting.

3. Bradwell Waterside – Sea Wall – Ramsey Island – St Peter's Way – Tillingham – Bradwell-on-Sea – Bradwell Waterside. 9¾m. *Enjoyable.*

Short Walks

1. Maylandsea – Sea Wall – Lower Mayland – St Peter's Way – Maylandsea. 3½m. *Rather developed.*

2. Steeple – Steeple Creek – Sea Wall – Steeple. 3¾m. *A fine walk.*

3. Asheldham – St Peter's Way – Badnocks – Asheldham. 5m. *Mostly under plough.*

Contd pp. 113-14

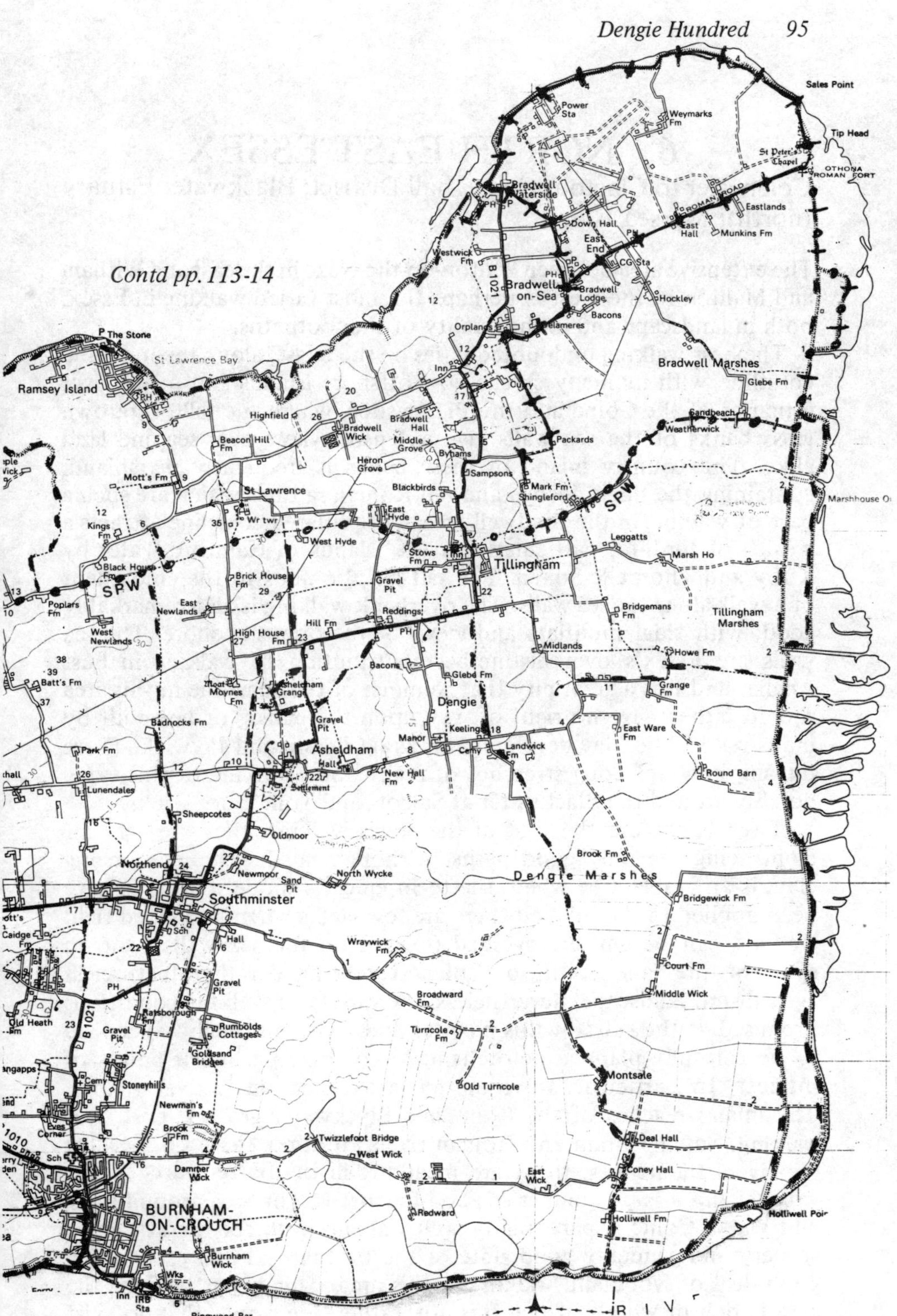

Contd pp. 86-7

6 NORTH-EAST ESSEX

Colchester to Clacton; Coggeshall District; Blackwater Estuary (north); Mersea Island

The extensive area between Walton-on-the-Naze in the east and Witham and Maldon in the west is perhaps the most varied walking in Essex, both in landscape and in the quality of the footpaths.

The best walking undoubtedly lies on the coast, along the indented coastline with its many creeks, low offshore islands and major river estuaries of the Colne and the Blackwater, where the tall overgrown grass banks of the sea walls give extensive views over sea and land alike. The country inland of these banks is frequently marshland, containing the duck decoys and red Roman saltings which are such a part of walking in the Bradwell area. This isolated coastline attracts a wealth of birdlife, particularly in the islands of Hamford Water by Kirby and Thorpe-le-Soken. The salt air also adds to the enjoyment of a walk along the sea walls. The riverbank walking is also remarkably good, with tidal mudflats and views of the opposite shore. The sea walls are Essex's own distinctive contribution to walking in East Anglia, and it is a great pity that so much of the coastline in this area should either have no right of way upon the banks, or be spoilt by industrial and holiday development, as at Clacton and Jaywick. There remain, however, long stretches of really good walking of this type, notably around the Blackwater at Salcott and Tollesbury Wick.

If sea banks are the best of the area's walking, they are very far from being the only good paths. Although north-east Essex, being clay, is an arable area where the techniques of modern farming have been applied to the full and there are few walks where ploughed field walking can be entirely avoided (except on the sea walls), and in spite of the land south of Colchester being a rather featureless agricultural landscape, nevertheless, the variety of walking conditions promised at the start of this chapter does exist, although walks need to be carefully planned beforehand to combine particular points of interest. In particular, there are some excellent little river valleys. The inland reaches of the Colne and Blackwater give the best river walking, but the Brain and Roman rivers are almost as good. Besides the rivers themselves, there are meadows in the flatter parts of the valleys, and a large number of good footpaths. The area around Earls and Wakes Colne is particularly well walked, both for the attractive scenery and generally good state of the footpaths. Finally, there is a good deal of woodland walking in this area. This is not because the area is rich in woods, which it is not; rather, the woods that do exist have more footpaths through them than, for example, west Essex. The woodland walking in the Layer-de-la-Haye and Markshall areas is particularly to be recommended. The paths included on the maps are in parts of the area regularly walked by the active Colchester-based rambling groups, and are mostly well signposted.

Only with the coming of the Romans did north-east Essex become regularly and widely settled. The Romans have left a wide scattering of remains in many of the villages along the paths, hardly surprising given the number of roads which converged here on the Roman *colonia* of Colchester. The oyster beds in the estuaries date from the Roman settlement, and many of the churches incorporate Roman brickwork or stand on a 3-4c villa site. There are fewer Anglo-Saxon monuments in the area, but the period undoubtedly saw an even greater expansion in the pattern of settlement than already existed in Roman times. Almost all the village names in the area are Old English – except Kirby and Thorpe, which suggest Danish influence.

By the middle ages the pattern of settlement was established. The ports, such as Colchester, Wivenhoe and Brightlingsea, were trading along the coast and across the North Sea, as well as supporting their own shipbuilding industry. Many of the cargoes were connected with the wool trade, shipping goods for such inland towns as Coggeshall and Earls Colne, where the proximity of the river had provided the resources necessary for the processes essential to the manufacture of cloth. These towns became the major market towns of the area and were supported by the network of smaller towns and humble arable villages of the surrounding country.

The ports and wool towns have all the architectural signs of medieval prosperity – half-timbered houses, large inns and grand churches, like Brightlingsea and Coggeshall. In the other villages, buildings remain generally very much more modest. The characteristic church of the area is Norman, flint and stone with some Roman bricks incorporated into the walls, altered piecemeal between the 13th and 15th centuries. Tudor brick towers are as typical of the district as the timbered belfry is of central Essex. In most villages, there is a manor house; this is in contrast to Suffolk, where independent farmsteads are more common.

Colchester to Clacton

It is difficult to avoid ploughed field walking in the agricultural regions lying inland.

Brightlingsea The name of the town is Anglo-Saxon, meaning Brihtric's island – and it is indeed very like an island, cut off on three sides by Brightlingsea and Alresford creeks. The marine atmosphere of the town has survived its later tourist development very well, and Brightlingsea still retains an active boat-building trade, producing catamarans for Olympic competitions. In the middle ages the most important port in Tendring Hundred. The imposing 15c church with its 100ft flushwork tower reflects this prosperity.

Colchester It is of course no part of this book to act as a general guide to major cities of East Anglia, since walkers are more concerned with the country than the town, but nevertheless, those outsiders intending to walk in the area should visit Colchester. The Norman castle keep, the largest in England, houses Colchester and Essex Museum; there are six medieval churches; Tudor, 17c and Georgian houses in the centre of the town; and the remains of Camulodunum, the old Roman capital, most notably the massive walls and the Balkerne Gate. Also of interest to the walker in the Stanway Green area are the remains of a Roman temple and theatre at the north end of Cheshunt Field, and Gryme's Dyke on the footpaths north to Beacon End. Both sites date back to pre-Roman times, and Gryme's Dyke is especially interesting as the best-preserved of five Iron Age ditches in the Lexden area. It is over 3 miles long, with a 50ft wide ditch and a 10ft rampart.

Elmstead Market Pretty centre about the main crossroads, totally ruined like the rest of the village by the volume of traffic that passes through it. The best of the village lies around the church, up a narrow road to the north.

Great Bentley The largest village green in the entire county covers 42 acres. The vicarage lies upon one side of the green, the church inconveniently upon the other. St Mary's has a Norman nave and chancel, but a 19c east end. In front of the altar are nine 13c tiles bearing animal figures including a stag and greyhound.

Great Holland A small and compact village; excellent views from the yard of its 19c church, across sloping fields to the sea.

Kirby-le-Soken The Danish names of Kirby and Thorpe, and the use of the term soke, imply that these settlements were originally made by Viking invaders penetrating up the creeks of Hamford Water. Certainly, they are the only two villages in the Hundred with Danish names. A small village with tidal streams rising and falling between banks of rushes and moss. Picturesque weatherboarded cottages, a 17c pub, the Ship, and an impressive church. North of the village lie the sea wall, creeks and mudflats of Hamford Water, some of the best walking in the area as a whole. The estuary has been declared a Site of Special Scientific Interest, and Skipper's Island further up the wall has a wealth of marine birdlife including kestrel and gadwall. The island is visible from the wall, so take binoculars.

Little Bentley The main hamlet lies north of the church and hall, about the crossroads and off the route. The church shows many typical features of these inland villages, including the Norman nave incorporating Roman bricks.

Little Clacton Village green, a nearby inn, the Blacksmith's Arms, and an active ramblers' group. As a result, the paths in this parish are well-used and signposted.

St Osyth Cottages spill down a little hillside to the boats, birds and open water of St Osyth Creek. The cottages themselves are mostly the simple weatherboarded type, but punctuated by the occasional brick and oversailing two-storey house.

St Osyth herself was an Anglo-Saxon princess, the daughter of King Frithewold. She was forced into a political marriage with Sigehere of Essex despite taking vows of virginity. Miraculously, she escaped Sigehere's attentions on their wedding night, and fled away to this little village to found a nunnery. She died in 653, beheaded by the invading Danes under Ingevar and Hubba after refusing to give up her religion. A fountain is said to have sprung from the spot where her head fell. In her honour, the village's name was changed from Chiche (winding creek) to St Osyth's. The 16c octagonal font in St Peter and St Paul's church contains carvings of her head and of an angel bearing her soul to heaven. The church is unusual, a Tudor Perpendicular building with brick piers and arches in the nave, common in Germany but rare in this country. **St Osyth's Priory** is the best-known building in the Hundred. It was founded in 1118 by Richard de Belmeis, bishop of London, as an Augustinian house. Its medieval reputation was poor, except as a centre for fox-hunting, but the priory was rescued from degeneracy in the early 16c by Abbot Vyntoner, and rebuilt so sumptuously that the lead on the roofs was valued at £1000 in the 1530s. Despite the revival in the abbey's fortunes, Vyntoner's successor had no doubts about obeying the royal command of dissolution: 'I am the king's subject, and I and my house and all is the king's.' The estate was handed to Lord Darcy, who adapted the priory as a country house only for it to be sacked in 1642 by a Protestant mob looking for the Catholic owner, Countess Rivers. The Tudor buildings were restored in the 18c, and the gardens and grounds laid out. The gatehouse is solid and square with a little arch as the gateway, the front a riot of flint flushwork. Open: daily in summer.

Tendring The capital of the Anglo-Saxon hundred has shrunk to little more than a hamlet. The dedication of the church to St Edmund King and Martyr confirms this Saxon greatness. Its large timber arch, framing the two doorways, provides a support for the hammerbeam of the roof – a very early, unusual and ingenious means of bearing the load.

Thorpe-le-Soken 15c inn, the Bell, and weatherboarded cottages in the High St and side roads. Georgian red brick Comarques, at the west end of Thorpe, once the home of the writer Arnold Bennett.

Thorrington A scattered village that reaches inland from the east end of Alresford Creek to the pleasant wooded hills by Tenpenny Heath, and east down the B1027 towards St Osyth. Weatherboarded cottages stand beside the creek about the old tide mill.

Weeley Victorian church down a splendid little lane, with old trees, ponds and a thatched barn. The pub is the Black Boy.

Wivenhoe The old port is best seen around the quay, with its weatherboarded buildings, its boatyards, its tangle of ropes, and smell of oil and tar. Just inland stands a delightful square and the church, mostly rebuilt after an earthquake in 1884. North-west of Wivenhoe stand the modern buildings of the University of Essex, occupying Wivenhoe Park, with the Vice-Chancellor's house between the two 18c lakes.

RECOMMENDED WALKS

1. Wivenhoe – Thorrington – Frating – Alresford – Wivenhoe. 8½m. HR.

A good walk in a difficult rambling area. There are some fine views over the Colne.

Start at the Rose & Crown on Wivenhoe Quay. Continue along the front E past the quays and cottages toward the shipyard. Go down The Folly and through the shipyard past the cranes to the far (E) side. Turn R (S) down its E side and pick up the bank of the Colne. The next 3½m of walking lie along the Colne bank. After ½m, the path is joined by the old railway line from Wivenhoe to Brightlingsea, which it follows for 1m past the woods of Alresford Grange to the point where Alresford Creek flows into the Colne estuary. The path from here continues SE to the minor road. Turn L (NNE) here very briefly but then R (SE) again at the footpath signpost. Keep on skirting the marshes and along the bank of the creek for a long mile until the path ends in a broad crossing track at the head of the creek. Turn R (ESE) here to the B road. Walk (NNE) up the road for ½m and then L (NW) at the crossroads down the B1027 for a further ½m. Eventually, turn R (N at a layby by Deep Dene; pick up the private road here signposted as a footpath past bungalows and into Christmas & Sons. Look N to a gap between a wall and a shed by a notice Strictly Private. Contract Yard. The footpath lies through this gap. It then veers between fences L (W) and R (N), and over a stile to a large meadow. Cross this ahead (N), just slightly R and uphill between the first and second pylons ahead. Cross the railway and continue to the edge of the orchard. Pick up a broad track ahead (N) between the trees. Where this ends, turn R (E) and round a bend L (N): continue ahead down this track and then a metalled driveway to the road. Continue N to the church, where take the road going W to the S of the churchyard. Follow this around a bend R (NNW by N) and on for ½m to the end of the hedge on your L. Turn L (WSW) here across the field (there is normally a division in the crops here) to the wood. Skirt a spur of wood on the S side and then continue WSW ahead through the trees. On the other side, continue up a hedge and then a cart track to the farm. Go through the farmyard and past the ponds to the farmhouse, then down the driveway to the road. Cross and take the side road on the other side. Follow this around a bend half-left (SSW by S). At the sharp bend L (ESE) by a white building, pick up an excellent dirt track just S of the house and follow W to the woods. Go through and pick up a broad farm track ahead (W) past a redbrick farmhouse and barn to the road. Cross and pick up a fine narrow grass track left between the crops (W). Continue back into Wivenhoe.

2. Wivenhoe – University of Essex – Elmstead – Crockleford Heath – Colchester. 8m. VHR.

An unusually shaped but enjoyable walk.

Start at Wivenhoe station. Exit on the N side and immediately turn L (NW) down a well-worn path between the trees and the wall. Follow the obvious path ahead to an underpass where you go under the line. Turn R (NW) alongside the line until the path meets the river bank. Climb onto this and continue ahead beside the Colne. Continue for 1m to the SE boundary of the University of Essex parkland. Cross the line here ENE and pick up a broad track ahead. Follow this past Wivenhoe Lodge and down the metalled driveway to the B1027. At the road, turn briefly R (SSE) for about 150yd to a footpath post on your L (E) side. Turn L (E) here down a field edge and then L (N) again up another hedge to the B1027. Turn R

Contd p. 109

Contd p. 102

Contd p.101

Great Bromley
Hamilton Lodge
Cowey Green
The Chase
Park Fm
Byes Fm
The Oaks
Mill Green
Little Bentley
Hospl
Tendring Heath
Tendring Green
Goose Green
Pilcox Hall
Clip Hedge Fm
Bentley Manor
Little Bentley Hall
TENDRING
Lodge Fm
A 604
Hare Green
Raven's Green
Bottles Hall
A 133
Balls Green
Morehams Hall
Grove Fm
Park Fm
Gurnhams
Hill Fm
New Hall
Frating Green
Crabtree Fm
Warren's Fm
Brett's Hall
Pestles
Frating Lodge
Mannings
The Cedars Fm
The Grange
Fisher's Fm
Hawk Fm
Elmstead Heath
Ivy Lodge
Admiral's Fm
Hall
Frating
B 1029
Blue Gates
Slough House Fm
Sturrick Fm
Brook Fm
Great Bentley
Risby's
Hockley
Hockley Pl
Alresford
Cockaynes
Tenderiny Fm
St Mary's Fm
Lufkins Fm
Gutteridge Hall
Brook Fm
Alresford Grange
Whitehouse Fm
Frating Abbey
Tye Homestead
B 1027
Motel
Alresford Hall
Moynes Fm
Coppice Fm
Norwood Lodge
Alresford Lodge
Thorrington
Aingers Green
College Fm
Hall
The Ford
Plumpton's Fm
The Lodge
St Osyth Wick Fm
Maldon Wood
High Birch
South Heath
Gatehouse Fm
Milton Wood
Sand Pit
Moverons
Hall
Sand Pit
Greatmarsh Fm
Hollybush Hill
Welches
Morses
St Osyth Heath
Lowermarsh Fm
Sand Pit
Frowick Hall
Riddles Wood
BRIGHTLINGSEA
Eastmarsh Point
Sand Pit
High Grove
Sand Pit
Lower Fm
Wellwick Fm
Flag Creek
Moat
Hurst Green
Jetty
Lamb Fm
Park Fm
Earls Hall
Tower
Westmarsh Point
Brightlingsea Creek
Cindery Island
Deer Park
Cemy
St Osyth Stone Point
Brightlingsea Creek
Martello Tower
St Osyth Creek
Priory
St Osyth
Point Clear
Warren Fm
Brazier's Fm
Daltes Fm
St Osyth Lodge Fm
St Clere's Hall
Sandy Point
Jetty
Lee Wick Fm
Wigboro Wick Fm
Whyers Hall Fm
Cockett Wick Fm
Mud & Sand
Ray Creek
Nature Reserve
St Osyth Marsh
Seawick
Bel-Air
Lee-over-Sands
Martello Tower
St Osyth Beach
Colne Bar
Colne Point

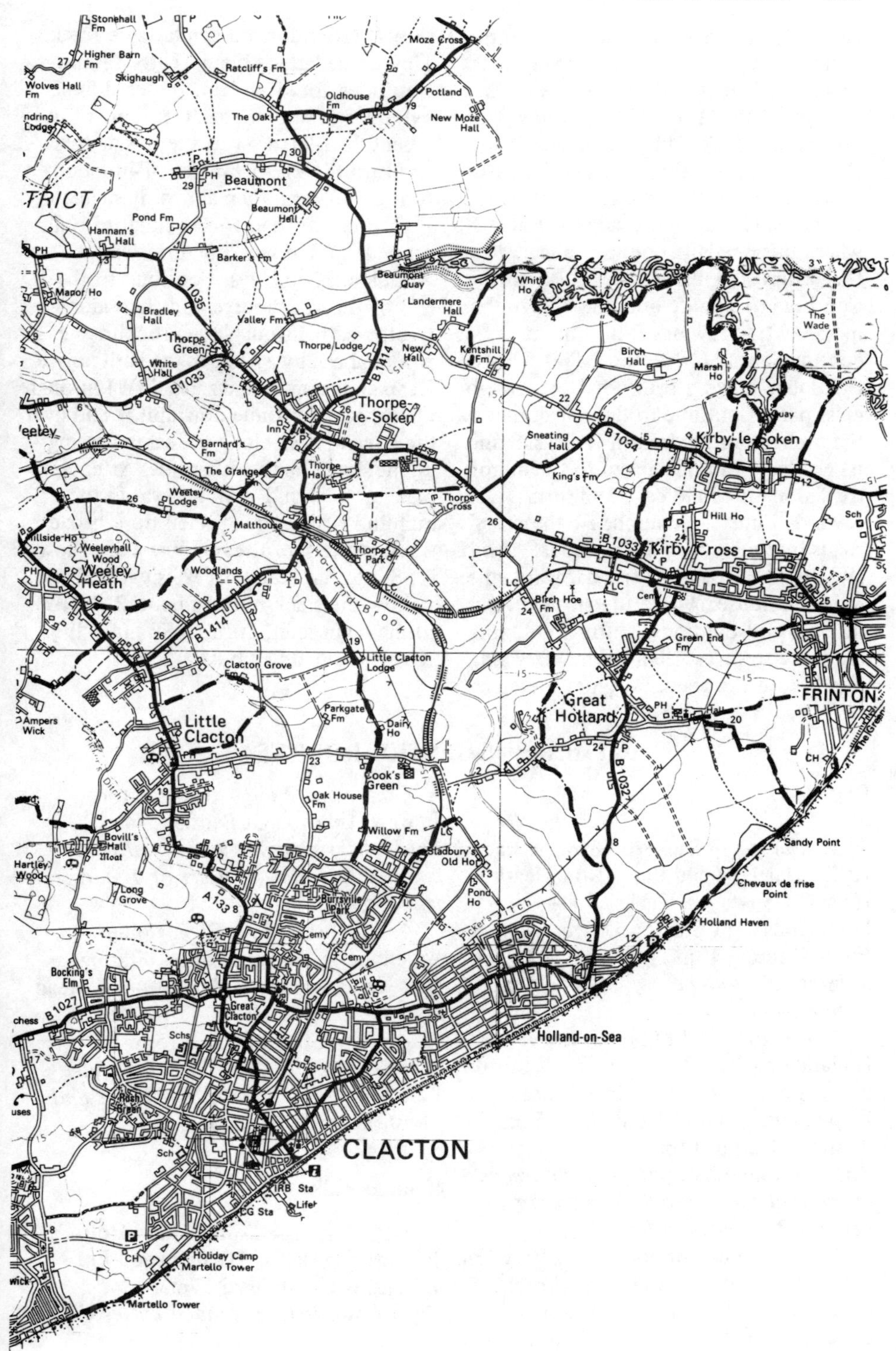
Stonehall Fm
Higher Barn Fm
Wolves Hall Fm
Skighaugh
Ratcliff's Fm
Moze Cross
Oldhouse Fm
Potland
The Oak
New Moze Hall
Beaumont
Beaumont Hall
TRICT
Pond Fm
Hannam's Hall
Barker's Fm
Beaumont Quay
Manor Ho
Bradley Hall
B 1035
Valley Fm
Landermere Hall
White Ho
The Wade
Thorpe Green
Thorpe Lodge
New Hall
Kentshill Fm
Birch Hall
Marsh Ho
White Hall
B1033
B1414
Thorpe-le-Soken
Weeley
Barnard's Fm
Inn
Sneating Hall
B1034
Kirby-le-Soken
The Grange
Thorpe Hall
King's Fm
Weeley Lodge
Thorpe Cross
Hill Ho
Sch
Malthouse
Hillside Ho
Weeleyhall Wood
Weeley Heath
Thorpe Park
B1033
Kirby Cross
Woodlands
Holland Brook
Birch Hoe Fm
Cemy
B1414
Green End Fm
Little Clacton Lodge
Clacton Grove
FRINTON
Great Holland
Ampers Wick
Parkgate Fm
Dairy Ho
Little Clacton
B 1032
Cook's Green
Oak House Fm
Bovill's Hall
Moat
Willow Fm
Stadbury's Old Ho
Sandy Point
Hartley Wood
Chevaux de frise Point
Long Grove
A 133
Burrsville Park
Pond Ho
Holland Haven
Cemy
Picker's Ditch
Bocking's Elm
B1027
Great Clacton
Schs
Holland-on-Sea
Sch
Rush Green
CLACTON
Sch
IRB Sta
CG Sta
Holiday Camp
Martello Tower
Martello Tower

(ESE) down this for a little over ½m to cottages on your L down a side lane. Go down this lane to a sharp bend R by two cottages. Turn L (NNE) here down a broad grass track. This soon bends slightly R and continues ahead to Fen Fm. Go down the pebbled driveway to the road and cross. Go down the side road here N; where this bends L, continue ahead down the signposted driveway of a farm. Continue to a white building. Where the metalled track swings R into the orchard, continue ahead (N) to the L (W) side of the house down a somewhat overgrown grass path. Continue to the NW corner of the orchard and then turn R (E) skirting its N edge. Continue ahead to the minor road along the field edge and turn L (N) towards Elmstead church. At the cross-roads by the large pink farmhouse, turn L (W) down a broad dirt track towards the redbrick house. Where the track divides just beyond the house, turn L (W) and continue towards Allen's Fm. After ¾m, just before the track becomes metalled, turn R (NE) down a similar side track. This immediately bends L (NW) and continues for over ½m, under double pylon wires to orchards. Continue round a bend half-left (W) to the minor road and turn R (N). At the next T-junction, turn L (SW) and then almost immediately R (N) on the road to Crockleford Hall. Turn L (W) down the driveway to Woodlands Nurseries. Continue to the R (N) of the glasshouses and then along a tractor path through the crops to the woods ahead by a Keep to the Path notice. Keep on the main track ahead (W) through the woods. Continue downhill W and over the stream, then along the same bearing up the slopes on the other side. After ¼m, pick up a path L (SW) towards the building visible ahead. Pick up a broad track to the L of the building and follow it SSW to the E edge of Welshwood Park. Follow the track round a bend R (WNW) to the main road. Turn L (SW) into the centre – or catch a bus.

OTHER SUGGESTED ROUTES

Day Walks

1. Clacton – Sacketts Grove – Earls Hall – Hartleywood Fm – Row Heath – Hillside House – Weeley Lodge – Woodlands – Lt Clacton Lodge – Willow Fm – Clacton. 13m.
Substantial stretches of metalled and concreted surface.

2. Clacton – Lt Clacton Lodge – Holland Brook – Thorpe Cross – Kentshill Fm – Skipper Island – Kirby le Soken – Kirby Cross – Gt Holland Gn – Sandy Point – Clacton. 14m.
An enjoyable walk taking in farm tracks, marsh wall and the well-worn coast path between Walton and Clacton.

3. Gt Bentley (station) – Crabtree Fm – Raven's Green – Lt Bentley church – Goose Gn – Tendring – Weeley – Gutteridge Hall – Welches – South Heath – Greatmarsh Fm – Thorrington – Frating Abbey – Gt Bentley. 14m.
Fairly heavy, along lesser paths and country lanes in the heart of Tendring Hundred.

4. Colchester – River Colne – Wivenhoe – Thorrington – Frating – Blue Gates – Elmstead Market – Elmstead church – Allen's Fm – Crockleford Heath – Welshwood Park. 15m.
Almost entirely along Recommended Walks: section between Blue Gates and Elmstead Market is difficult.

Medium Walks

1. St Osyth – Daltes Fm – Rouse's Fm – Earls Hall – Hartleywood Fm – Riddles Wd – St Osyth. 7m.
The outward stage is much better than the return.

2. Clacton – Sandy Point – Gt Holland Gn – Gt Holland Common – Burrsville Pk. 6m.
Likewise; buses needed from Burrsville Pk.

3. Thorpe Cross – Skipper's Island – Sea Wall – Kirby Cross – Thorpe Cross. 8m.
This excellent walk with its mudflats and wildlife can also be started from Kirby Cross station; in that case, walk it the other way around to leave the roadwork at the end.

4. Kirby Cross – Gt Holland Common – Lt Clacton Lodge – Thorpe Cross – Kirby Cross. 7m.
Easy.

5. Weeley – Weeley Hall – Weeley Lodge – Woodlands – Lt Clacton – Hartleywood Fm – Maldon Wood – Gutteridge Hall – Weeley. 8m.
Some problems.

6. Hythe Quay West – Rowhedge – Fingringhoe Mill – Donyland Wood – Friday Woods – Berechurch – Bourne Pond and Mill (NT) – Hythe. 9m.
Combination of river, wood, and town walking including two of Colchester's best known mills. When the red flags are flying the Army is using Donyland Woods; at such times return to Hythe Quay via Rowhedge.

7. Fox Street – Crockleford Heath – Elmstead – A137 – Fox Street. 7m.
A good walk through arable farmland.

Short Walks

1. St Osyth – St Osyth Creek – Stone Point – St Osyth. 4m.
Easy; but necessitates returning along the same path.

2. Lt Clacton – Hartleywood Fm – Row Heath – Lt Clacton. 4m.
A lot of road.

3. Gt Bentley – Gurnhams – Ravens Gn – Crabtree Fm – Gt Bentley. 5½m.
Variable.

4. Brightlingsea – Sea Wall – Hollybush Hill – Greatmarsh Fm – Morses – Brightlingsea. 4½m.
Can be marshy.

5. Wivenhoe – Colne Wall – Alresford Ford – Alresford Grange – Wivenhoe. 4½m.
The return is by a pleasant metalled lane – but there were signs of possible widening when I was there.

6. Hythe Bridge – River Bank to Wivenhoe – Wivenhoe Park – Hythe. 4m.
Generally easy although the river bank can be heavy going in wet weather.

7. Broadlands (off Ipswich road) – Myland Hall – Brinkley Grove – Mile End – Turner Road – Cowdray Ave – Broadlands. 3m.
An easy stroll around High Woods with fine views of Colchester, well worth appreciating as building developments are scheduled for the area.

8. Maypole Green – Berechurch Hall Camp – Roman River – Friday Woods – Kingsford Bridge – Maypole Green. 4m.

Coggeshall District

Attractive country, with generally good paths. River walking along Colne valley, with occasional meadows and woodland.

Birch Excellent wooded walking between here and Layer-de-la-Haye.

Bradwell Often known as Bradwell-juxta-Coggeshall to distinguish it from its namesake in Dengie Hundred. The village lies in woodland on the winding banks of the Blackwater. There is an excellent pub.

Chappel and **Wakes Colne** A pair of pleasant villages straddling the river, and providentially on the branch line to Sudbury. The Stour Valley Railway is here, displaying vintage locomotives. Open: weekends. Its most prominent feature is the enormous bridge nearly 400yd long by which the steep little valley is bridged, which makes a marvellous landmark for those walking in the valley. The country between here and Earl's Colne is quite beautiful, especially south of the river with the fine paths through Chalkney Wood.

Coggeshall During the 15-16c, Coggeshall was heavily involved in the wool industry, and has several buildings that record that involvement – the Fleece Inn (real ale) in West St being one. Also in West St is a fine half-timbered house, Paycocke's. Thomas Paycocke was the town's leading clothier at the end of the 15c. The house is owned now by the National Trust. Open: Wednesdays, Thursdays and Sundays in summer.

Copford Excellent village inn, the Alma. 12c church incorporates Roman material and also some of the earliest medieval bricks in England. Superb 12c wall-paintings remain.

Earls Colne Most of the village, with its thatched, timber-framed and weather-boarded cottages, lies off the paths, but a short walk from here combines well with a look about the High St. There are several good pubs in the village, including the Bird in Hand on our route. This path also passes the site of the old priory, founded at the beginning of the 12c by the de Veres but replaced by the present 18c redbrick house. South-west of the village stands the old airfield, with rights of way following three of the old runways. The airfield was run by the USAAF for daylight bombing of enemy airbases, and later housed units of the Special Operations Executive. Now, it is returned to arable use. Beyond the airfield lie the woods of Markshall, the best wooded walking in this district.

Easthorpe The little Norman church is dedicated to the Anglo-Saxon St Edmund. The country around here is very flat, open and arable.

Inworth Excellent pub (real ale) and a little church with some faded 13c murals above the arch separating nave from chancel.

Kelvedon The site has produced archaeological finds from prehistory right through the Roman period into Anglo-Saxon times. St Mary's church nave roof is decorated with figures of musicians.

Layer Breton, Layer-de-la-Haye Good views over Abberton reservoir.

Layer Marney There was once a village here, on the low slopes overlooking the valley of Layer Brook. Now, the site is only occupied by a handful of buildings, a church and Layer Marney Tower – a soaring 16c brick gatehouse of eight storeys, higher than any other in England. It is enormously tall. It was built in the early 1520s, shortly before the deaths of the first and second Lord Marney. Their deaths brought an end to the line, and called a halt to the building of the hall which the sumptuous gateway was to have led to. The monuments of the two lords as well as one of their 15c ancestors lie nearby in St Mary's church. Layer Marney Tower is open: Thursday and Sunday afternoons in summer, also Tuesday afternoon in high summer.

RECOMMENDED WALK

1. **Birch – Layer de la Haye – Birch Green – Layer Marney – Birch. 10m. HR.**

A walk for the energetic, and one that is best kept for dry weather as many of the pathways are used by horses and can be muddy after rain.

Starting at Birch church, go through the churchyard R of the church and take the path NE through the small swing gate, following the path through the wood (ENE) to a metalled road with a small lake on the L. Go straight across the road (ENE), along a path which swings R (SE) and then L (NE) alongside a wood, crossing a bridge over Roman River. Continue up the hill to Olivers. At the clearing turn R (S) over a stile, following a path down the hill and back over Roman River by the bridge. Follow the path through woods, branching L (SE). Continue SSE over a small brook, up the hill and through to the B1026. Turn R (SW), walk through the village for a long 1m, taking the path R (W) signposted to Layer Breton. Following the hedgeline for approx. 400yd, continue straight across the field in a general westerly direction, picking up a farm track heading due W into Birch Green. Take the sign-posted path WSW at the junction, leaving a house with moat on the L. Continuing SW along the hedgeline, turn L (SE) at the road and then R (SSW) by the public footpath sign to Layer Marney. After walking 250yd along the hedgeside path go straight (W) across fields towards the Tower, leaving Wick Fm L (S). Follow public footpath signs W past the Tower and church, turning R (N) at the end of the track and then L (W) along the hedgerow, walking towards houses on a hill. Here take the metalled road NW over crossroads then turn R (NNW) onto a well-signposted path through the wood. At the end of the wood turn R along the B1022, walk as far as the layby past the White Horse, then turn R (E) onto a path beside the hedge. Continue R (E) down the road by a bungalow and then L (E) along a farm track beside the farmyard. Follow the track NE until it stops, then walk across a field taking the gap through the hedge L of the house opposite. This path leads N to a track branching first L (N) then R (E) before reaching a road. Turn L (NE then NNW) back to Birch church.

SUGGESTED ROUTES

Weekend Walk

Lexden (Colchester) – Gryme's Dyke – Chest Wood – Birch – Layer Breton – Layer Marney – The Rampart – Messing – Prested Hall – Kelvedon (overnight stop). Kelvedon – Coggeshall Hall – Coggeshall – Essex Way – Gt Tey – Fordstreet – West Bergholt (Whitehouse Fm) – Lexden. Day 1: 12m. Day 2: 12m.
A fairly leisurely weekend taking in many sites of historical and archaeological interest.

Day Walks

1. Earls Colne – Chalkney Wood – Florries Fm – Palmers Fm – Houchins Fm – Coggeshall – Bungate Wood – Burtons Gn – Greenstead Gn – Stonebridge Hill – Earls Colne. 13m.
Some arable but mostly good paths.

2. Coggeshall – Bouchier's Grange – Markshall – Earls Colne airfield – Tilekiln Fm – Chalkney Wood – Swanscombe Fm – Wakes Colne – Penlan Hall – Fordstreet – Essex Way – Coggeshall. 15m.
This can be reduced to 11m by starting at

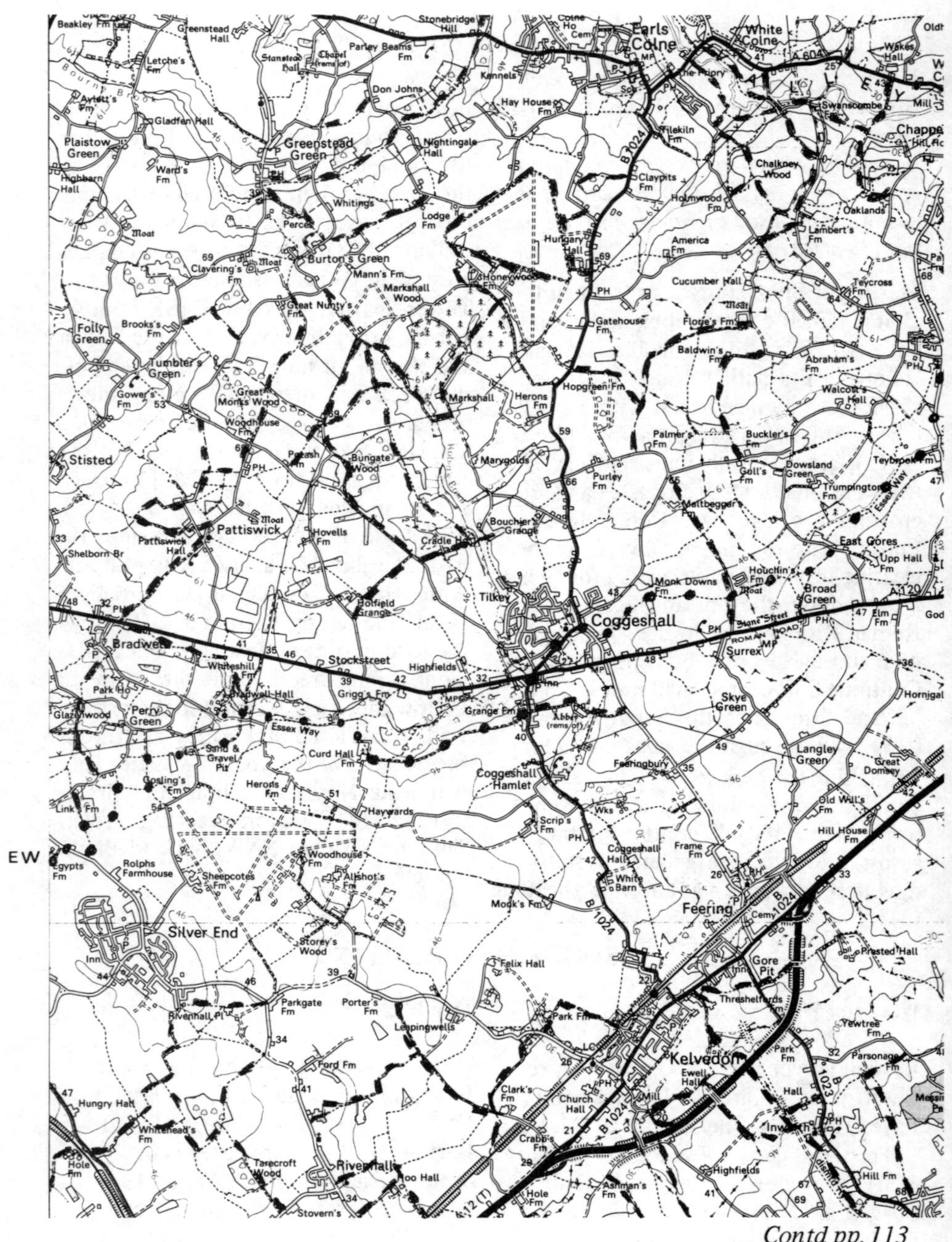

EW

Contd pp. 113

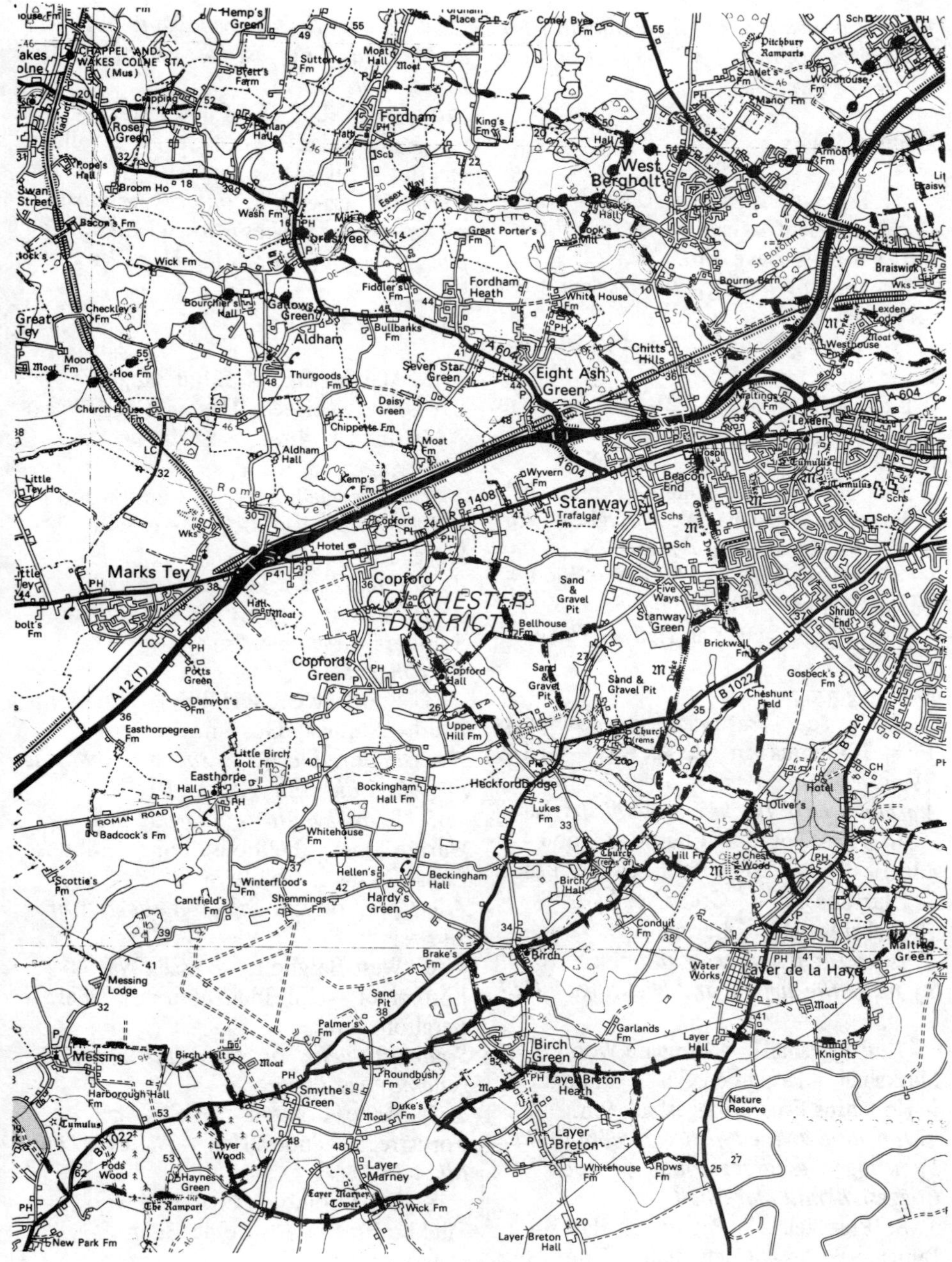

Hemp's Green
CHAPPEL AND WAKES COLNE STA. (Mus)
Brett's Farm
Sutton's Fm
Moat Hall
Coney Byes Fm
Pitchbury Ramparts
Scarlet's Fm
Woodhouse Fm
Manor Fm
Rose Green
Fordham
King's Fm
West Bergholt
Armoury Fm
Pope's Hall
Broom Ho
Swan Street
Essex Way
River Colne
Wash Fm
Bacon's Fm
Fordstreet
Great Porter's Fm
Bourne Barn
St Botolph's Brook
Braiswick
Wick Fm
Fiddler's Fm
Fordham Heath
White House Fm
Lexden Lodge
Checkley's Fm
Bourchier's Hall
Gallows Green
Westhouse Fm
Great Tey
Aldham
Bullbanks Fm
Chitts Hills
Moor Fm
Hoe Fm
Thurgoods Fm
Seven Star Green
Eight Ash Green
Maltings Fm
A 604
Lexden
Church House Fm
Daisy Green
Chippetts Fm
Moat Fm
Aldham Hall
Little Tey Ho
Kemp's Fm
Wyvern Fm
Beacon End
Roman River
B 1408
Stanway
Trafalgar Fm
Schs
Wks
Copford Pl
Hotel
Sch
Marks Tey
Copford
COLCHESTER DISTRICT
Sand & Gravel Pit
Five Ways
Stanway Green
Bellhouse Fm
Shrub End
Potts Green
Copford Green
Copford Hall
Brickwall Fm
A 12 (T)
Damyon's Fm
Sand & Gravel Pit
Gosbeck's Fm
B 1022
Cheshunt Field
Easthorpegreen Fm
Upper Hill Fm
Little Birch Holt Fm
B 1026
Easthorpe Hall
Bockingham Hall Fm
Heckfordbridge
Hotel
Oliver's
ROMAN ROAD
Badcock's Fm
Lukes Fm
Whitehouse Fm
Hill Fm
Chest Wood
Scottie's Fm
Winterflood's Fm
Hellen's
Beckingham Hall
Birch Hall
Cantfield's Fm
Shemmings Fm
Hardy's Green
Conduit Fm
Malting Green
Messing Lodge
Brake's Fm
Birch
Water Works
Layer de la Haye
Sand Pit
Palmer's Fm
Garlands Fm
Layer Hall
Messing
Birch Holt
Roundbush Fm
Birch Green
Knights
Harborough Hall Fm
Smythe's Green
Layer Breton Heath
Tumulus
Duke's Fm
Nature Reserve
B 1022
Layer Wood
Layer Breton
Pods Wood
Haynes Green
Layer Marney
Whitehouse Fm
Rows Fm
The Rampart
Layer Marney Tower
Wick Fm
New Park Fm
Layer Breton Hall

wakes Colne and using the Houchin's Fm – Florries Fm route. All the paths around here are enjoyable.

Medium Walks

1. Layer-de-la-Haye – Chest Wood – Cheshunt Field – Gryme's Dyke – Hill Fm – Layer-de-la-Haye. 6m.
A great deal of historical interest and some lovely woods.

2. Malting Green – Blind Knights – Birch Gn – Layer Marney – Smyth's Gn – Birch – Chest Wood – Malting Gn. 9¾m.
Variable.

3. West Bergholt – Essex Way – Fordstreet – Wakes Colne – Penlan Hall – Fordham church – West Bergholt. 9m.
Some delightful riverside walking.

4. Wakes Colne – Chalkney Wood – Pattock's Fm – Gt Tey – Essex Way – Fordstreet – Penlan Hall – Wakes Colne. 9m.
Mostly good paths.

5. Gt Tey – Pattocks Fm – Lamberts Fm – Houchins Fm – Essex Way – Gt Tey. 7½m.
Variable: farm tracks and arable paths.

6. Earls Colne – Chalkney Wood – Florries Fm – Hopgreen Fm – Markshall – Burtons Gn – Greenstead Gn – Stonebridge Hill – Earls Colne. 9½m.
This excellent walk can be reduced to 7m by using the airfield and Nightingale Hall path.

7. Coggeshall – Bungate Wood – Markshall – Hopgreen Fm – Palmers Fm – Houchins Fm – Coggeshall. 9m.
This can be divided into two 6½m walks by using the direct route between Coggeshall and Markshall.

8. Bradwell – Pattiswick Hall – Bungate Wood – Coggeshall – Essex Way – Bradwell. 7½m.
An excellent and mostly easy walk.

9. Gryme's Dyke – Cheshunt Field – Birch Hall – Heckford Bridge – Copford Hall – Bellhouse Fm – Oldhouse Fm – Gryme's Dyke. 7m.
Easy walking through woodland but the arable field of the last part can be muddy in wet weather.

10. Chitts Hills – Cook's Mill – Fordham Bridge – Fordstreet – Fordham Heath – Chitts Hills. 6m.
Excellent walk along one of the most picturesque stretches of the Colne valley, part of which includes the Essex Way.

Short Walks

1. Malting Gn – Blind Knights – B1026 – Layer-de-la-Haye – Chest Wood – Malting Gn. 4m.
Patchy.

2. Layer-de-la-Haye – Chest Wood – Hill Fm – Birch church – Layer-de-la-Haye. 3m.
A charming and well-used little walk.

3. Messing – Smyth's Gn – The Rampart – Messing. 5m.
Very pleasant.

4. Stanway Gn – Hill Fm – Cheshunt Field – Stanway Gn. 4m.
This can be reduced to a 3m stroll by using the woodside path S of the B1022.

5. Stanway Gn – Stanway Hall – Warren Lane – Bellhouse Fm – Oldhouse Fm – Stanway Gn. 4½m.
A bit patchy especially on the return journey.

6. West Bergholt – Essex Way – Fordstreet – Fordham church – West Bergholt. 5m.
Some problems on the return, but generally very good.

7. Wakes Colne – Penlan Hall – Fordstreet – Pope's Hall – Wakes Colne.
Likewise.

8. Earls Colne – Chalkney Wood – Tilekiln Fm – Earls Colne. 3½m.
A very pretty walk.

9. Hungary Hill – Hopgreen Fm – Florries Fm – Chalkney Wood – Hungary Hill. 5½m.
Variable.

10. Gt Tey – Swan St – Fordstreet – Gt Tey. 5½m.

Likewise. Takes in the Essex Way.

11. Burtons Gn – Markshall – airfield – Lodge Fm – Burtons Gn. 4¼m. *A great contrast of paths and country, for such a short walk.*

Blackwater Estuary (north)

Sea and river wall walks; river valley and woodland inland.

Goldhanger There is a decoy pond by the creek, together with red mounds marking the remains of Roman salt workings.

Great Braxted Braxted Park has absorbed the picturesque little church, and hidden it behind woods and beautiful old red brick walls. Magnificent old inn, the Du Cane Arms.

Heybridge At the head of the Blackwater estuary, with a number of old cottages, and a mill – mostly spoilt by the traffic which thunders through the village.

Little Braxted Just above the junction of the Blackwater and the Brain, with only a handful of scattered cottages, but including a Tudor hall, a Georgian miller's house and watermill, and a tiny 12c church.

Rivenhall Mostly modern, a commuter's village on the outskirts of the town, but the neo-Gothic church contains some fine medieval stained glass, brought over from St Martin of Tours during the French Revolution by an English curate.

Salcott Some magnificent sea wall and marsh walking to the east. The mainly half-timbered cottages have a forsaken look. The church is Victorian.

Tollesbury The square by the church has little shops and an old weatherboarded lock-up. Church font inscribed: Good people all I pray take care, That in ye church you do not sware, As this man did . 'This man' was one John Norman, and his penalty was to pay for the font. South of the church are good views over the Blackwater estuary. The sea wall here is again particularly good walking, and brings the rambler round to Tollesbury's picturesque harbour and old sheds at the east end of the village. The pub is the Hope, with an unusual sign showing Noah receiving the dove with a sprig in its beak.

Tolleshunt D'Arcy Two D'Arcy brasses remain in the church to show how the village got its name. 16c hall with moat crossed by Elizabethan bridge. Little pub in the village.

Tolleshunt Major Weatherboarded cottages, church lying with hall to east of village.

Wickham Bishops A large and mostly modern village with an excellent pub, the Mitre. The old church stands unused between the equally defunct railway and the Blackwater. The country is especially pleasant, with fine woods and views from Beacon Hill over the flatter lands to the south-east.

Witham The largest town in this district, with some light industry and much new development, but still retaining timber, blue brick and Georgian houses in High St, Bridge St and Newland St.

Contd p.108

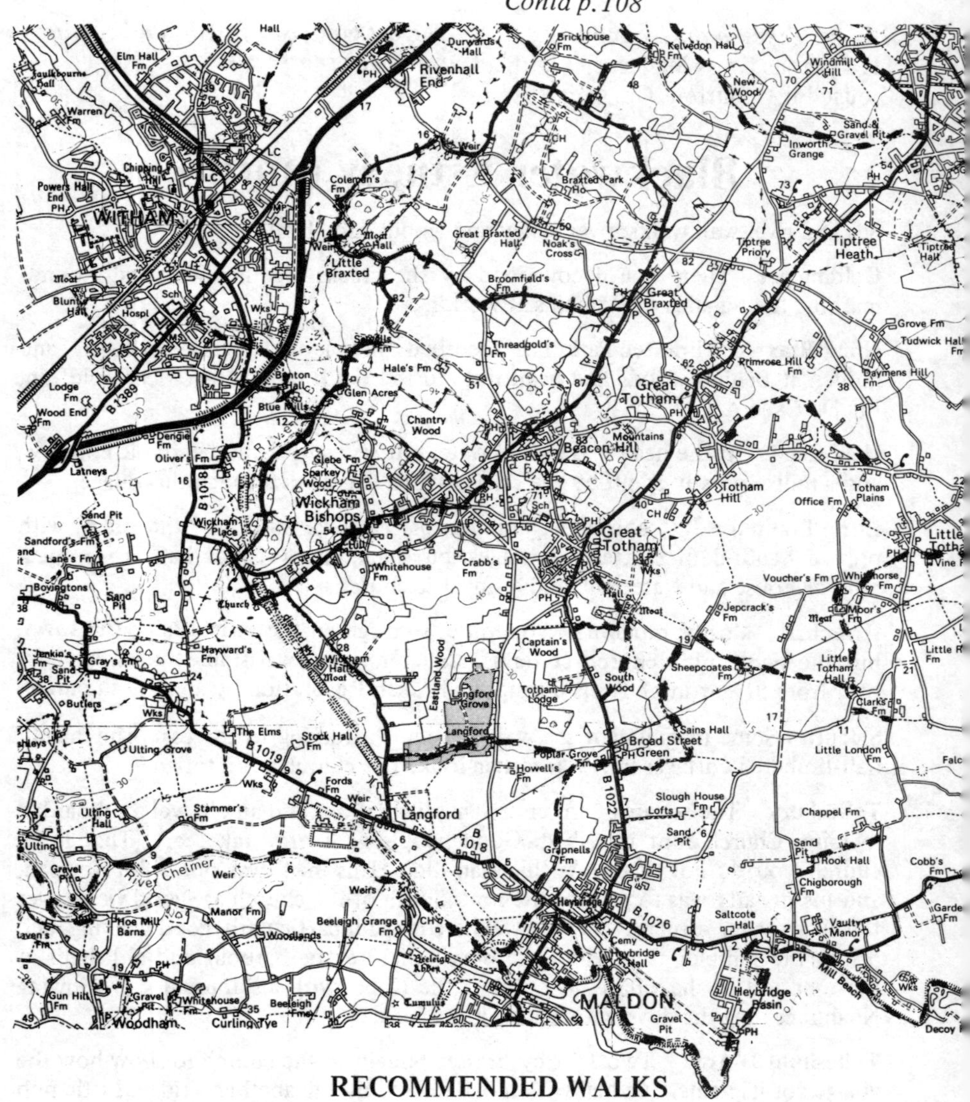

RECOMMENDED WALKS

1. **Witham – Wickham Bishops – Gt Braxted – Witham. 10m. HR.**

Shorter walks:

Witham – Wickham Bishops – Lt Braxted – Witham. 7m. R.

Lt Braxted – Gt Braxted – Lt Braxted. HR.

The S half of the walk includes a number of metalled surfaces.

Start at the red brick bridge over the Blackwater on the Gt Totham road. Turn R (SSW) by the Private Fishery sign onto a path separated from the E bank of the river only by bushes. The path follows this often rather overgrown path for 1m to the point where the next road (the B1018) crosses over the river. Climb up to the road and turn L (SSE) to the telephone box, where the road bends L (E). Pick up a broad cart track between

Contd pp. 94-5

crops from here to the old church. Turn L (ENE) here over the old railway line and down a cart track under telegraph poles to the road. Cross and go down the main driveway of Fontenay Orchards, again following telegraph poles through the orchards NE to the road. Turn R (ENE) up the road to a T-junction. Turn L (N) here up Station Rd and then R (E) down Church Rd. Go past the church and through Wickham Bishops. At the fork in the road, turn down the R fork E (sign-posted to Gt Totham) and continue to a junction opposite the Mitre pub. Turn L here and then almost immediately R (down Handleys Lane). At the end, continue NE down the signposted path under trees. Go down this and then a driveway to Kelveden Rd. Take the road N from the crossroads (by the war memorial) and then turn R (ENE) down Braxted Rd. Keep on this lovely wooded lane for 1m into the centre of Gt Braxted by the Du Cane Arms. The long and short walks divide here. (If on the short walk, walk W out of the village; pick up a signposted path just opposite Sexton's Fm, and cross the field WNW to the N edge of the woods ahead. Skirt the woods to Broomfields Fm and go down the driveway to the minor road; turn R (NW) up the road till it bends R by a large gravelled layby, pick up a grass field edge path S of the houses and continue NW. The path follows hedges around the N side of a lake and then turns half-left (SW) along a field edge under telegraph poles to the R (W) of the houses.) If on the long walk, pick up a signposted grass path immediately E of the Du Cane Arms; follow this NNE down hedgerows to the road. Cross half-right and pick up a signposted farm road skirting the red brick wall of Braxted Park. Follow past a gateway (where the metalled surface swings L) NNE to the edge of the wood. Turn L (NW) here along a path through the wood to its S edge, then half-right (NNW) through the trees again and along their E side. Eventually, pick up a lovely unmade lane half-left (WNW) skirting the park to a minor road. Turn L (SSW). At the T-junction, take the road R (W). Shortly after crossing the Blackwater, turn L (WSW) down a broad track. This was being concreted when I walked it, and the route may be changed. The right of way continues WSW as shown on the map. Turn L (SSE) at the minor road. Follow around bends over the Blackwater and past two houses (where the short cut rejoins the path) to a sharp bend L (ESE) just before a farm. At this point, continue ahead down a signposted concrete farm road to the L-hand edge of a wood. Skirt the wood on its N side to its SW tip. Turn half-left there and cross the cornfield S to the large gap between the trees ahead. At that gap, turn briefly R and L to avoid the front lawn of the house and then R again down the metalled driveway to the road.

2. **Tollesbury – Decoy Fm – Shinglehead Point – Tollesbury. 7m. VHR.**

Easy walking along cart tracks and sea wall, with many good river and marshland views.

Start at Tollesbury church. Pick up the road immediately to the W (Church Lane). Where this forks, take the L (E) fork and continue to the entrance to Bohun's Hall. Continue S down the broad cart track ahead for 1m. This goes past Decoy Fm and onto the sea wall. Turn L (SE and then E). The walk follows the sea bank for the next 5m, including two winding detours around Mill Creek and a part of Tollesbury Wick Marshes. Continue past Shinglehead Point, NW to Woodrolfe Creek and then SW to the headwaters of the creek. The bank eventually returns to Tollesbury by the old ship sheds and modern block of flats. Turn L (WSW) at the road and return into the centre of the village.

OTHER SUGGESTED ROUTES

Day Walks

1. Messing – Smyth's Gn – Roundbush Fm – Birch – Hill Fm – Chest Wood – Malting Gn – Blind Knights – Layer Breton – Layer Marney – The Rampart – Messing. 14½m.
This can be reduced by omitting Messing or Malting Gn.

2. Witham – Blue Mills – River Blackwater – Wickham Bishops – Gt Braxted – Braxted Pk – Hole Fm – Clarks Fm – Porters Fm – Parkgate Fm – Rivenhall Place – Whiteheads Fm – Rivenhall Rd – Witham. 13m.
Rather too much road at first, but some pleasant paths – and excellent pubs.

3. Heybridge – Sea Wall – Goldhanger – Decoy Fm – Tollesbury – White House Fm – Brook House Fm – Tolleshunt Fm

– Tolleshunt Major – Lt Totham – Lt Totham Hall – Sheepcoates Fm – Sains Fm – Heybridge. 18m.
This excellent walk along sea banks and (mostly) farm tracks can be reduced by 2½m by using the path between Lt Totham Hall and Chigborough Fm, or by 5½m by taking the Lt Totham Hall – Goldhanger route.

Medium Walks

1. Silver End – Whiteheads Fm – Rivenhall Rd – Rivenhall – Clarks Fm – Snivelling Lane – Parkgate Fm – Rivenhall Place – Silver End. 6½m.
Some arable work to be done.

2. Salcott – Quince's Corner – Sea Wall – Salcott. 7½m.
Excellent sea-bank walking.

3. Heybridge – Sea Wall – Chigborough Fm – Lt London Fm – Lt Totham Hall – Sheepcoates Fm – Sains Fm – Heybridge. 8m.
A bit patchy.

Short Walks

1. Rivenhall – Rivenhall Rd – wood by Whiteheads Fm – Silver End Rd – Rivenhall. 4m.
Easy but a lot of road.

2. Goldhanger – Sea Wall – Chigborough Fm – Chapel Fm – Goldhanger. 5m.
Not quite as good as some sea wall walks.

3. Tollesbury – Sea Wall – Tolleshunt D'Arcy Rd – Tollesbury. 4m.
A lot of road.

Mersea Island

There is a footpath round the island, linked by a short stretch of road beside the shore at West Mersea. The total distance is about 12 miles.

West Mersea Full of sailing holidaymakers in the summer, but pleasant at all times, with seasonal caravans mainly out of sight.

East Mersea Off the path, but still much as it was a hundred years ago when Baring-Gould, then rector, wrote *Mehalah*, a haunting story of these Essex creeks and saltings.

7. CENTRAL ESSEX

Chipping Ongar to Chelmsford (south); Chipping Ongar to Chelmsford (north)

The area covered by this chapter is bounded by Chelmsford, Brentwood, Chipping Ongar and Pleshey. The overlying boulder clay left behind after the Ice Age forms a plateau of water-resistant ground, with undulating hills and valleys etched into it by the surface water draining away as streams and rivers. Like central Suffolk and Norfolk, it was heavily forested from the end of the Ice Age right up to the middle ages. Epping Forest (admirably covered by Fred Matthews' walks pamphlets, and so not a part of this chapter) is all that remains of this original covering. Apart from some clusters of more recent woodland around Mill Green and Billericay, the area is remarkable for its lack of large wooded expanses. This hilly plateau, with its streams and rivers, is now generally dominated by arable farming. Man's impact on this region is comparatively recent: prehistoric man with his stone and later soft metal implements could make little headway in clearing the Essex forests, and seems to have confined his few settlements to river valleys such as the Wid, by Billericay. Even Roman remains are doubtful evidence of Roman settlement, for in many cases, they consist only of Roman bricks or tiles incorporated into the walls of medieval churches, and this material may have been brought for some miles to the site of the church. Such Roman settlement as there was seems to have concentrated in the three river valleys of the area, the Roding, Wid and Can: several settlement sites have been discovered on the Can, especially in the Boyton and Chignall St James area.

The earliest Saxon settlements were also in the valleys, and along the line of the Roman road south-west of Chelmsford. The succession of -ing place names between Chelmsford and Brentwood is impressive. The gradual clearance of the forests in the six centuries following the arrival of the Anglo-Saxons seems by 1066 to have led to the establishment of most of the villages currently on the map. By the middle ages towns like Writtle, Chelmsford, Brentwood and Pleshey had developed, along with a few large and prosperous villages like Blackmore. Prosperity, of course, was relative. Generally speaking, this part of the county did not share in the great cloth-based wealth of the 14th and 15th centuries that so developed Norfolk and Suffolk. The arable sufficiency of this area was not enough to create more than a few market towns, like Chipping Ongar. The result is very visible today in the Pleshey district, where the villages are small, very often no more than a few cottages. Frequently, they have declined in size during the last 150 years, particularly with the advent of mechanised farming and the attraction of better-paid employment in Chelmsford. In the south of the area there are plenty of large villages, but this is mostly a product of the last two centuries, as the architecture shows, and particularly a commuter-based phenomenon of our own age. There are therefore very considerable differences between walking in the two districts, with the northern providing much more isolated country than that to the south. The footpaths are generally better in the southern district, where there are more people to walk them and where the several rambling groups of the area are based. In either district, the signposting is excellent.

Walking consists of quite a lot of arable work, tempered by the large numbers of paths and the attitudes generated by the long tradition of rambling that exists in central Essex. The landscape is fairly varied, at least in terms of hills and valleys. To the north, there are many isolated farms and hamlets, and no large villages; to the south there are some large modern villages but also a few where the influx of money has preserved the great original beauty of the buildings from decay. Architecturally the area is very distinctive, a constant reminder of local expertise, originally acquired in the middle ages, in building in timber. The churches very often have timber porches and roofs, and there are many with wooden towers and belfries, or shingled spires. The lower prosperity of the area during the middle ages might account for the plainer church interiors, and complete absence of stone. Houses too are typically in timber, either wood-framed or weatherboarded. The grander buildings, of which there are remarkably few in the area, are sometimes of red brick, particularly if Tudor in date like Ingatestone Hall. The result is a very simple and attractive rural scene, unmistakably Essex.

The future of this area as walking country must be in some doubt. In the southern district in particular, creeping development must in the long term threaten the remaining stretches of isolated countryside. The best way to keep the footpaths open is to walk them.

Chipping Ongar to Chelmsford (south)

Good footpaths, good signposting. A more populous district than the northern section, with strong rambling traditions.

Bellhouse and **Ramsden Heath** The country between them is pleasantly wooded, with little hills and pasture.

Billericay Too large to be visited in a walk, but an interesting town nevertheless. Chapel Street and High Street have many fine buildings. The Pilgrim Fathers assembled at 57-9 High Street before boarding the *Mayflower*. The Cater Museum has a collection of prehistoric, Roman and Anglo-Saxon finds. Open: afternoons except Sunday. **Norsey Wood** The country between the Ramsdens and Billericay contains some excellent woodland walking. Of these woods, Norsey Wood is the most interesting, because it was the site of a battle in 1381 between royal troops and supporters of the Peasants' Rebellion. 500 peasants were killed and Billericay, a centre of the revolt, taken.

Blackmore Now a very fashionable village, with a fine 15c inn, the Bull. In the middle ages it was a tanning and horse trading town, with its own canonry known as Jericho. After the dissolution of the latter in 1527, a palace was built for Henry VIII's mistress Elizabeth Talbois and their bastard son Henry Fitzroy. When the king was not at court, the more frivolous courtiers would say that he had gone to Jericho. It is a lovely spot, with green pastures and shady trees beside a brook inevitably known as Jordan. The splendid church stands here. The complex structure of oak struts, beams and cross-pieces that supports the three-storey tower is, unusually, visible. St Lawrence, to whom the church is dedicated, is shown being roasted on a griddle in an 18c panel.

Brentwood Large and modern, and difficult to get out of onto good footpaths. Weald Country Park to the west of the town.

Chipping Ongar A contradictory place, the last outpost of the London Underground, and still a market town. The High Street and church bounded the medieval town. The church has a peep-hole from the archorite's cell. Ongar Castle survives as a mound immediately north of the church. Originally there was also an outer bailey 80 ft wide, on the town side. David Livingstone stayed here during his training as a missionary, and preached at the Nonconformist chapel.

Doddinghurst and **Stondon Massey** Old villages generally ruined by unenterprising modern development. The Elizabethan composer William Byrd lived at Stondon Place, and is thought to be buried in the churchyard. **Paslow Wood Common**, north-east of Stondon, has in the Black Horse a splendid pub, although walkers would do well to be mindful of the plush carpeting.

Greensted The Saxon church was constructed of rough-cut logs split down the centre and inserted into grooves in a beam running along either side of the nave. The marks of the adze are still visible upon the logs. Local tradition says that St Edmund's body was kept here briefly on its journey from London to Bury Abbey; and the wooden covers of the church bible are meant to have come from the tree where the king was martyred.

Hylands Park a Council-owned country park, open to all. There are fine paths, and few visitors on weekdays. The house was built in 1728.

Ingatestone Despite the modern suburban development and traffic which besets the village, the High Street remains chiefly Georgian. Its -ing name suggests an early Saxon history. The church is unusual, built of stone and brick, possibly to emphasise the importance of the medieval town under its manorial lords. Monuments of the Petres include an alabaster tomb-chest in the chancel to Sir William Petre, the son of a Devon tanner who rose to be Henry VIII's principal secretary of state. Thomas Cromwell's protégé made good as a commissioner for the dissolution of the monasteries, and was rewarded with the manor of Ingatestone. **Ingatestone Hall** is the mansion he built here. It originally had three courtyards and a great hall. Now, only part of the inner court survives. The hall is a splendid red brick building; there is a lovely gateway, some fine lawns and gardens with brick walls surrounding them, and a beautiful façade with gables and mullioned windows. The interior houses the Essex Record Office, open to the public and giving exhibitions of county history during the summer months. There is a Long Gallery and also a Priest's Hole, for the Petres were a Catholic family. Father Paine was betrayed here by the apostate spy, George Elliott. The fourth Lord Petre died in prison after the Titus Oates affair: the ninth led the campaign for the Catholic Relief Acts of the 1780s, and the Emancipation Act of 1829. Their religion kept them out of public life, and too poor to alter their beautiful house.

Margaretting The church tower is supported on ten posts, with a ground floor, belfry and shingled spire. Look also at the curious carvings on the font and the tree of Jesse in the east window. The Red Lion is one of a number of pubs.

Mill Green The Cricketers pub stands beside the huge triangular green, with its grass and bushy woodlands. The wooded country to the north of here is some of the best walking in the district. They complement the wooden belfries of the area and remind the walker of the huge forests that once covered this part of Essex.

Navestock Heath A large green with a pub (the Plough) beside it. Ultra-slim wooden church spire, 14c tombs of the Waldegrave family in the chancel.

Navestock Side Large green used mainly as a cricket pitch, with a little timber pavilion on one side and the Green Man inn. Good views over wooded, rolling countryside.

South Hanningfield A few cottages and a tiny medieval church behind the manor house, with timber belfry and porch. A barn stands by the church.

Stanford Rivers In the middle of some remarkably hilly and unpopulated country, with generally good walking.

Stock A beautiful village, despite much modern bungalow development. To the east is a well-preserved windmill; in the centre by the crossroads are two old inns, and a general purpose shop called Stock Lock and Barrel; and the village green, almshouses and church. The country around Stock is wooded and rolling, with several farms and an isolated little church at St Mary, Buttsbury. **Buttsbury** was originally larger than Stock, but has now declined to a handful of cottages.

West Hanningfield has suffered from new development. The church contains work of every period in the middle ages. The country around here is extremely arable. The village's most prominent feature is its reservoir. Built in 1958, this covers nearly 900 acres and cost £6 million. It has wooded banks, and is well-stocked with fish; nearly a hundred different species of birds are to be found here.

Writtle Still separate from Chelmsford, perhaps because they were for so long rivals during the middle ages. King John had a palace here, marked by the dry moat half a mile north of the church, and there was also a Hospital of the Holy Ghost with several chantries. Writtle Green, with its cricket pitch and cottages, is attractive.

RECOMMENDED WALKS

1. Stock – Hanningfield Reservoir – Stock. 4m. HR.

An easy short walk along well-defined paths and quiet lanes. This walk may be linked to the next route to create a longer (12½m) circular route. **HR.**

Start at the Cock inn. Walk E down Mill Rd and then turn off L (NE) down Mill Lane. Continue to the N end of a row of modern houses. Turn R (E) over a stile opposite No. 33 by the Private Property notice and cross the field diagonally E to the minor road by Steel's Fm. Turn R (SE) up the hill past Lt Steels and then turn L (E) down Seaman's Lane at the house and bridleway notice. Continue down this delightful lane for ¾m, with trees and fields on either side. The metalled surface eventually gives way to a dirt track. Turn R (SSW) just before the reservoir over an iron gate and into a meadow, with the plantation of the reservoir on your L (E) side. (If you reach the Danger. Deep Water notice, you have gone too far down the lane.) Continue over the first meadow to another iron gate. From here, the footpath continues S over the next two meadows past the L-hand corner of one wood and then the R-hand side of the reservoir plantation. Go over the stile here and cross the next (fourth) meadow to the R-hand edge of the next wood. Turn R (W) here and skirt the next field to the edge of the trees. Turn R (W) again and continue along a well-trodden path to the road. Turn R (NW) and walk up the road for 60yd to the next bend. At this point, leave the road L (W) past the footpath signpost and over the iron gate. Continue across to the woods to the R of the white weather-boarded house and weeping willow. Pick up the pebbled driveway of the house half-left (WSW) between woods and a mature hedge to the narrow road (Whites Hill). Turn R (NW) over a crossroads and on to a side road coming in from the L. Turn L (SW) briefly down this lane but almost immediately turn R (WNW) down the path leading to the first cottage on that side of the road (with a corrugated iron roof). Continue past this on its N side, go over a stile and across the next field. Cross another stile and go down a narrow path to the road. Walk R (N) up the road for 35yd and pick up a good path L (W) between hedges immediately N of the Sunnybrook Fm entrance. Continue ahead to Stock church and turn R back into the centre of the village.

2. Ingatestone – Margaretting Hall – Stock – Ingatestone. 8½m. HR.

This walk follows easy arable paths between the attractive villages of Stock, Margaretting and Ingatestone.

Leave Ingatestone down Lt Hyde Lane (NW). Where this bends L (W) by The Grange, take the narrower lane (also Lt Hyde Lane) R (NE). Follow towards farm buildings on the hill, but turn off L (N) down a signposted track towards Handley Barns. Where this bends L over a brook, follow but immediately go R through a gap in the hedge and R again (E) along a field edge path N of the brook. Follow the brook to a little wood: walk through it on its S edge and rejoin the stream. After a short distance, cross the stream onto its S bank and follow it WNW under the A12. The right of way here continues along a well-trodden path ESE to the B road. Turn L (NE) past the Red Lion and service station to signposted path R (SE) opposite Pennys Lane school. Cross a stile into meadows and continue between the hedge and the stream. Follow the stream to the railway line, cross and continue to a bridge over the river Wid. Turn L and follow the river ENE to the top of the field (the official right of way however crosses the field). Where the Wid bends sharply L, continue ahead (SE) over a rough stile and through a hedge into meadows. Continue up the L side of this field past a track L (to a wooden barn) and past more hedges on to the road. Turn briefly R (SW) but leave the road at the next bend down a broad sign-posted bridleway under trees. Where this path ends in a broad crossing farm track, turn L (SE) through Fristling Hall and down the pebbled driveway to the minor road. Cross and go through the gap in the hedge immediately opposite. Turn sharp R (SE) alongside the road and then ahead to the wood. Skirt the wood to a crossing lane and turn R (S) to the B1007. Turn R (SW) into Stock. Leave the village R (W) via Back Lane (just S of The Cock). Continue to the end of the metalling and then down a shingle lane. Where this divides, turn L (SSW) towards farm buildings. Continue down this broad track for 1m to a minor road. At the road, continue ahead (S) to a sharp bend L (ESE) and a side road S by the church. Pick up a narrow grass path R (WNW) across the field to the stream. Follow the stream briefly R (NW) to a little bridge over the Wid and then pick up the path ahead (W) past isolated trees to the R of Ingatestone Hall visible up the hill. At the narrow road, turn L (S) to visit the hall; then return down the road and continue WNW into Ingatestone.

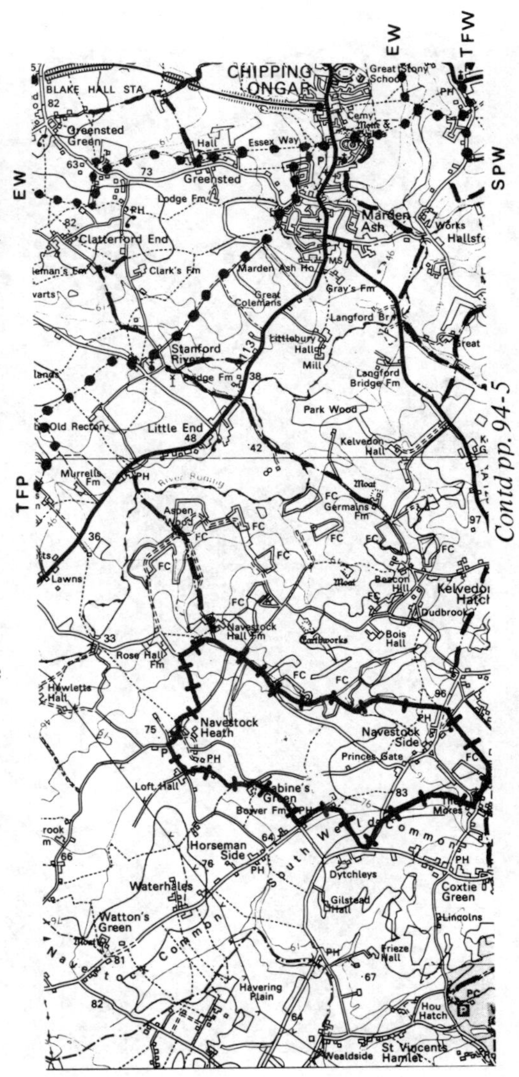

Contd pp. 94-5

3. **Mill Green – Parsons Spring – Highwood – Wells & Sheds – Mill Green. 6¼m. VHR.**

Shorter walks:

Mill Green – Parsons Spring – Highwood – Mill Green. 4m. VHR.

Edney Common – Wells & Sheds – Highwood – Edney Common. 4m. HR.

Delightful wooded walking around the little village of Mill Green.

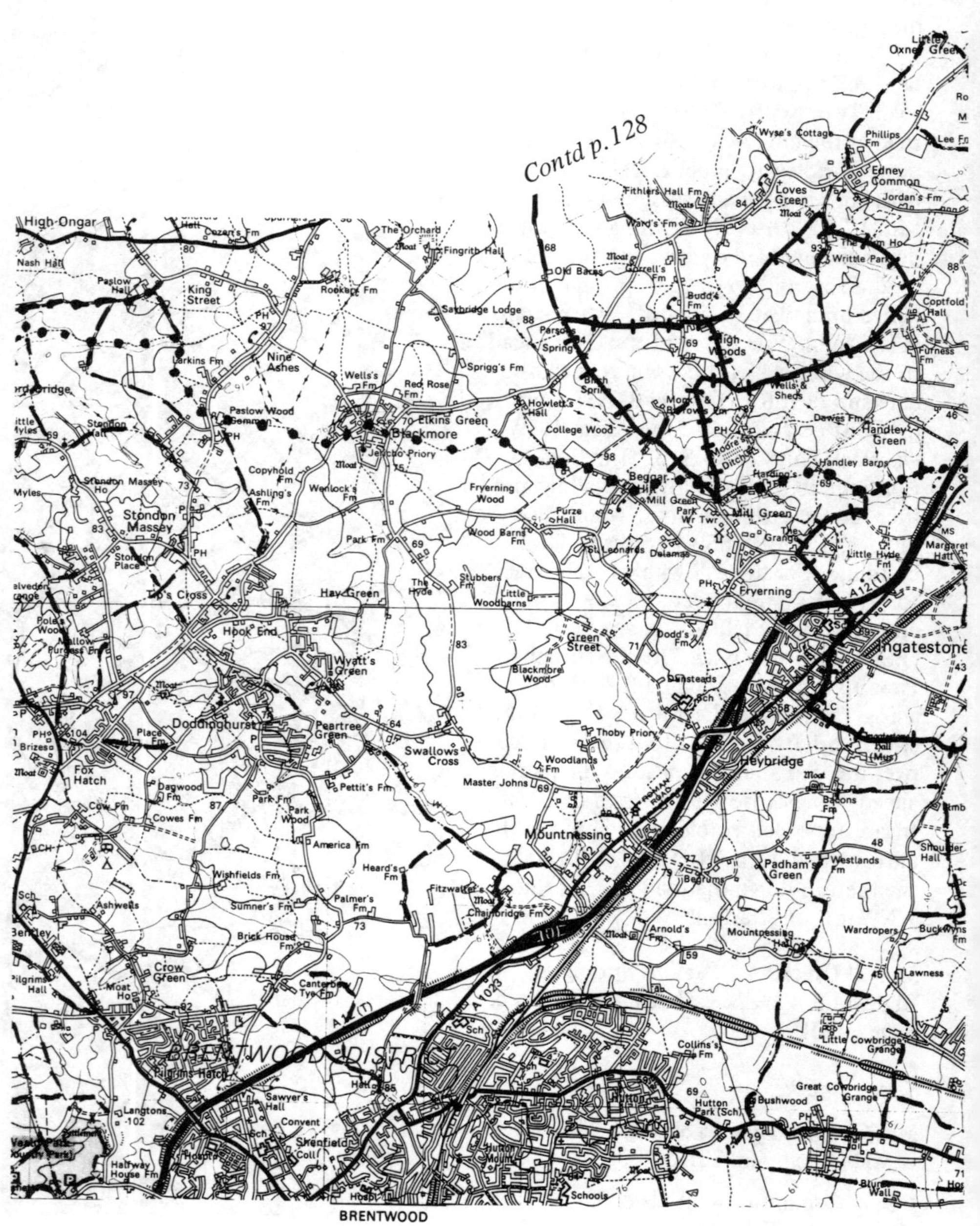

Contd p.128
High Ongar
Nash Hall
Paslow Hall
King Street
The Orchard
Fingrith Hall
Rookery Fm
Saybridge Lodge
Nine Ashes
Larkins Fm
Wells's Fm
Red Rose Fm
Sprigg's Fm
Paslow Wood Common
Elkins Green
Blackmore
Jericho Priory
Howlett's Hall
College Wood
Copyhold Fm
Ashling's Fm
Wenlock's Fm
Stondon Massey
Stondon Place
Fryerning Wood
Furze Hall
Wood Barns Fm
Park Fm
Hay Green
Tip's Cross
Hook End
The Hyde
Stubbers Fm
Little Woodbarns
Green Street
Wyatt's Green
Blackmore Wood
Doddinghurst
Peartree Green
Fox Hatch
Swallows Cross
Thoby Priory
Woodlands Fm
Master Johns
Pettit's Fm
Dagwood Fm
Cow Fm
Cowes Fm
Park Fm
Park Wood
America Fm
Heard's Fm
Wishfields Fm
Ashwells
Sumner's Fm
Palmer's Fm
Fitzwalter's Fm
Chainbridge Fm
Brick House Fm
Crow Green
Pilgrims Hall
Moat Ho
Canterbury Tye Fm
BRENTWOOD DISTRICT
Pilgrims Hatch
Langtons
Sawyer's Hall
Convent
Shenfield
Halfway House Fm
Mountnessing
Begrums
Arnold's Fm
Mountnessing Hall
Padham's Green
Westlands Fm
Wardropers
Collins's Fm
Hutton Park (Sch)
Hutton
Bushwood
Great Cowbridge Grange
Little Cowbridge Grange
Lawness
Schools
Heybridge
Ingatestone
Fryerning
Dodd's Fm
St Leonards
Mill Green
Mill Green Park
Beggar Hill
Handley Barns
Handley Green
Little Hyde Fm
Margaret Hatt
Bacons Fm
Shoulder Hall
Buckwyns Fm
Moore's Ditch
Wells & Sheds
Dawes Fm
High Woods
Budd's Fm
Old Barns
Fithlers Hall Fm
Ward's Fm
Loves Green
Wyse's Cottage
Phillips Fm
Edney Common
Jordan's Fm
Lee Fm
Writtle Park
Coptfold Hall
Furness Fm
Oxney Green
A12(T)
A1023
A129
BRENTWOOD

Writtle
A 122
Sch
New Rollestons Fm
Shakestons
Crem
Widford
CH
Hospl
Bumpstead's Fm
PC
Hylands Park
Elm Fm
Southwood Fm
King Wood
MS
Lodge Fm
Webb's Fm
Killigrews
Moat
Galleywood
Bearman's Fm
Durrant's Fm
White's Place
Lower Green
Margaretting
Crondon Hall
PH
Margaretting Tye
Canterburys
Oldbarn
Crondon
Temple Fm
Forest Lodge
West Hanningfield Hall
Tinsley Fm
Patten's
SPW
Crondon Park
Clovile Hall
Fristling Hall
Forest Wood
Foxborough Fm
Wr Twr
Tye Green
Ramsey Tyrrells
Keelings
Slough House Fm
West Hanningfield
Greenwoods
Stock
Steel's Fm
Water
Terrells
Lilystone Hall
Great Prestons
Hanningfield Reservoir
Brocks Fm
Greenacre Fm
Hall Fm
South Hanningfield
Whitelilies Fm
Little Blunts
Great Blunts
Crowsheath Fm
Common Fm
Forty Acre Plantn
Poplars Fm
Queen's Park
Brock Hill
Lodge Fm
Sudbury's Fm
Hunt's Fm
Ramsden Heath
Downham
The Grange
Norsey Wood
Cox Green
De Beauvoir Fm
Ramsden Hall School
Meepshole Wood
Downham Hall
Kent Hill
Outwood Fm
Ramsden Park Fm
BILLERICAY
Ramsden Bellhouse
Greens Fm

Start at The Cricketers in Mill Green. Pick up the signposted bridleway just opposite it at the entrance to Mill Green Park. Follow the well-used grass path up the L-hand side of the green and continue down a rough lane ahead (NW) past red brick houses. Follow this with woods on your R to a fork in the tracks by a white house and an open field ahead. Take the L fork here NW past an old barn and between hedges to the wood. Where the path forks again just before the woods, take the R-hand path ahead. (This path can be extremely muddy in wet weather, and is used a lot by horses.) Continue down good leafy paths NE to the minor road. Cross and continue down a concreted track ahead. Follow this to the very edge of the trees on your R and then turn R (E) down an excellent grassy path through the N part of the wood to another road. Cross and continue E down the farm road to Barrow Fm. Where this curves L past the duckpond to the farmhouse and barn, continue ahead down a broad signposted cart track. This skirts the N edge of the woods and then continues to the minor road. Turn L (N) here and then R (E) down Cock Lane. At Sunny Side, pick up the signposted cart track half-left (NE) skirting the trees. (If on the short walk, however, take the R fork to its end and then pick up a signposted field edge path ahead SSE: the official right of way crosses the field diagonally.) Skirt High Woods on their NW side. At their NE corner, continue straight ahead (NE). This path runs alongside a belt of trees. At the end of this belt, turn R (SE) to the lane. Turn R (S) down the road past the little bungalow and then L into the concreted farmyard. Go through this and pick up a broad dirt track across the field ESE towards the woods. Continue SE through the woods. After ¾m, before the Coptfold Hall track, pick up a narrower path R (SW) through the woods. This returns you to the Writtle Park lane. Turn L and then R (W) to the minor road at Wells & Sheds. Walk WSW along this. After ¾m, the road bends half-left (SW). A narrow bridleway leaves at the very crown of the bend ahead (WSW) into the trees and through to another minor road. Turn R (WNW) here to the next bend R, and pick up a broad signposted track between crops to the woods. Turn half-left (S) through the woods back to Mill Green.

4. Navestock Side – Navestock Hall – Navestock Heath – Bentley – Navestock Side. 5½m. HR.

Variable walking in some excellent countryside.

Start at the Green Man in Navestock Side. Walk W down the broad path immediately N of the pub. Continue to the woods ahead. Skirt the wood on its S side and keep on half-left (WSW) with the stream on your R (N) side. At the crossing stream, turn R (WNW) along it to the N edge of the woods. Turn L (W) here along the N edge of one wood and then the S edge of the next to the minor road. Turn R (NW) for ½m past side roads R and L. Turn R (N) just before the bend L (SW) in the road, if visiting Navestock church. Return and continue SW along the road over the white bridge to a footpath signpost just before the black and white chevrons. Turn L here across the field in the direction of the sign (SSE by S); pick up a field edge ahead to the road. Turn R (SW) into Navestock Heath. Walk down the driveway to the Plough. Turn R (S) just before the pub along a hedge beside the village green and pick up a cart track L (SE) just N of a white house. Follow to Sabine's Green. Turn R at the footpath signpost and go over the stile. Continue SW down a good field edge path and then a grass track over the field to the pink building ahead. At the minor road, turn L (NE) to a sharp bend L (N) in the road. At that point, pick up an obscurely signposted footpath over a little wooden bridge and low fence into a meadow S of a red-tiled barn. Cross to the barn, then turn half-right and pick up a field edge path SE to another minor road. Walk briefly E up the road and then L (NE) where the road forks. Continue up the road to Pantile Hall. Cross the road and pick up a splendid track through the wood over a gate. (Note: the owner of the wood, a keen conservationist, has had many problems with people disrupting the wood's wildlife. Please observe the Country Code at all times.) The path continues for ½m ENE into the wood and then turns R (ESE) to the road. Turn L (NNE by N) along the main road past the church. Where the road forks, take the L fork ahead (NNE) marked to Ongar. Continue to the last house before the A road and there turn L (NNW) down a footpath signposted to Navestock Side Green. Go past a white weatherboarded cottage and over a stile. Go straight (rather than diagonally) over three cornfields NNW using gaps in the hedges as guides. Continue into Navestock Side.

OTHER SUGGESTED WALKS

Day Walks

1. Billericay – Meepshole Wood – Ramsden Heath – De Beauvoir Fm – Wickford – South Hanningfield – West Hanningfield – Gt Prestons – Norsey Wood – Billericay. 15m.
The paths are mostly good; a lot of roadwork.

2. Billericay – Norsey Wood – Gt Prestons – Slough House Fm – Foxborough Fm – Forest Lodge – Margaretting Tye – Margaretting – Lt Hyde Lane – Ingatestone – Ingatestone Hall – Elmbrook Fm – Queen's Pk – Billericay. 15m.
This can be reduced to 13m by using the Stock-Margaretting Hall route, or to 11½m by omitting Margaretting and Ingatestone entirely (using the Stock-Elmbrook Fm path).

3. Brentwood – Weald Country Park – Bentley – Navestock Side – Kelvedon Hatch – Tip's Cross – Doddinghurst – River Wid – Fitzwalter's Moat – Brentwood. 12½m.
Rather varied.

4. Writtle – Edney Common – High Woods – Mill Gn – Ingatestone – Ingatestone Hall – Stock – Margaretting Tye – Killigrews – Hylands Pk – Writtle. 15m.
This can be reduced by 3m by using LDFP to cut out Ingatestone and Stock.

5. Chelmsford – Chipping Ongar (Day 1 of the Weekend Walk, second section of this chapter). 13m.
Return by bus.

6. Chelmsford – Writtle – Oxney Gn – Edney Common – High Woods – Mill Gn – Ingatestone – Ingatestone Hall – Mountnessing Hall – Bushwood – Brentwood. 13½m.
Good. Return by train.

Medium Walks

1. Chelmsford – Ingatestone (as in Day Walk). 9m.
Interesting and varied.

2. Writtle – Hylands Pk – Southwood Fm – Coptfold Hall – Edney Common – Oxney Gn – Writtle. 6m.
This can be extended by 2m to take in High Woods.

3. Billericay – Elmbrook Fm – Ingatestone Hall – Mountnessing Hall – Bushwood – Billericay. 8m.
An interesting walk.

4. West Hanningfield – Gt Prestons – Ramsden Heath – De Beauvoir Fm – Brock Hill – South Hanningfield – West Hanningfield. 9½m.
Good tracks but a lot of road (round the reservoir).

5. Chipping Ongar – Greensted Green – Stanford Rivers – Marden Ash – Chipping Ongar. 6m.
Takes in the delightful Saxon church at Greensted.

6. Chipping Ongar – LDFP – Paslow Wood Common – Gt Myles – Langford Bridge – Chipping Ongar. 6¾m.
The pub at Paslow Wood Common is a good resting place.

7. Doddinghurst – Stondon Massey – Paslow Wood Common – Gt Myles – Pole's Wood – Fox Hatch – Doddinghurst. 7½m.
New development, country paths.

Short Walks

1. Edney Common – Coptfold Hall – Southwood Fm – Lee Fm – Edney Common. 4½m.
Easy paths.

2. Galleywood – Crondon Hall – Killigrews – Galleywood. 4m.
Takes in a lovely Tudor hall.

3. Stock – Slough House Fm – Crondon Hall – Stock. 5¾m.
Easy tracks.

4. Margaretting – Margaretting Tye – Margaretting Hall – Margaretting. 3m.
Can be extended to 3½m to take in the Crondon Pk path.

5. Ingatestone Hall – Mountnessing Hall – Buckwyns Fm – Elmbrook Fm – Ingatestone Hall. 5m.
A pleasant walk along field paths and farm tracks.

6. Mountnessing Hall – Bushwood – Gt Cowbridge Grange – Lt Cowbridge Grange – Mountnessing Hall. 4¾m.

7. Billericay – Norsey Wood – Hunt Fm – Meepshole Wood – Billericay. 4½m.
Fair paths.

8. Ramsden Heath – Crowsheath Fm – Whitelilies Fm – Common Fm – Ramsden Heath. 3¼m.
Takes in the very edge of the reservoir.

9. Ramsden Heath – Downham Hall – Brock Hill – Crowsheath Fm – Ramsden Heath. 4¾m.
Some road in the centre of the walk.

10. Wickford – South Hanningfield – Poplars Fm – Wickford. 4½m.
This can be reduced still further (3m) by using the Poplars Fm-Brock Hill path.

11. South Hanningfield – Poplar's Fm – Flemings Fm – South Hanningfield. 3m.
A pleasant variation on the last walk.

12. Weald Park – Coxtie Green. 3¾m.
The park is the finest thing about Brentwood.

13. Blackmore – Paslow Wood Common – Nine Ashes PH – Blackmore. 4m.
Part of St Peter's Way and a splendid pub.

14. Stondon Massey – Pole's Wood – Gt Myles – Lt Myles – Paslow Wood Common – Ashling Fm – Stondon Massey. 5½m.

15. Chipping Ongar – Greensted Green – Greensted Church – Chipping Ongar. 4m.
An excellent walk.

Chipping Ongar to Chelmsford (north)

Well signed, and necessarily so since villages are sparser and more scattered. The country is therefore more isolated, and somewhat heavier going.

Beauchamp Roding Several unpretentious little cottages, and a rather decayed 14c church.

Berners Roding This, like all the tiny villages along the Roding river, is a reminder of how simple life was in this isolated corner of Essex, until the arrival of the commuter.

Fyfield On the willow-shaded banks of the Roding, in imminent danger of being swamped by a tide of new development: in the middle ages it was a town, and seems set to become one again.

Good Easter Characteristic Essex cottages stand around the green in front of the church.

Great Waltham There are more than eighty buildings in the parish from before 1714, including the 15c Six Bells. Langleys is 17c, the home of the Everards and later the Tufnell family who live there today. Their coloured monuments can be seen in the old church. The nearby guildhall is timber-framed, with tall chimneys.

Pleshey Pleshey is still dominated by the castle that made the village so important in the middle ages, and from which Geoffrey de Mandeville defied King Stephen. No stonework remains, but there are extensive earthworks including a 50ft high mound 900ft in circumference, within a moat. The bridge crossing this is the only relic of the stone castle. An outer ditch 45ft wide can also be seen ringing the entire village. Thomas, Duke of Gloucester, founded a college of chaplains here in the late 14c; here too he was seized by his nephew Richard II, and carried off to Boulogne. Two years later, Richard's own half-brother was executed for treason, by Henry IV. The physical evidence of all this vanished in the Elizabethan period, but the atmosphere remains. The village is small, along a main road. A Tudor house has barn and dovecote. There are two pubs, the Leather Bottle does real ale, the White Horse has an attractive patterned exterior.

Roxwell A large village that has grown up beside the Chelmsford-Bishop's Stortford road. Most of Roxwell is fairly modern.

Shellow Bowells The church is a rare example of 18c ecclesiastical architecture.

Willingale I walked here just after the village had been announced as a possible site for the third London airport. I was carrying a compass, binoculars and an Ordnance Survey map of the district, as well as a notebook in which I was busily making notes. I was almost pleased to be looked at with such suspicious hostility. The village is small, with rather too may new houses to be really picturesque. Its churchyard contains two churches, Willingale historically comprising two parishes: Spain and Doe – the names are from Hervey d'Espagne and William d'Ou, the Norman knights who divided the manor between them after the Conquest. A path passes between the two churches and past a little pub, The Bell.

Writtle See *South of Chipping Ongar – Chelmsford*.

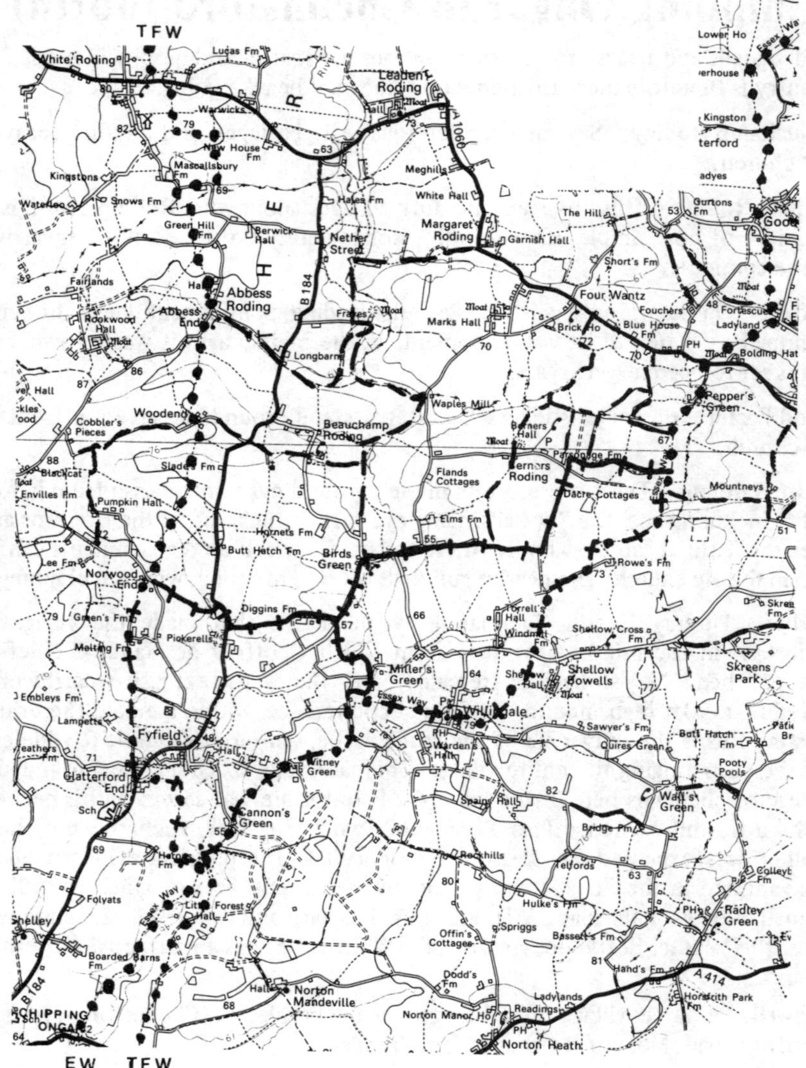

RECOMMENDED WALKS

1. **Fyfield – Norwood End – Miller's Green – Fyfield. 6½m. HR.**

This may be combined with the following walk to make a circular 13m route. Some difficult walking in the heart of west Essex countryside.

Walk SW down the main street in Fyfield and turn off R (W) down the minor road signposted to Moreton. Turn R (N) at the footpath signpost down the driveway immediately after the Gipsy Mead restaurant. Where this drive swings L (NW) to the red-roofed building, continue ahead (N) down an overgrown grass track L of a mature hedge. Where this in turn bends, go ahead across the grassy wasteland beyond. Cross the stream. Turn briefly L

Contd p. 151

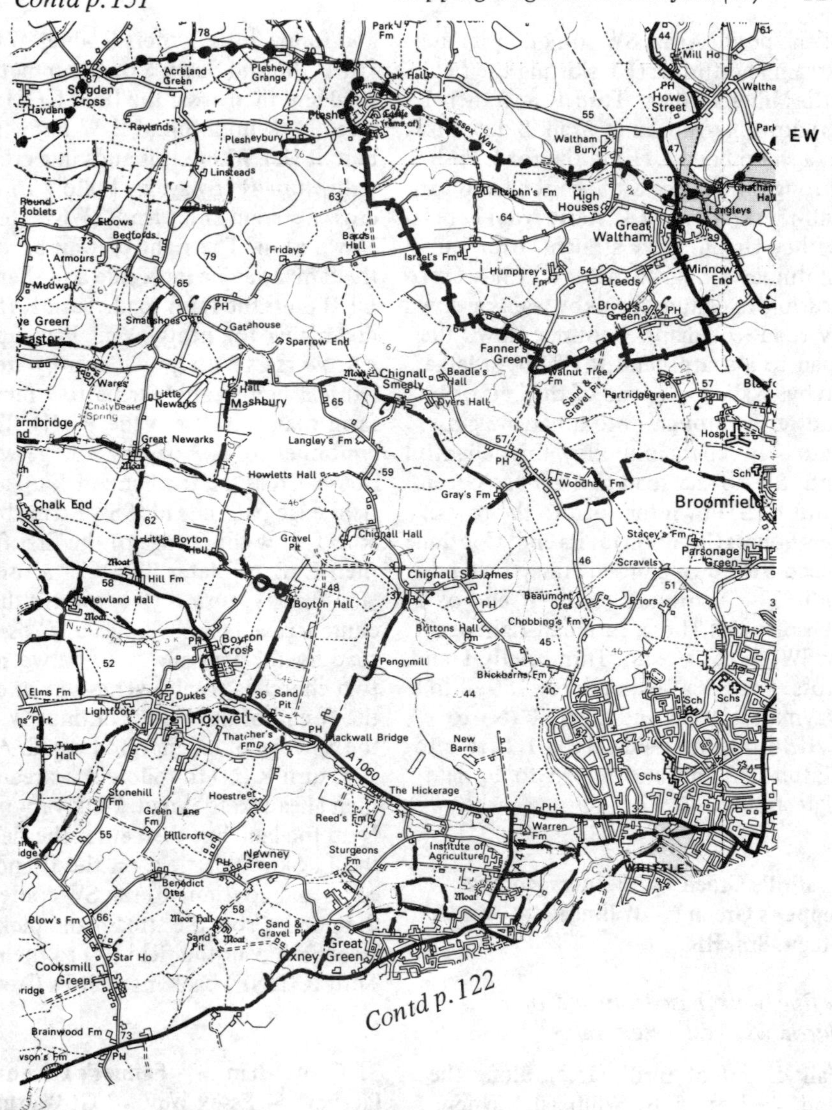

and then R (N) up field edges to a broader track. This continues generally N past Malting and Green's Fms to Norwood End. At the lane, turn R for 100yd to a footpath signpost. Continue SE down a green lane and then hedges to the wood. Cross this L (NE) and down a field edge next to red-roofed houses to the road. Walk R (S) down the road toward the white barn. Turn L (E) at the footpath signpost down a concrete and then a broad grass track ahead. Where this ends, continue E down a hedgeside path and then across two fields to Diggens Fm. Continue E down the farm road to the minor road. Turn R here for 50yd to double gates by two horses' heads and a curious arched pair of garages. Turn L through the forecourt and pick up a broad grass track between two fences under telegraph lines. This continues over a stile and across the field to the R (W) of the pond. At its SW corner, cross the stream and turn L (E), skirting the field into Miller's Green. Turn R and then L (S) down narrow lanes. Walk S down this to a sharp bend L (E) in the road. Push through the hedge S of the road and turn half-right (WSW). The route from here to Withey Green goes straight over an enormous ploughed field; it is however possible to eliminate this by walking down by road (see map). Continue down the road to a sharp bend R (W) by a large layby. Walk to the end of the belt of trees and push through onto a narrow grass path between them. Follow this delightful path SW to the road at Cannons Green. Turn L (S) down the road to the row of new houses (Tighoon) at its end. Continue ahead SW down a broad grassy field edge path. This continues to the W end of a belt of trees. There, turn half-right again (WSW) to the stream. Turn briefly L and cross. Follow a field path for 150yd to a waymarked tree and then R (N) to Fyfield playing fields. Turn L here into Clatterford End and return to Fyfield high street.

2. **Bird's Green – Berners Roding – Pepper's Green – Willingale – Bird's Green. 8m. HR.**

A fine walk based on one of Fred Matthews' west Essex walks.

Walk E out of Bird's Green along the road signposted to Willingale. Where this swings R (S), continue ahead (E) down the Berners Roding road. Where this in turn bends sharply L (N), continue ahead (E) down a broad signposted pebbled track with a grass strip in the middle. (Ignore the second signpost pointing you S.) This excellent path continues past a pottery, to a wood, and then ahead between the trees. A little later, the path leaves the trees and continues ahead along field edges to a crossing metalled farm road. Turn L (N) and follow into Berners Roding. Walk R (E) at the end down a rough unmetalled road and then cross the field L (N) to the trees. Pick up a broad E-W farm track here R (E). Where this ends in a crossing path, turn R (S) again. Follow for ¼m, cross a stream and turn R (WSW) towards Rowe's Fm. The right of way passes by the farm away on its N side and then turns L (S) onto the farm road. Turn R (SW) down this for nearly ½m. Pick up a narrow grass path grown over by trees L (S) just before another narrow metalled farm road joins from the R (N). This continues to the road by a large white house. Cross the road and pick up a fair field edge path ahead (SSW). This bends R to follow the S edge of the first field, then L (S and later SSW) for a further ¼m. Finally, turn R (W) towards the two church towers of Willingale. Cross the road by the Bell and walk between the two churches to an overgrown stile at the W end of the yard. Continue W along the S hedge of an enormous field. After ½m, turn R (N) to follow the stream and then ahead to the road. Walk very briefly N up the lane but then enter the field on the L. Skirt this field on the E and N edges and continue to the SW corner of the pond. Cross the stream and pick up a grass path over the field (N) to the road. Turn R (NNE) back into Bird's Green.

3. **Gt Waltham – Fanner's Green – Pleshey – Essex Way – Gt Waltham. 8m. VHR.**

Shorter walks:

Pleshey – Fitzjohn's Fm – Fanner's Gn – Pleshey. 5m. VHR.

Gt Waltham – Fanner's Gn – Fitzjohn's Fm – Gt Waltham. 6m. VHR.

Much very pleasant walking taking in the splendid villages of Pleshey and Great Waltham.

Start at Great Waltham church and walk S down South Street to a sharp bend R (WSW) by new houses and a large triangle of green. Go through a gap in the hedge ahead just L of Little Garth. Continue over a stile and down a well-trodden field edge path SSE by S. This crosses a stream and continues ahead up the slope to a farmhouse and road. Turn R (W) to the next sharp bend R (N) in the road. At that point, pick up a signposted green lane L (S) over a gate and along to the NW corner of the wood. Turn R (WSW) here and follow hedgeside paths for a long ½m. Eventually you enter a huge field by a large bank with a belt of trees upon it. Turn R (N) here across the cornfield to the road and then L (WSW) to Fanner's Green. At the T-junction, turn R (NNE by N) for a short distance to cottages and a corrugated iron hut; at this point, turn L (WNW) down a signposted No Through Road. Follow to the white gates where the road becomes private but the right of way for walkers continues. Pick up a rougher cart track WNW and then bending R (N) to a crossing track by an orchard. Turn L (WSW) down a green lane past a white thatched cottage and duckpond. After 350yd, turn off this R (N) down another grassy lane between hedges. Continue ahead to the narrow road. Cross and continue down the signposted green lane (only the post of the sign remains) NNW to the W side of the wood. Pick up another green lane L (W) at its NW corner. This ends in a concrete farm road. Turn R (N) and follow for ½m till it bends sharp R (E). Cross into a cricket field and follow its L (W) side to regain the hard track by the castle moat. Turn L to the road opposite the pink cottage and turn R (ENE) down the Street. Follow through Pleshey to a Z-bend notice by the sewage works. Take the L of two signposted footpaths on the R of the road. This skirts the wire netting fence on its W and N side (can be overgrown with nettles) and then becomes a good grass path beside the stream. The path swaps to the N bank after ¼m and continues beside it. After another ¼m, there is a bridge back over the stream. The long and short walks divide here. (If on the short walk, cross and follow the field edge S to Fitzjohn's Fm; turn L (ESE) at the junction of farm tracks before the farm and follow to the road. Turn R and then L (S) down the side road past Humphrey's Fm, then R (SSW) towards Fanner's Green; pick up a broad cart track R (W) at the footpath signpost where the road crosses a stream.) If on the long walk, continue along the N bank of the stream to the reservoir and then along a broad rutted cart track skirting it to the S and E. (You are requested to keep off the reservoir banks themselves.) Cross the road by the white house just N of the ford and pick up the signposted route opposite. The path from here follows field edges SE with the brook on your R to the A130. Turn R (S) into the centre of Great Waltham.

OTHER SUGGESTED ROUTES

Weekend Walk

Chelmsford – Gt & Lt Oxney Gn – Edney Common – High Woods – Mill Green – St Peter's Way – Blackmore – Chipping Ongar (overnight stop). Chipping Ongar – Essex Way – Fyfield – Good Easter – Pleshey – Gt Waltham – Blasford Hall – Broomfield. Day 1: 13m. Day 2: 15m.

Varied walking along well-used paths, with several beautiful villages en route.

Day Walks

1. Roxwell – Roxwell Brook – Radley Gn – Old Barns – Mill Gn – Wells & Sheds – Edney Common – Gt Oxney Gn – Newney Gn – Roxwell. 13m. *Mostly good.*

2. Chipping Ongar – Fyfield – Willingale – Wall's Gn – Radley Gn – College Wood – LDFP – Chipping Ongar. 16m.
Strenuous but worthwhile.

3. Willingale – LDFP – Good Easter – Mashbury – Roxwell – Wall's Gn – Willingale. 13m.
This may be reduced to 11m by using the river Can path to omit Good Easter and Mashbury.

4. Gt Waltham – LDFP – Pleshey – Good Easter – Mashbury – Chignall Smealey – Fanner's Gn – Broad's Gn – Gt Waltham. 13m.
A good day's walk round some excellent villages.

Medium Walks

1. Chipping Ongar – LDFP – Willingale – Offin's Cottages – Norton Mandeville – High Ongar – Chipping Ongar. 9m.
A lot of minor road walking.

2. Willingale – LDFP – Mountneys – Elms Fm – Patience Bridge – Wall's Gn – Willingale. 6¾m.
Some difficult patches.

3. Fyfield – Miller's Gn – Bird's Gn – Beauchamp Roding – Woodend – Norwood End – Lampetts – Fyfield. 7½m.
A varied walk taking in parts of LDFPs.

4. Roxwell – Boyton Hall – River Can – LDFP – Mountneys – Patience Bridge – Roxwell Brook – Roxwell. 8½m.
This can be reduced to 7m by using the Gt Newarks-Newlands Hall path.

5. Good Easter – Mashbury – Little Boyton Hall – Newlands Hall – Mountneys – LDFP. 8m.
Mostly good walking with some fine views.

6. Pleshey – Fanner's Gn – Chignall Smealey – Mashbury – Good Easter – LDFP – Pleshey. 9m.
A delightful walk, though with some problems.

Short Walks

1. Chelmsford – Writtle – Chelmsford. 3¼m.
Well walked.

2. Beauchamp Roding – Bird's Gn – Diggins Fm – Norwood End – Wood End – Beauchamp Roding. 5¼m.

3. Roxwell – Newland Brook – Patience Bridge – Roxwell. 5m.
Excellent; stream banks.

4. Roxwell – Boyton Hall – Gt Newarks – Newland Brook – Roxwell. 4½m.
Good paths.

5. Pepper's Gn – River Can – Newland Hall – Mountneys – Pepper's Gn. 5m.
Very pleasant country and some appreciable slopes.

6. Good Easter – Mashbury – River Can – Farmbridge End – Good Easter. 4½m.
The usual mixture of arable and stream-bank paths.

8 WEST ESSEX

Bishop's Stortford to Thaxted; North of Harlow (the Ash Valley); Harlow to Dunmow

This chapter covers three networks of walks on the western borders of Essex, connected together to make a single huge pattern of footpaths from Harlow to Thaxted. Some of this large area extends into Hertfordshire to cover the particularly good walking countryside in the valley of the river Ash.

Heavy land extends over most of the area as an agricultural plateau. In the extreme north and north-west of the area the ground becomes higher and turns into the foothills of the chalky north Essex highlands. Most of the area is subject to the heavy arable cultivation that can be found generally throughout the county. The three main river valleys contain some splendid water meadows, particularly in the Much Hadham area on the Ash and around Wallbury Camp on the Stort. Forest predominated until the wholesale clearances of the Anglo-Saxon and medieval periods. Now there is relatively little woodland in the area, and most of the surviving woods are small. The one major remnant of the original forest is Hatfield Forest. How far this is really original is a matter of dispute. Most of the forest was in fact felled at the beginning of our own century, but there survive enough ancient hornbeams and oaks among the new silver birch coppices to give this a remarkable atmosphere of authenticity. It is the one area in Essex open to large-scale walking which can give an impression of the original deciduous forests.

Prehistoric settlement was mainly in the Hatfield district, where there was a well-drained hill on which forest cover was light enough to be fairly easily cleared. Otherwise, settlement concentrated in the valleys of the Ash, Chelmer and Stort. The best evidence of this, of course, lies in the Iron Age fort on Wallbury Camp, on the Stort. The area's only other fort of this type, Portingbury Hills, lies very close to the Roman road known as Stane Street, now metalled as the A120; the presumption therefore is that the road must have started life as a major pre-Roman track. The Romans also constructed another major road in the extreme east of the area, running NNE through Great Dunmow. This survives today as the B184. Otherwise, the Roman presence in the area seems to have been fairly limited, to judge by what remains: mainly tiles and bricks in the area's churches. This relative lack of population seems to have set the pattern for subsequent centuries. Even after the clearances, most of the settlements remained small, so that an isolation-loving order like the Cistercians would have no hesitation in picking a village like Tilty for one of their foundations. There were medieval castles and market towns, of course: Great Canfield and Great Easton keep their earthwork motte-and-baileys to this day, while Thaxted and Hatfield Broad Oak were important centres of population, the former even having its own corporation and MPs, but in general there are few market towns and a large number of little villages. A village in this area is often a small central hamlet about the church and manor house, with two or three other Ends or Greens in the surrounding countryside and many isolated single farmsteads. This is most noticeable on the highlands between the river valleys; but of the three valleys themselves only the Stort, with its concentration of rail and road links to London, can claim large, nucleated villages and towns.

The most walkable country, the largest villages and the grandest and most picturesque buildings are generally to be found in the valleys of the Ash, Stort and Chelmer, and particularly in the first two of this trio. Riverbank paths vary considerably from the well-trodden Stort towpath through water meadow to arable, but are normally good. Paths in the surrounding area are also normally of a fairly high standard relative to those on the higher land. The routes on the uplands between the valleys are much more likely to be arable headlands and even middles, but it would be wrong to define even this as poor walking. West Essex has a long tradition of walking, with some active local groups and even weekend ramblers from London. Signposting is good, and farmers are generally used to people walking on their land. Arable paths are therefore better than those in many other parts of East Anglia, with some reasonable headlands and even grass strips left across fields. In the Hatfield Broad Oak parish this awareness of rambling has even led to the erection of some signposts in the fields directing walkers to the route which they should take.

The buildings of the uplands are generally fairly simple. Churches are mostly small, although constructed of flint and rubble rather than the timber of central Essex. There are few cottages, these very often thatched. Manor houses are quite numerous, particularly in the Thaxted district but they are large farmhouses rather than squires' manors, often isolated from the main village. In the valleys the villages are larger and contain more ambitious ecclesiastical and domestic building. Domestic building is of course in timber or brick, and therefore reaches two peaks, in the 15th and 16th centuries with timber-framed housing, and in the Georgian red brick of the eighteenth century. Inevitably, the valleys have been most affected by building in our own century.

Bishop's Stortford to Thaxted

Pleasant villages set among rolling, wooded farmland; threatened by the growth of Stansted airport.

Broxted A hill village, charming as its name, badger's place. The church is small and stone, with Roman tiles in its walls and a wooden belfry. Nearby stands a group of old buildings including a 17c brewing house.

Chickney Set in delightful agricultural country. Church nave and oval churchyard go back to Saxon times. The churchyard is kept by the Essex Naturalists Trust as a reserve for typical Essex wild flowers like the sweet violet, cowslip, oxslip and goldilocks. Rarer plants like the hare's ear are also being introduced here.

Elsenham A commuter village with some thatched white cottages and an octagonal wellhouse. The Norman church lies south-east, in the grounds of the Hall, which was owned by the Gilbey family, the vintners, and also the founders of Elsenham's jam-making company. The combination of this with its position on the railway line has led to a great deal of characterless 1930s development.

Great Dunmow The market town of the area, and the only settlement of any size for miles around. The High Street is very pleasant, with the excellent Saracen's Head coaching inn. There are some good houses and shops, making it a fine place to be combined with a short walk as a day's visit.

Great Easton Much larger in the middle ages, when a motte-and-bailey castle stood here. Earthworks survive south of the church.

Henham The village stands on top of a hill (its name means high place), and was selected by Neolithic man as an encampment within and above the dense forests of the district. As far as is known, it has been continuously inhabited ever since.

Little Easton Inside the church are some remarkable medieval paintings including a 12c seated prophet, and an early 17c south chapel containing many monuments of the local Maynard family. The last of them, Daisy, countess of Warwick, was Edward VII's mistress, and the path passes her home, Easton Lodge, now mostly demolished. West of the village lies the Second World War airfield, where the USAAF flew Marauders on precision bombing raids during the years of 1943-4. RAF Stirlings later trained here in preparation for the Arnhem mission and then the Rhine crossing at Wesel. Country walking here sometimes seems to bring back those days, because of the noise of aircraft flying overhead from Stansted airport.

Manuden The crossroads and main street display a classic grouping of thatched white cottages and timbered houses with overhanging storeys. William Waad, buried in the church, was the builder of nearby Battails Hall and a noted Jacobean public servant. It was he who supervised Guy Fawkes's torture in 1605, and escorted Walter Raleigh to trial.

Quendon and **Rickling Green** Now one village, the latter having migrated over the centuries from its original isolated position one mile north-west about the church and hall. A Norman castle stood here.

Stansted Mountfitchet Now a small town and growing rapidly under the triple influence of the railway, airport and proximity to Bishop's Stortford. It has been an important place since the road was sited through here in Roman times. The Norman Mountfitchets constructed Stansted castle in the 12c. Remains of earthwork and rubble are visible to the north of the railway station. There is an excellent pub in Lower Street, where the footpath leaves Stansted north for Norman House wildlife park. The park contains a large collection of birds, including flamingoes, cranes and pheasants as well as more ordinary ducks and geese. The planned expansion of the airport threatens this – as much else in the district.

Thaxted Outstanding on every count. In the middle ages it was a centre of the cutlery industry, and later of the Jacobean weaving trade. Thaxted therefore, although now a village, has the buildings of a town: Clarence House, a superb example of red brick Queen Anne; the priory; the Recorder's House; and so on. The best building is the guildhall. Preserved and restored to its present appearance by the expenditure of £65 000 in Architectural Heritage Year, it is a supreme example of late medieval corporate building. The ground floor is open, for markets, but also includes an old lock-up containing two huge hooks for pulling thatch from burning houses (Thaxted means thatched place). The rest of the building is supported on enormous wooden posts, cross-beams and a massive central pillar. The town council met in the panelled room on the first floor, leaving the second floor as a schoolroom. On top of the hill stands the splendid church with a superb square tower and a soaring spire held up by some dainty flying buttresses. Inside, the church is rich in work of the 14-16c. It is notable for its perfect symmetry: aisles, transepts, chapels and porches complement each other to make up a mirror image along an imaginary central axis. There are some splendid arches and arcades, no fewer than six original medieval doors, magnificent hammer- and tie-beam roofs, unique wood-encased font and altar screens with delicate 15c carving, some fine stained glass, and equally attractive modern tapestries and banners.

Tilty Little remains of the Cistercian abbey constructed here in the 12-13c, except for the church, originally the gatehouse chapel of the abbey. Traceried east window includes a giant stone wheel and five lights.

Widdington Around Widdington are a number of isolated halls and farmhouses. South of Prior's Wood, toward Little Henham, stands 13c Prior's Hall, with a large barn of similar age. North-east of Widdington on the path to Debden is Widdington Hall, which is 15c. Half a mile to the east stands Mole Hall, a moated Elizabethan mansion whose grounds contain one of the most pleasant small wildlife parks in England: muntjac deer, otters, wallabies, racoon, coatimundi can be found alongside macaws, cranes, geese and ducks. Open: all year. Further east, towards Thaxted, are three more manor houses: Thistley Hall, Amberden Hall with its wet moat and New Amberden Hall, itself several centuries old. The country between here and Thaxted is typical of the district, with some fairly steep little hills, broad views and little hamlets like Hamperden End and Cutler's Green.

RECOMMENDED WALKS

1. **Tilty – Broxted – Henham – Chickney Sucksted Gn – Tilty. 10m. HR.**

Shorter walks:

Tilty – Broxted – Chickney – Sucksted Gn – Tilty. 5½m. HR.

Henham – Chickney – Henham. 4½m. HR.

Mostly broad paths, but some difficult fieldwork around Chaureth Hall.

Start at Tilty church. At the end of the lane, continue N ahead past the old abbey and across the stream by the disused mill. Turn L (WNW) along the stream, with woods to either side. The path follows the stream for 1¼m to the B1051. Turn L (SSW) and round a bend R (W) to the church. Leave the churchyard on its S side and follow a path S to the village. At the minor road, turn L (WSW). Where the road forks, keep on the R street N to the T-junction and turn L onto the B road again. Follow this around sharp bends R (NNE) and L (W). After a short distance, turn R (NNE) down a narrow metalled lane signposted to Chickney Hall. Where this divides by the white gate, take the signposted cart track L (NNW). Walk down the cart track and turn L (W) down a field edge just before the start of the trees on your R. Follow to the NE corner of the woods and cross them WSW. Pick up a broad cart track between crops (the official right of way may however lie slightly to the N). Go through the first crossing hedge and turn half-right (WNW) along a field edge path to the R (N) of the old grain silo and wooden barn. Walk down the farm road to the signpost and there turn L (WSW) down a hedgeside path under telegraph lines. Follow to the S end of village street and turn R (NNW) to its end. Turn R (N) up the main road. At the T-junction, bear L (NNW). Where the road bends L (W), turn R (NNE) by the black wooden barn and brick gateway. Continue down the unmade track. At Henham Lodge Fm, turn sharp R (SE) down another farm track to the minor road. Turn very briefly L (E) along the road and then L (NE) down a broad and dead straight cart track – the line of the old railway. At the minor road, turn R (SE) and leave the road where it bends R (SW), down a signposted cart track. Follow this SSE back to Chickney (1m). At the white gates, turn L (NE) to the church. Leave the churchyard ENE across the field. The path continues on this bearing (fieldwork needed) to the L (NW) of Chaureth Hall Fm. Cross a second stream N of the farm and turn L (N) paralleling it to the minor road. Turn R (SE and later E) into Sucksted Gn. Cross the B road and pick up a good grass track between hedges on the other side. This continues for 1m to Tilty Hall Fm. Turn L (ENE) down the farm drive and then R (S) back into Tilty.

2. **Stansted – Manuden – Uppend – Farnham – Stansted. 7½m. HR.**

Shorter walks:

Stansted – Manuden – Bentfield Gn – Stansted. 6½m. HR.

Stansted – Farnham – Hazel End – Stansted. 5m. HR.

An arable walk taking in Stansted and the beautiful village of Manuden.

Start at Stansted station. Walk NNE up the B1351 past the junction with the Elsenham road. Turn R (NNE) down Lower St at the Dog & Duck. Continue past the Gall End notice to the end of the metalled surface. At the 3-way footpath post, take the broad middle track between hedges. Continue to the SW corner tip of the belt of trees ahead. The official right of way keeps on N from here to the minor

Contd p. 160

Contd p. 145

Rook End
Slough Fm
Debden Green
Woodhams
Yardley Hall
Goddard's Fm
Terrier's Fm
Boyton End
The Hall
Swayne's Hall
Mole Hall
Wildlife Park
Monk's Fm
Roother's Fm
Millhill Fm
Thaxted
Thistley Hall
Hamperden End
Woodruff Fm
Water Hall Fm
Richmond's in the Wood
Cutlers Green
Amberden Hall
Legget's Fm
Loves Fm
New Amberden Hall
dismantled railway
Priors Hall
Cherry Green
Lovecotes Fm
Sibleys
Stan Brook
Dairygreen Fm
Stanbrook
Henham Lodge
Buckingham's Fm
Dovehouse Fm
Richmond's Green
Broxted Hill
Hammer Hill
Armigers
Sharpes Fm
Springate
Monk Street
Woodend Green
Sucksted Green
R. Chelmer
Sibley's Green
Greenend Fm
Church Hall
Broadfans Fm
Handley Fm
Moat Hall
Pledgdon Hall
Tilty Hill Fm
Wolsey's Fm
dismantled railway
Little Cambridge
Church End
Church Hall
Hyde Fm
Pelegates Fm
Greenarbour
Duton Hill
Blamster's Hall
Gallows Green
Pledgdon Green
Broxted
Pennington Hall
Sand Pit
Wood Fm
The Grange
Tilty
Abbey (remains of)
Broxted Hall
Mill End Green
Brick End
Moor End Fm
Goodfellows
Little Rakefairs
Home Fm
Loppingdale
Dapifers
Great Easton
Andrews Fm
Gaunt's End
Woodgates End
Bigod's Wood
Mott's Hall
Chapel End
Molehill Green
Broxted Hill
Perrydeans
Easton Fm
Bigods
Flemings Hill Fm
Tye Green
UTTLESFORD DISTRICT
Butcher's Pasture
Maysland
Waltham Hall
Brookend
Easton Lodge
Lower Hall
Colchester Hall
Teagles
Wr Twr
The Grange
Elmbridge Fm
High Ho
Little Easton
Coopers
B 184
The Parsonage
Bamber's Green
Sheering Hall
Ravens Fm
Fanns
GREAT DUNMOW
HCW

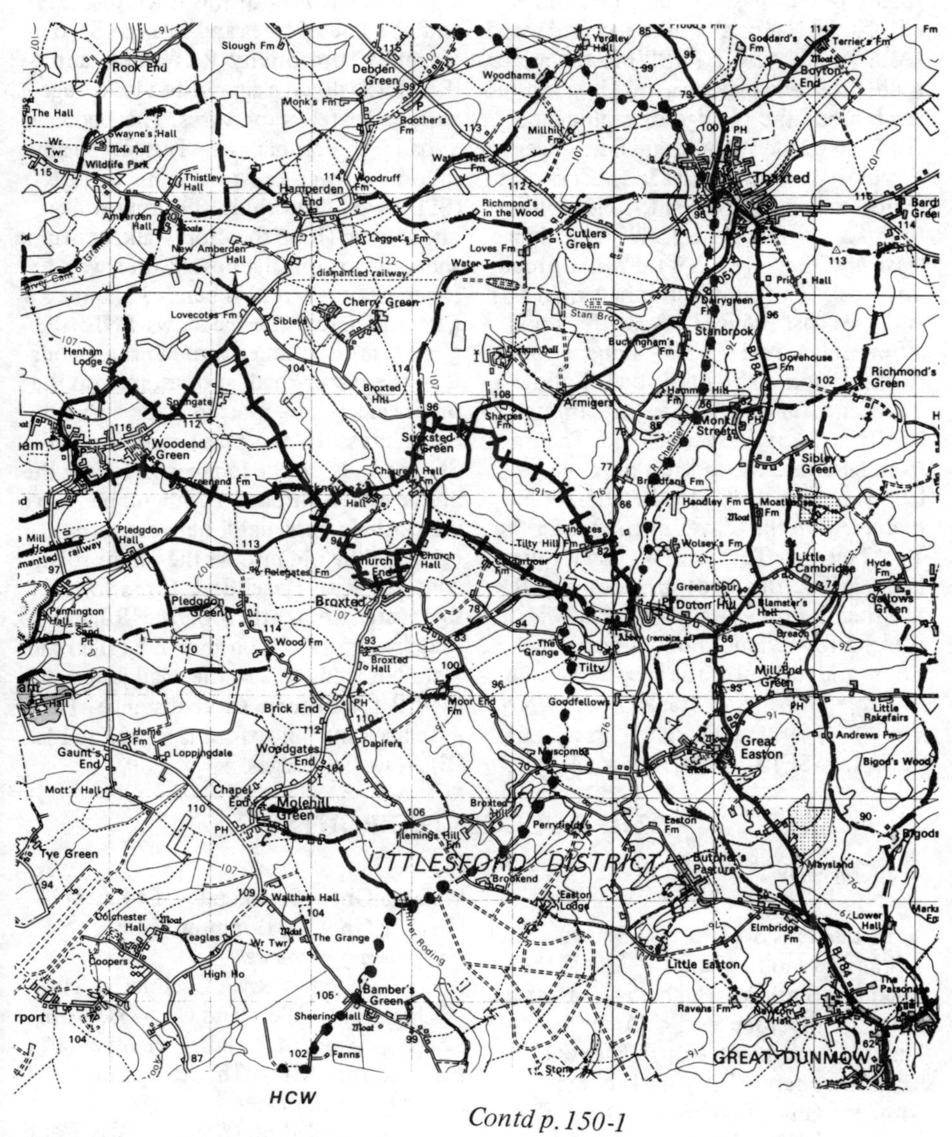

Contd p.150-1

road; but most walkers seem to turn R (ENE) along the S side of this belt and then L (NNE) past woods L (W) and R (E). At the NW corner of the second wood (Alsa Wood), turn L (WSW) to the minor road. Cross and pick up a broad signposted track along the N edge of a ploughed field. Continue WNW along field edges for the most part to the B1383. Cross and continue W down the side-road; follow round a sharp bend L (SSW) and then leave the road R (WNW) down a broad dirt track. This soon bends half-right (N) and goes past the R (E) edge of a wood. After ½m, turn L (WSW) along a good track, opposite the hard road. Follow a ditch and then a field edge, turning briefly L (S) in the second field. The track from here into Manuden is normally well trodden. Turn L (S) to the church and then pick up the Clavering road, past the Yew Tree inn. Turn off (W) down Butt Lane. Where this ends, bend briefly R and then L at the first building down an even narrower lane. Follow past Clock House and the end of the metalled surface: pick up a broad grass track ahead (WNW and WSW) for ½m. Pick up a grassy cart track L (SSE) to a narrow road by Mallows Gn. Cross the green down a rough track to the R of the 3 cottages. Follow the R fork of this track to the N end of a line of trees and turn L (S) to Uppend. Turn briefly R (W) here and then L (S) down a signposted field edge path under telegraph wires. This becomes a road into Farnham Gn. Turn L (E) and follow for over ½m to a sharp bend R (SSE by S). The short and long walks divide here. (If on the short walk, continue ahead down the signposted driveway to Saven End: where this bends L, go over a gate and across the meadows ENE: the good track continues through the woods E to the minor road, and resumes on the other side as a signposted track between crops; cross the Stort and continue into Stansted.) If on the long walk, follow the minor road S through Farnham; pick up a signposted grass path between crops opposite the old inn. At the minor road, continue E to Hazel End. Cross to the signposted footpath S of the R-hand thatched cottage. Continue E to the road. Walk NE along this to the road junction, then R (SSE) for a short distance. The path back into Stortford is signposted L (E) along field edges.

OTHER SUGGESTED ROUTES

Weekend Walk

1. Bishop's Stortford – Stansted Hall – Stansted Mountfitchet – Alsa Wood – Elsenham Station – Henham – Amberden Hall – Hamperden End – Cutler's Gn – Thaxted (overnight stop). Thaxted – River Chelmer – Tilty – Brookend – Bamber's Gn – Takeley – B183 – Bush End – Hatfield Forest – Bishop's Stortford. Day 1: 13m. Day 2: 14m.
Can be fairly heavy walking, but takes in some delightful villages (including Thaxted) and Hatfield Forest.

Day Walks

1. Gt Dunmow – Gt Easton – Tilty – Molehill Gn – Brookend – Lt Easton – Pharisee Gn – Gt Dunmow. 13m.
Fairly heavy in places.

2. Thaxted – River Chelmer – Tilty – Chickney – Woodend Gn – Henham Lodge – Amberden Hall – Hamperden End – Cutlers Gn – Thaxted. 12m.
Fairly heavy in places.

3. Stansted Mountfitchet – Alsa Wood – Bellington Hall – Manuden – Mallows Gn – Uppend – Patmore Heath – Upwick Gn – Level's Gn – Farnham – Hazel End – Stansted Mountfitchet. 13m.
An interesting extension of the Recommended Walk.

Medium Walks

1. Gt Dunmow – Tilty – Muscombs – Brookend – Lt Easton – Pharisee Gn – Gt Dunmow. 9¾m.
This can be reduced to 8½m by omitting Tilty.

2. Chickney – Tilty – Muscombs – Church End – Chickney. 6m.
This can be extended to 8m to take in Molehill Gn.

3. Molehill Gn – Moor End – Muscombs – Bamber's Gn – Molehill Gn. 6m.
Heavy.

4. Bamber's Gn – Canfield End – Bury Fm – Pharisee Gn – Lt Easton – Brookend – Bamber's Gn. 9m.
Likewise.

5. Henham – Lt Henham – Widdington – Amberden Hall – Sibleys – Chickney – Pledgdon Gn – Henham. 8¾m.
A 6½m walk can be had by using the Sibleys-Woodend Gn path back into Henham.

6. Quendon – Lt Henham – Henham – Elsenham Station – Bollington Hall – Rickling Hall – Quendon. 9½m.
Takes in parts of the Harlow-Cambridge-Harlow LDFP.

Short Walks

The walks below can only be a fragment of the total available in the area.

1. Manuden – Farnham Gn – Mallows Gn – Manuden. 4m.
Rather a lot of metalling.

2. Henham – Lt Henham – Widdington – Prior's Wood – Henham. 4¾m.
Very pleasant.

3. Henham – Amberden Hall – Sibleys – Woodend Gn – Henham. 4½m.
Likewise.

4. Widdington – Prior's Wood – Henham – Amberden Hall – Widdington. 5m.
A certain amount of road on the return.

5. Widdington – Rook End – Widdington. 3m.
The gentlest of walks.

6. Chickney – Woodend Gn – Pledgdon Gn – Chickney. 3½m.
A few small problems.

7. Broxted – Coldarbour Fm – Tilty – 63 – Broxted. 3m.
Easy.

8. Tilty – 63 – Muscombs – Tilty. 4m.
More roadwork required.

9. Gt Easton – Muscombs – Lt Easton – Gt Easton. 5m.
Takes in the old air base.

North of Harlow (the Ash Valley)

The Ash valley is delightful, the best walking in this chapter.

Albury North of the village is Albury Hall, delightfully wooded, and a pleasant thatched pub, the Catherine Wheel, at Gravesend.

Eastwick 13c marble knight lies under the church tower.

Furneux Pelham Famous among real ale enthusiasts as the home of Rayment's brewery, now a subsidiary of Greene King. Inside the church (where 'Time Flies. Mind your Business' is picked out in gold letters on the west tower) there is stained glass by Morris and Burne-Jones.

Hunsdon An attractive street-village stretching along the B180. The hall and church lie together south of the village. Hunsdon House today is less than a quarter of the original mansion built for Henry VIII in 1525. The veranda is Jacobean, the rest Victorian. St Dunstan's began life in the 13c, but only the heavy-timbered north porch has survived the rebuilding of Tudor and Jacobean times.

Little Hadham A parish of several scattered hamlets including Westland Green, Hadham Ford, Green Street and Bury Green. The church has a Carolean three-decker pulpit, box pews and textual wall-paintings in the north chapel. To the east stands the Elizabethan Hadham Hall, now a school. The village has a number of good timber-framed cottages, particularly in Church End, about the crossroads.

Much Hadham Village of exceptional character, with main street of great interest, including one of the finest 13-15c churches in the district with a lovely tie-beam roof; Much Hadham Hall, a five-bay house with a hipped roof; the Red House on the other side of the road; the pargetted 17c Bull Cottage, Old House and Green Shutters; the timber-framed Morris Cottage (home of William Morris's sister); and Georgian Moor Place. The Palace, a long H-shaped house with brick gables north of the churchyard is the 17c refacing of a medieval building owned by the bishops of London.

Patmore Heath Nature reserve is remarkable as an area of acid grasses rare in this district. Open: daily.

Widford The water meadows of the river Ash lie to the north-west.

RECOMMENDED WALKS

1. **Furneux Pelham – Whitebarns – Patmore Heath – Hole Fm – Furneux Pelham. 8m. HR.**

Quite a lot of metalled surface.

Start at the church and pick up a metalled lane immediately to the E running N to Whitebarns. (This is signposted at the S end.) At Whitebarns Fm, follow the main track R (ENE) for ¼m to a narrow road (Violets Lane). Turn R (S) down this lovely lane for 1m back into the village. Cross the main street and continue S down the side road to Barleycroft End. At the T-junction, turn L and follow the road E and S to a road junction by a little wood. Pick up a cart track into the trees just S of the junction and follow ESE to another minor road. Turn R (S) here and follow round a bend R (SW) along the N edge of the woods. Walk through Patmore Heath, turning R (N) at the T-junction on the Furneux Pelham road. At the N edge of the village, turn L (W) down a track signposted to Furneux Pelham and Albury. Follow along a field edge and up the N edge of the L-hand wood. Continue W along field paths and pick up the Hole Fm driveway. Turn R (N) at the farm down to the minor road. Turn L (W) for ½m to a large wood N of the road. Continue to its W edge and then pick up a farm track R (N) through blue gates. Skirt the wood and continue ahead to the farmhouse. Pick up another farm road here R (NE) to the SW corner of the next wood. Leave the track here and skirt the wood on its S edge. At the far corner, continue ENE back into Furneux Pelham.

2. **Hadham Ford – Bury Gn – Green Tye – Much Hadham – Hadham Ford. 9m. HR.**

This route may be combined with part or whole of the following Widford walk to make a circular route of 11½-13m. **HR.** *A great variety of paths including the* *lovely Ash river, and the village of Much Hadham.*

Start at the Nag's Head. Walk S on the Much Hadham road and then L (ESE) down a narrow lane. After ¼m, go round a corner and past a signposted path R (S) just before woods. Go on a short distance and then leave the road L (NE) over a stile toward the wood. Before the wood, the path veers R (ENE and ESE) along field edges into Bury Gn. At the road, turn R (S) to the green and pick up the lane L to Lower Fm with the No Through Road notice. This quickly becomes a broad cart track and then a narrower grass bridleway SE to a B road, turning R (SSW) just after crossing the pylon lines. Turn L (E) along the road to a bend L by black-and-white chevrons. At that point, leave the road R (S) along a hedge and across a field to a small copse. Turn R (WSW) through the copse. At its SW corner, walk diagonally (S) across the next field. Turn R (NW) again and pick up a much better track L (S). This ends after ½m in an E-W crossing track. Turn R (W) to the N tip of Mathams Wood. Leave the cart track L (SSW) on the well-defined path through the wood. Pick up the old airfield perimeter track R (SW) to the road. Turn R (NW) and then L (SSW) down a pebbled track signposted to Sacombs Ash. Follow along a fence toward the farmhouse and the clump of trees about it. 20yd after the end of the fence, turn R (WNW) down a good grass path under the pylon wires and across the prairie. Cross the stream. Continue WNW along hedgeside paths into Green Tye. Turn R (N) up the side street to the village road. Turn L (WSW) past the pub and pick up the signposted bridleway R (NW). Where this broad track bends R (NNE), turn half-left (W and NW) along field paths downhill to the woods ahead. Pick up a path L (W) through the woods and then L again (SW) between the trees and the stream. At the road, turn R and then L at the first fork. Cross the Ash. At the T-junction, continue ahead (WNW) on a path into Much Hadham. Walk N up the village street and then R (E) at the B180 back over the river. Take the signposted footpath L (N) over a stile and along the line of trees to the riverbank. Follow the river upstream until the path ends in a minor road. Continue ahead (NNE by N) into Hadham Ford.

3. **Allen's Gn – Widford – Hadham Cross – Green Tye – Allen's Gn. 7½m. HR.**

Shorter walks:

Widford – Hadham Mill – South End – Widford. 4½m. HR.

Allen's Gn – South End – Hadham Mill – Green Tye – Allen's Gn. 6m. HR.

Start at the Queen's Head. Walk S to the church and then S again down a footpath signposted to Chandler's Lane. Continue to and past the W edge of the wood to a broad E-W crossing track. Turn R (W) to a signpost by the farm cottages. Turn briefly L (S) here along the metalled surface and then R (W) again down a grassy field edge path at the next signpost. Follow a ditch SW to Fiddler's Brook; walk first on the N, then the S, then the N side of the ditch. Turn briefly R at the brook and cross. Continue W along a field edge to the lane at the top of the hill. Turn L (S) to and along the minor road. Pick up a broad cart track R (W) opposite a barn. Cross the pylon lines; where the track bends L (S) shortly afterwards, turn half-right (WNW) towards the woods ahead. The path here turns briefly L (W) and then goes through the wood WNW to the SE corner of the second wood. Skirt this on the N side. At the NE corner, continue ahead (W) along a fair track to the B180. Turn R (NNE) for ½m through Widford to Nether St. Turn L (WNW) to the Ash. Turn R (NNE) down the track before the river. The route follows the

Contd p.145

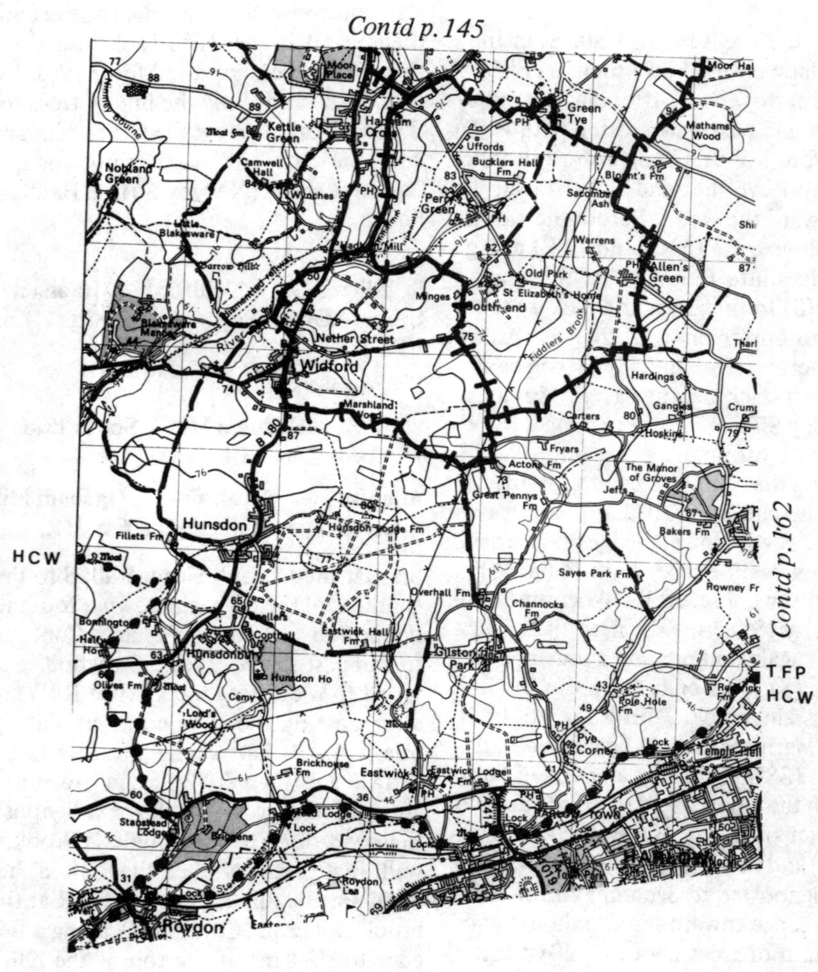

Contd p.162

Contd p. 138

Contd p. 144

fields E of the river back to the B road. Cross and walk E down the South End side road. The long and short walks divide here. (If on the short walk, follow the road into South End: turn R (SSW) down the lane to Acton's Fm, leaving it down a cart track where the main lane swings R (WSW) to Nether St.) If on the long walk, turn L (ENE) down the Hadham Mill lane. At the SW corner of the woods, turn L again (NE) between the Ash and the trees. Follow this well-defined path all the way to Hadham Cross. Cross and pick up the path to Green Tye and Sacombs Ash (see the walk above). At the Sacombs Ash track, turn R (SSW and SE) into Allen's Green.

OTHER SUGGESTED ROUTES

Day Walks

See Day Walks 1 and 2, Bishop's Stortford – Dunmow.

3. Albury – Albury End – Hadham Ford – Bury Gn – Stortford Park – Upwick Gn – Patmore Heath – Furneux Pelham – Patient End – Albury Hall – Albury. 12½m.
Some excellent tracks.

Medium Walks

The Bishop's Stortford Footpaths Association have been very industrious over the last few years in devising and publishing walks of short to medium length. I will therefore limit myself to a few of my own invention, and to recommending readers to obtain their excellent booklets.

1. Hadham Ford – Bury Gn – Stortford Park – Upwick Gn – Patmore Heath – Albury – Albury End – Hadham Ford. 9m.
This can be reduced to 7m by taking the Bury Gn – Upwick Hall path.

Short Walks

Again, the walks below can only be a fragment of the total available in the area.

1. Much Hadham – Kettle Gn – Lt Brakesware – Ash Path – Much Hadham. 5m.
Excellent.

2. Much Hadham – Green Tye – Southend – Hadham Mill – Much Hadham. 5m.
Likewise.

3. Much Hadham – Dane Bridge – Bury Gn – Hadham Ford – Ash – Much Hadham. 4¾m.
The third of this fine trio.

Harlow to Dunmow

Some beautiful and historic villages in fairly heavy arable countryside; forest droves and narrow country lanes are the best paths.

Great Canfield Dominated by the considerable earthwork remains of its medieval castle, with a 45ft high motte nearly 100yd in circumference. The boundaries of the outer bailey can still be traced south-west of the church. St Mary's is Norman, with some fine decoration on the doorways and a 13c mural of the Madonna and Child in one of the three little arches behind the chancel arch. There are several 16c brasses of the Wyseman family.

Great Dunmow See p.135.

Great Hallingbury The hall dates back to Tudor times and was for a long time the home of the Parker family. One Parker was Admiral of the Fleet at Sluys in 1340, in the decisive defeat of the French navy. Another achieved even greater fame as Lord Mounteagle, who blew apart the Gunpowder Plot after receiving a curious warning letter in 1605. The letter, and Mounteagle's part in the affair, has long been a matter of dispute. Many modern writers believe the Plot to have been known to Salisbury at least since the beginning of 1605. If this were so, the Catholic Mounteagle would be his agent and the plotters mere dupes. St Giles's church lies slightly away from the wooded village. It is much restored, but has a pleasing tall spire, a chancel arch made out of Roman bricks and an attractive modern mosaic of the Walk to Emmaus.

Harlow is no place to take in as part of a walk, although the New Town is in many respects one of the better modern towns developed as a result of the 1946 Act. Old Harlow church has a magnificent collection of Tudor and Stuart brasses. For the rambler, there are several ways of leaving the town: the Town Trail and Forest Way to the south and Stort towpath to the north offer easy ways into the countryside about the town.

Hatfield Broad Oak Once an important market town, and still has many 16-17c houses with gables and robustly-carved woodwork along the main street. The medieval priory remains as part of a precinct wall, some old fishponds, and a parish church that was once the monastic chapel. This has an 80ft tower, a Norman north wall and 14c nave and chancel arches. Internal fittings include the gallery of corbel portraits in the nave, an 18c candelabra with thirty-six branches, a rare library, and a wooden effigy of the priory's founder, Alberic de Vere, Earl of Oxford.

Hatfield Forest Like Epping Forest, this large expanse of deciduous woodland is a survivor of that which once covered the county until medieval clearances. Although most of the old trees have disappeared during felling operations early in this century, many ancient oaks, hornbeams and horse chestnuts remain, including the famous Doodle Oak, a thousand years old and still standing. A great deal of new woodland, particularly silver birch, has grown up to take the place of the felled trees. The coppices are separated by broad rides and open areas of grassy parkland ideal for walker and picnicker alike. Apart from a small area of marsh fenced off by the Essex Naturalists' Trust for snipe, ringed snakes and orchids, the whole 1049 acres of forest are open to visitors. Wildlife includes some muntjac deer, which escaped from Woburn Park in the 19c and have set up home here. Also to be seen is the prehistoric ring-fortress on Portingbury Hills. There are five access points for walkers into the Forest: the east one is the busiest, since it also receives cars. Most of the car-borne visitors get little further than the small area around the lake and pavilion (Shell House). It is therefore not only an excellent place for walkers, but also surprisingly deserted.

Hatfield Heath I can recommend the White Horse inn as a fine traditional pub.

Little Hallingbury The best part of the village lies around the church, where a stained glass window with pictures of St Etheldreda and Alan of Walsingham is a reminder of the church's connection with Ely during the middle ages.

Matching Two greens, several medieval and early modern houses, and a 17c moated barn. Wedding Feast House was built in the middle ages by one Mr Chimney, for the feasting of bridal couples too poor to use their own place.

Sawbridgeworth Centres on a square of small roads, with many good brick or overhanging timber houses, notably Market House at the corner of Knight and Bell Streets, and the White Lion opposite it. In an area brimming with tomb monuments, no church has a greater number or variety than St Mary's.

Sheering East window of church famous for the rare beauty of its stained glass: the crowned Madonna and the eight orders of the Heavenly Host.

Spellbrook Scattered and small. Magnificent 15c thatched pub, the Three Horseshoes. **Wallbury Camp** is the most impressive of Essex's Iron Age hill forts, with a double rampart and enclosure of 30 acres. The trees that make it such a magnificent site also prevent the towpath walker from appreciating it in any detail.

Takeley Despite its noisy position by the airport and A120, Takeley remains attractive with church incorporating Roman tiles, plus work from every century after 1066. Font cover with canopies and pinnacles, echoes pinnacled oak pulpit standing nearby. Many recognisably Tudor and earlier barns and houses throughout the village.

Thorley Ribbon development from Bishop's Stortford has been threatening this little hamlet for a long time, but at present its fine Early English church still has a predominantly rural atmosphere. Note the nearby set of stocks.

RECOMMENDED WALKS

1. **Bishop's Stortford – Gaston Green – Bishop's Stortford. 5m. VHR.**

The towpath of the Stort is the finest part of the walk.

Start at Bishop's Stortford. Walk SSE down the main street; where the A roads fork, turn R (SSW by S) over the river and then turn L (SSE by S) down Twyford Rd. Follow across the railway line. Where the lane bends R (S), pick up a broad pebbled track half-left (SSE by S) to the lock. Cross and walk down the road for a short distance. Turn R (SSW) down a tarmac driveway. Turn L (SSE by S) onto the field just before the thatched cottages and follow the line of the crops up the hill with telegraph poles away to your L. Cross the little road and continue through a gate just L (E) of Jarian. Go down the driveway of the boarding kennels; where this track bends R to the house, continue ahead down the grass path S. This exits via a private driveway onto Dell Lane. Turn R (S) down the lane until it bends sharp R (W). At that point, pick up a path ahead sign-posted by Windy Walls. Go down the line of the hedge, then down across meadows via a stile. Cross the stream and continue S via field paths to Gaston House. Pick up an unmetalled drive ahead to the narrow road and turn R (WSW by W) to the mill. Cross the mill stream and continue to the lock. Turn R (N) before the lock along the towpath of the Stort. Follow back into Bishop's Stortford.

2. **Bishop's Stortford – Sawbridgeworth – Hatfield Forest – Bishop's Stortford. 13m. HR/VHR.**

Walk down to Twyford Lock as in the previous route. Turn R (W) immediately after the bridge onto the grass towpath and past the footpath notice. Follow the towpath for 3m to Sawbridgeworth. (The right of way follows the E bank to the A414, then crosses to the W bank.) After ¼m on the W bank, turn L (E) down a minor road over the river and railway line. Where this ends in a T-junction, turn L (NNE by N) for 40yd up Lower Sheering Rd to a stream at the next bend opposite Windsor House. Turn R (E) down a grass path beside the stream. Continue to Quicksbury Fm visible up the slope ENE and pick up a farm track E to and over the M11. Continue E and then turn L (NNE) along a field edge to the minor road by the bungalow. Cross the road half-right and continue N to the W edge of the wood. The path goes up the edge of this and then a second small wood. At the N end, cross a ditch and follow it N toward the M11. (The right of way however cuts off the corner of the field NNE by N.) Turn R down a track towards Stone Hall Fm and skirt it on the L (N) side to the road. Turn L (NNW) along this to the M11 bridge. Turn R (E) down a driveway to a large brick barn with blue doors. Go over a stile and continue ENE over the meadow past the large isolated tree to the stream. Cross. The path ENE here is part of the Three Forests Way, and is normally well defined. Ignore all side paths and maintain the ENE bearing for 1m. Turn L (N) there down a green lane to Monk's Wood and the enormous village green. Cross this due N over one road to the road at the extreme N edge of the green. Turn R (E) along the road skirting Wall Wood and past one public footpath sign to the Forest Way signpost and National Trust notice on your L by a bend R in the road. Go down the indicated drove NNE between the trees. The recommended path through the forest is the broad grass ride past Forest Lodge and Warren House. Turn L (WNW) just after Warren House and continue along a narrower ride until it ends in a NE-SW ride. Turn L (SW) to the edge of the forest and then R (N) to Beggar's Hall. Walk down the farm road to the village street by the Hop Poles inn. Turn R (N) and then L (W) at the sign-posted footpath to Harps Fm. Where the tracks divide before the farmhouse, go between the farm buildings. Where this broad cart track ends, continue WNW to the stream. Cross this at the little bridge and turn L (WSW) along it to the motorway. Go under the M11 and follow the stream for a short distance. Where the stream bends sharp L (SW), continue ahead (W) and then half-right (NW) to the golf course. Cross this on the signposted route NW and WSW to the hospital.

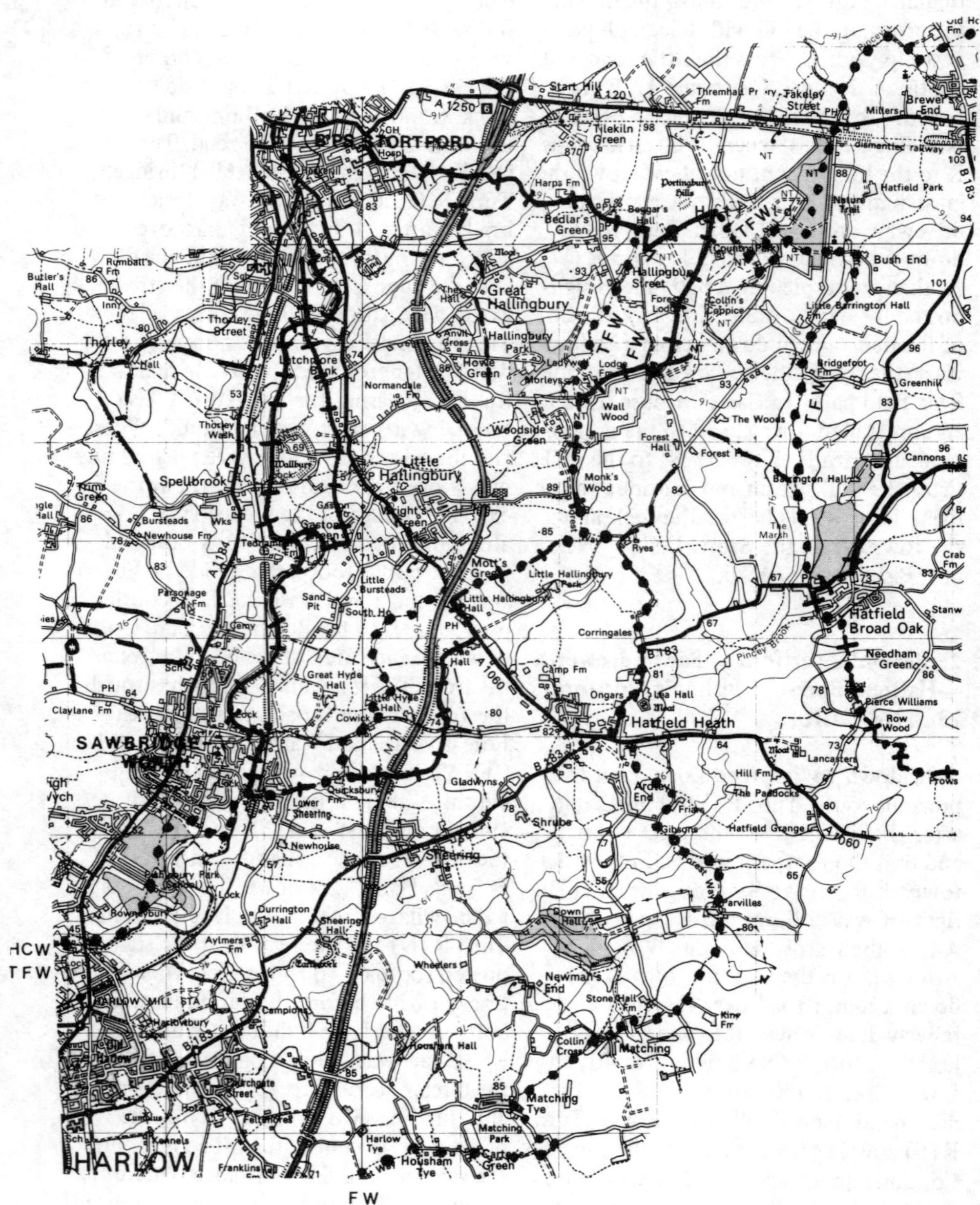
B'PS STORTFORD
Start Hill
Tilekiln Green
Takeley Street
Brewer's End
Hatfield Park
Nature Trail
Harps Fm
Beggar's Hall
Bedlar's Green
Bush End
Hallingbury Street
Great Hallingbury
Collin's Coppice
Little Barrington Hall
Rumball's Fm
Butler's Hall
Thorley Street
Thorley
Latchmore Bank
Hallingbury Park
Howe Green
Bridgefoot
Greenhill
Normandale Fm
Wall Wood
The Woods
Thorley Wash
Woodside Green
Forest Hall
Cannons
Spellbrook
Little Hallingbury
Monk's Wood
Barrington Hall
Trims Green
Bursteads
Newhouse Fm
Gaston Green
Wright Green
Ryes
The Marsh
Parsonage Fm
Little Bursteads
Mott's Green
Little Hallingbury Park
Sand Pit
South Ho
Little Hallingbury Hall
Hatfield Broad Oak
Corringales
Needham Green
Great Hyde Hall
Little Hyde Hall
Camp Fm
Ongars
Lea Hall
Pierce Williams
Claylane Fm
Cowick
Row Wood
Hatfield Heath
SAWBRIDGEWORTH
Lancasters
Hill Fm
Gladwyns
The Paddocks
Quicksbury
Lower Sheering
Ardley End
Friars
Prows
Shrubs
Gibsons
Hatfield Grange
Newhouse
Sheering
Parvilles
Durrington Hall
Down Hall
Sheering Hall
Aylmers Fm
Wheelers
HCW
TFW
Newman's End
HARLOW MILL STA
Campions
Stone Hall Fm
Harlowbury
Collin's Cross
Matching
Housham Hall
Churchgate Street
Matching Tye
Matching Park
Harlow Tye
Housham Tye
Carter's Green
HARLOW
FW

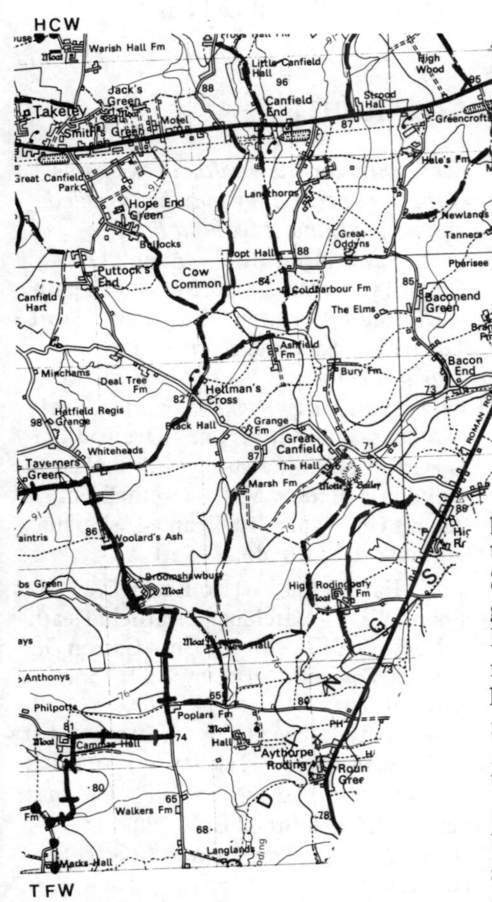

3. Hatfield Broad Oak – Cammas Hall – Taverners Gn – Hatfield Broad Oak. 7m. HR.

Fine walking in this isolated arable area.

Start at Hatfield church. Walk SSW along the village street and take the first turning L (ENE) down Cannons Lane. Turn R (S) opposite No. 16 down a signposted path. Walk alongside the fence and then pick up a good track left between crops. Continue past the hedge and telegraph wires and then along a field edge ahead to the first of the waymark stones. Continue to the farm (huge green barns) and road. Cross the lane half-right and pick up the signposted footpath between the gate-posts. Continue SSE to the next gate and thence to the W edge of Row Wood. Skirt the wood on its W and S sides. A good track leaves from here E, S and E to Prows Fm, where it turns R (SE) onto the minor road. Turn L and follow this narrow lane E, round a sharp bend L (N) and on round two more bends to Cammas Hall. At the next sharp bend L (W) by the red brick house (Cammas Cottage), turn R (E) down a cart track. This marches along beside a hedge under telegraph wires to another minor road. Turn L (N) to the sharp bend R (E) in the road by Poplar's Fm. Pick up a good path straight ahead (N) up a field edge; this skirts one wood, then continues to and through another. Continue N beyond the wood to a broad E-W farm track. Turn L (W) to the narrow lane and then R (NW) for 1m past Broomshawbury and Woolard's Ash. Before Aldbury's Fm, turn L (W) down a broad signposted green lane. Follow to Taverners Gn. The right of way from here officially leaves from the footpath notice opposite, through an overgrown hedge and along the moat edge. Most walkers however go L (S) to the next gateway and then R (W) into the field. Follow this field edge along the trees to your R to the end of the field. Turn half-left (WSW) across the second field to the stream. Follow along the fields on its N bank back into Hatfield Broad Oak.

OTHER SUGGESTED ROUTES

Weekend Walk

1. Bishop's Stortford – River Stort Towpath past Sawbridgeworth and Harlow to Roydon (overnight stop). Roydon – Stanstead Lodge – Olives Fm – Fillets Fm – Widford church – River Ash path – Much Hadham – River Ash path – Hadham Ford – Bury Gn – Thorley Houses – Bishop's Stortford. Day 1: 12m. Day 2: 12m.
An excellent leisurely weekend along the area's two best river paths.

Day Walks

Roydon is connected to Bishop's Stortford by train; either of the daily stages of the first Weekend Walk can therefore be used as a day walk.

The first two Day Walks begin in the Bishop's Stortford – Dunmow district, but are mainly in the Ash valley.

1. Bishop's Stortford – Towpath – Sawbridgeworth – Allen's Gn – Green Tye – Much Hadham – Hadham Ford – Bury Gn – Stortford Park – Wickham Hall – Bishop's Stortford. 18m.
This walk is too long on this clay soil for any but the most energetic. It is however divisible into four smaller day walks. One is the Recommended Walk. The others are: Bishop's Stortford – Sawbridgeworth – Allen's Gn – Thorley Houses – Stortford Park – Wickham Hall – Bishop's Stortford (15m); Bishop's Stortford – Thorley Wash – Thorley – Thorley Houses – Bury Gn – Stortford Park – Wickham Hall – Bishop's Stortford (13m); Sawbridgeworth – Allen's Gn – Much Hadham – Hadham Ford – Bury Gn – Thorley – Towpath – Sawbridgeworth (15m). *These are only the main alternatives; with such a wealth of walkable paths in the area, they may be curtailed or extended almost without limit.*

2. Sawbridgeworth – Allen's Gn – Green Tye – Much Hadham – Ash path – Widford – Hunsdon – Eastwick – Stort Towpath – Sawbridgeworth. 16m.
This too can easily be reduced to two much shorter day walks: Sawbridgeworth – Allen's Gn – Actons Fm – Overhall Fm – Harlow Mill – Sawbridgeworth (12m): Roydon – Harlow Mill – Overhall Fm – Allen's Gn – Much Hadham – Ash path – Hunsdon – Roydon (15m).

3. Harlow Mill – Housham Tye – Forest Way – Matching – Hatfield Heath – Ryes – LDFP – Mott's Gn – Gaston Gn – Stort Towpath – Harlow Mill. 15m.
Road at first.

4. Hatfield Broad Oak – Taverners Gn – Hellmans Cross – Takeley – Frogs Hall Fm – Gt Canfield – New Hall – Cammas Hall – Hatfield Broad Oak. 14m.
A good walk taking in some deserted hamlets.

Medium Walks

The Bishop's Stortford Footpaths Association have been very industrious over the last few years in devising and publishing walks of short to medium length. I will therefore limit myself to a few of my own invention, and to recommending readers to obtain their excellent booklets.

1. Bishop's Stortford – Stort path – Thorley – Thorley Houses – Bury Gn – Stortford Park – Wickham Hall – Bishop's Stortford. 9m.
Fairly heavy.

2. Sawbridgeworth – Allen's Gn – Moor Hall – Thorley Washes – Stort – Sawbridgeworth. 8m.

A fine walk, though with some road at first.

3. Harlow Mill – Housham Tye – Matching – Sheering – Stort – Harlow Mill. 9m.
Takes in part of the Forest Way.

4. Gt Hallingbury – Forest Hall – Bridgefoot Fm – Hatfield Forest – Bedlar's Gn – Gt Hallingbury. 8m.
An excellent walk taking in the Forest.

5. Hatfield Broad Oak – Bridgefoot Fm – Hatfield Forest – Woodside Gn – LDFP – Pincey Brook – Hatfield Broad Oak. 8m.
Likewise.

6. Hatfield Heath – Pincey Brook – Hatfield Broad Oak – Forest Fm – Woodside Gn – Lt Hallingbury Park – Hatfield Heath. 6½m.
A good variation.

7. Hatfield Heath – Ryes – Mott's Gn – Sheering – Matching – LDFP – Hatfield Heath. 9m.
Good walking, with some road.

8. Gt Canfield – Hellmans Cross – Whiteheads – Broomshawbury – Poplars Fm – Gt Canfield. 6½m.
An amalgam of BSFA footpaths.

Short Walks

Again, the walks below can only be a fragment of the total available in the area.

1. Sawbridgeworth – Harlow Town (by towpath). 5½m.
This can be shortened by stopping at Harlow Mill station rather than Harlow Town.

2. Harlow Town Trail (Passmores, Tye Green and Sewards). 5m.
A series of cards on this are available from Harlow Council.

3. Bury Gn – Upwick Hall – Stortford Park – Bury Gn. 5½m.
Generally good paths.

4. Gt Hallingbury – Bedlar's Gn – Hatfield Forest – Woodside Gn – Gt Hallingbury. 4¾m.
Rather a lot of road on an otherwise splendid walk.

5. Hatfield Broad Oak – Forest Fm – Woodside Gn – Pincey Brook – Hatfield Broad Oak. 5½m.
A pleasant little walk.

6. Gt Canfield – New Hall – Marsh Fm – Gt Canfield. 4½m.
Good.

7. Bishop's Stortford – Stort Path – Sawbridgeworth. 4½m.
Easy walking between railway stations.

8. Takeley – Hellmans Cross – Canfield End – Takeley. 5¾m.
Arable.

9 NORTH ESSEX HIGHLANDS

Saffron Walden to Haverhill; Saffron Walden to Royston

This chapter covers footpaths in no fewer than four counties, Essex, Suffolk, Cambridgeshire and Hertfordshire, but it lies mostly in Essex, and is therefore included in this section of the book. It is generally a good walking area, particularly for ramblers like myself who do most of their walking in the flatter lands of Cambridgeshire, to the north. Highlands is rather a misleading term, since no part of this area is more than four hundred and ninety feet above sea level, and the average must be more like three hundred and seventy-five feet. Nevertheless, this district includes the highest points in both Cambridgeshire and Essex, and is the watershed of East Anglia: from this low ridge the Saffron Walden and Linton Cams flow north-west to Cambridge, the Great Ouse and the Wash. Only a few miles to the south rise the Chelmer, Stort and Ash, flowing down through Essex and Hertfordshire to the Thames estuary. To the east, on the other side of Haverhill, the Stour begins its course through Suffolk and Essex to Manningtree. With the exception of the Saffron Walden Cam, however, these streams are, at their sources, too small to carve out any significant valleys. The area is therefore a remarkably uniform upland plateau, founded on a bedrock of chalk, covered with a thick layer of chalky boulder clay deposited during the glaciations of the Late Pleistocene age. Boulder clay is a mixture of clay, rocks, sandy material and chalk, and the last is particularly predominant here, as a glance at any of the fields will show. This is certainly not chalk downland, and there is none of the springy turf that can be found further to the south-west, along the chalk ridge, but it is a lighter and more walkable ground than pure clay, and the chalk also complements the natural slope of the land in creating fairly dry conditions.

The landscape rolls gently, with the hills never quite becoming level upland. The presence of clay indicates that the area would have become forested very shortly after the departure of the ice, and also that the streams draining off the rainwater from the land would remain on the surface. The forests were probably lighter and more easily cleared here than in the middle of Essex, possibly accounting for the presence of early settlements in the area.

The landscape today still shows features of the original appearance. The hills and streams are still there, and so are a great number of woods particularly in the Chrishall and Langley district west of

Saffron Walden. It is now predominantly arable, with very little pasture or heath. The fields are mostly rather smaller than those on the Cambridgeshire plains, and usually retain their original mature hedges as field boundaries. It is therefore fairly easy walking, by the standards of East Anglian arable, as well as being an interesting and varied landscape with continual gentle slopes with views over the flatter lands, particularly to the north. These reminders of the area's relative height are always present, and give the walker an illusory feeling of altitude, especially between Saffron Walden and Royston.

The earliest example of prehistoric settlement comes from Therfield Heath, in the extreme west of the area, with its Neolithic long barrow and several Bronze Age round tumuli. Hoards of metal found in the villages between here and Saffron Walden confirm this Bronze and later Iron Age occupation, and it seems probable that the forest clearings of the time were used not only for agriculture but also the smelting of metals. The greatest prehistoric monument in Essex itself is Ring Hill, at Audley End: one of the largest and originally most impressive of Iron Age hill forts in this part of the world. Ring Hill lies in the valley of the Cam, and it was here that settlement concentrated. Similarly, most evidence of early habitation in the district east of Saffron Walden is to be found along the other branch of the Cam, above Linton, which is particularly rich in Roman remains (to be expected, with the Via Devana from Colchester to Cambridge coming down the valley). The villa at Horseheath lies very close to the road; but the best site, the famous Romano–British barrows known as the Bartlow Hills, lies some distance away from the Via Devana on the banks of the river itself. Settlement would therefore seem to have followed more than one route into the forested interior.

During this early period, the impact of man was undoubtedly accelerated by the Icknield Way. It is clear from the presence of flints from Grimes Graves in great numbers at the south-west end of the Way that there was a great deal of traffic along this easily traversable chalk belt. The routes comprising the Icknield Way through Cambridgeshire and Essex are far from certain, and many would consider that the main crossing of the Cam would have been further north than my own route, Whittlesford Mill being the most likely. It is, however, certain that the Way entered Cambridgeshire in the Royston district, and probable that at least one of the various local routes would have passed through Chrishall to a crossing of the Cam at the significantly named Ickleton. An even more southerly route to Ring Hill is also favoured by the great archaeologist of the area, Fox. Great Chesterford is certainly a likely Roman crossing, having been inhabited continuously since the Neolithic age and being a major Roman town from the first century AD.

Anglo-Saxon settlement in the area also began in the valleys. Increasingly, however, the Saxons cleared the forests and established new villages within the newly cultivated land. This quiet revolution in land use is not the only evidence of the Saxon period: in the early Anglo-Saxon times the boundaries of the three kingdoms of East Anglia, Essex and Middle Anglia met here, most likely at Great Chesterford. Heydon Ditch is one of the four great earthworks in Cambridgeshire by which the East Anglians defended the chalk belt from western invasion.

Throughout the middle ages the villages of the river valleys remained larger and more prosperous than those on the uplands. Their grand churches, halls and ambitious domestic building of all periods still look prosperous, with Saffron Walden and Newport the most attractive market town and village respectively. In upland villages the churches and manor houses are mostly small, and there are none of the large houses that can be found in the valley of the Saffron Walden Cam. That apart, they are mostly very attractive small villages, many – like Arkesden – having declined in population since the 19th century.

As a walking area the highlands are a bit neglected by most ramblers, the main walking groups being based in county towns to the north or south. The district west of Saffron Walden is better known among walkers, and attracts ramblers from other parts of East Anglia, and from London. Signposting is not as excellent in this part of Essex as elsewhere in the county, but is generally good by the standards of East Anglia as a whole. The paths vary considerably, and include some across ploughed fields. Most, however, are eminently walkable, either along headlands or some splendid hedged tracks like the green lane from Ickleton Grange to Royston.

Saffron Walden to Haverhill

Small villages off the beaten track, with handsome, larger Saffron Walden and Newport in the Cam valley. Relatively easy fieldwork and generally good signposting.

Ashdon A Roman villa has been discovered on Great Copt Hill, complete with seven rooms and hypocausts. The village also disputes the claim of Ashington near Southend to be the site of Edmund Ironside's famous battle of Assandun against Canute, in 1016. There are many attractive cottages, a windmill north-east of the village, a 15c timber-framed Guildhall and All Saints church.

Bartlow Bartlow Hills lie south of the church across the old railway line, a fine set of Romano-British burial mounds. There were seven of them originally, and four remain as overgrown humps in the surrounding woods. Unlike the familiar Bronze Age round barrow, these are not gentle, broad slopes but tall and steep-sided, unmistakably artificial. Their 19c excavation was tragic: found to be walled graves with splendid bronzes, enamels, glassware and pottery, these treasures were transferred for safe keeping to Easton Lodge in Dunmow. A few years later, the Lodge burned down, taking all its contents with it. Roman house sites have been discovered in some numbers within the village. There is a fine old village pub, some isolated houses and a delightful 12c church.

Castle Camps South of the village along a splendid track is the church and Castle Farm. West of the church lies an extensive series of mounds, ditches and moats remaining from the 12c castle built here by Aubrey de Vere, first Earl of Oxford, and maintained by the de Veres until the 16c. The church actually stands within the castle bailey, and has fine views. Beyond Castle Farm stands the old Second World War airfield. This flew fighters during the Battle of Britain and later housed the first hush-hush Mosquito squadron during 1942. One casualty of the airfield was Wigmore Pond, the highest point in Cambridgeshire and an Anglo-Saxon settlement site. The site remains as two parallel lines of trees, but the pond itself is no more.

Debden In rich and attractive countryside, with many woods. A number of excellent 16-17c houses and farms, and the church standing among Spanish chestnuts. The Hall was demolished in 1936, though its parkland and lake remain, the latter feeding Debden Water. A few years later the RAF arrived, and the fighters from here played a leading part in the Battle of Britain. The station was later transferred to the Americans, whose P-47s were the first to enter German airspace, in 1943. A De Havilland Venom still stands outside the airfield, north of the village. For long the HQ of the RAF Police Training Unit, there are rumours that it will be restored to operational use.

Great Chesterford On the main railway line to Cambridge, and very close to a junction of the M11. There are several good pubs, including the Plough and the Station – the latter being the old railway station, rather than just a hotel. Old Roman settlement north-west of the houses among fields was a large town, extending over some 37 acres, and grouped around the military fort. The walls were still visible into the 19c.

Great Sampford Many pretty gabled cottages, especially to the south of its unusually lavish 14c church.

Hadstock In little valley, with nice cottages by the church. St Botolph's name indicates an early foundation, and it is a Saxon building of the most primitive kind, remodelled four centuries later. There are some fine wall-paintings, rugged exposed stonework and a huge Anglo-Saxon oak door. This bore until recently a human skin nailed upon it, the remains of a Dane flayed alive for desecrating the church during the Viking invasion of the early 11c. South of the village stands Little Walden airfield, where the US Army Air Force flew bombing missions in 1944-5. The concreted rights of way here are part of the old airfield roads.

Newport A village almost to rival Saffron Walden. It is a typical street village, along the A11 and therefore regrettably busy. The 15c Monk's Barn and Priory have overhanging eaves; the pargetted Crown House, traditionally linked with Nell Gwynn, has a plaster crown outside to denote Charles II's proprietorial interests. The church contains much fine medieval work, including a 13c portable altar in one of the transepts bearing the earliest English oil paintings on wood. Newport's grammar school was founded in the late 16c, the building is more recent. The scholastic diet was then limited to Latin, Greek and Hebrew, learned by rote over an immensely long working day; the day has shortened, but the high standards remain.

Radwinter The Red Lion and the church stand at the crossroads, the mainly 19c church with 14c nave roof and porch.

Saffron Walden A flourishing centre since the Bronze Age, colonised by the Romans and with an Anglo-Saxon cemetery containing enough British burials to imply a Celtic survival into the early Saxon period. This is confirmed by the name Walden, which means valley of the Britons. (Saffron refers to the cultivation of the saffron crocus in the middle ages, for use in dyeing and in medicine.) Saffron Walden museum contains a wealth of prehistoric and historic remains from all over our area. Open: daily. 12c castle remains still visible today; the town also constructed its own defences, the battle ditches west of the centre. A large number of splendid houses remain from the 15-18c, particularly in Bridge St, High St and Middelton Place. The Youth Hostel and Eight Bells pub are both medieval; so is the pargetted Sun inn on Church St corner, which was the Parliamentary military HQ at the end of the Civil War. 15c St Mary's is magnificent. The stately tomb chest of Thomas Audley occupies the south chapel. **Audley End House** The moderately sized stone building, symmetrical and Jacobean behind a magnificent green lawn, was once however a palace of which James I remarked: 'Too much for a king, but it might do very well for a Lord Treasurer.' That was Thomas Howard, who helped James to his throne and was rewarded in 1603 with office and the Earldom of Suffolk. He built the mansion on the site of the medieval Walden Abbey, a 12c Benedictine monastery which at the Dissolution had fallen into the hands of Thomas Audley, Speaker of the Reformation Parliament. Audley had pulled down the abbey and erected a hall which his Howard grandson now in turn demolished for a grander design. The present appearance reflects 18c pruning and a fortune spent by Lord Braybrooke on restoration and decoration. Open: afternoons except Monday, April to September. The grounds were landscaped by Capability Brown and several engaging follies include a Temple of Concord east of the house, the Springwood column on the golf course and another, circular temple to the west, on top of Ring Hill fort. The latter is an early Iron Age earthwork of great size and importance, with 50ft ditches enclosing 16 acres of defended ground. Nearby stands Audley End village, a tiny hamlet south of the Lion Gate, with 18c estate cottages complementing the College of St Mark, a row of late Elizabethan almshouses.

Sewards End No doubt originally a typical Essex end, or hamlet, of a main village isolated in the country at the end of a road, but now connected by the B1053, and grown into a small village.

Shudy Camps Many Roman house sites, and an extensive Anglo-Saxon cemetery. In those days, Shudy Camps must have been a large vill; today, it is little more than a group of little cottages and a simple little 15c church clinging to the sides of the Georgian park. The monuments of the Dayrell family can be seen in St Mary's.

Wendens Ambo On the railway line to London. Burials from Bronze Age through to Anglo-Saxon times have been discovered. Roman bricks have been re-used in St Mary's church, built just after 1066. The murals of the life of St Margaret were executed in the 14c. Wenden means beautiful valley; it is little changed.

Wicken Bonhunt The traditions of craftsmanship of previous centuries are maintained by a carpentry firm based here; there is evidence throughout the little village.

Wimbish A tiny hamlet, surrounded by a great number of fine old farmhouses. The moated site of the Tudor manor house and 14c church lie in the centre of the parish.

RECOMMENDED WALKS

1. **Shudy Camps – Castle Camps – Wigmore Pond – Ashdon – Bartlow. 7½m. HR.**

This C-shaped walk connects two villages on the same bus route between Cambridge and Haverhill. Good walking in an isolated corner of north Essex.

Start at Shudy Camps church. Walk SE through the village towards the T-junction S of Shudy Camps. Just before that junction, turn L (NE) down a fine green lane known locally as the bridlepath. Follow to Castle Camps. Turn R (S) at the village street to the T-junction. Turn L (E) here and then R (S) again opposite a white gate. Cross a small field and then turn R (W) down a splendid grass path SW to the church at Castle Fm. Walk SE from the church beside a red brick wall to the farmyard entrance. Skirt the farmyard on its R (W) side and go over a farm gate into pasture. Continue ESE to the perimeter track of the old airfield and turn R (SSW). (The right of way lies SE and then SW in the fields beyond; the farmer however prefers walkers to use the concrete track.) Follow the perimeter road towards the high radio aerial and clump of trees. Shortly after a bend L (SE) in the track, turn R (SW) across the field to the two lines of trees. This is the site of Wigmore Pond. Continue ahead (SW) to the road. Turn R (NE) to the aerial and pick up a bridleway L (SW) just S of the aerial. Continue along this to the farm road. Turn R (WNW) down the road past the farm. Where the lane veers R (N) to Camps End, continue L (WNW) on a farm track to Winsey Fm. Turn NW along a cart track and then leave it where it bends abruptly L (SW). Keep on here NW down a good grassy footpath. Where this ends in a broad E-W crossing track, turn L (W) beside the stream. Walk down this for ¾m to Sandons. Pass the house. After about 200yd, take the signposted field edge path R (N). Turn R (E) at the top of the field to the NE corner and then L (N) to the windmill at the top of the hill. Pick up a metalled road; but where it bends L (W) almost immediately, keep on NW down a field edge and over the field to the white gates of Walton Pk. Walk up the driveway past the house and through a belt of trees. Turn half-right (NE) along a splendid ride. Where this broad track turns sharp L (W), continue uphill for 20yd and then L (WNW) down a cart track to the Ashdon-Bartlow road. Turn R (N) into Bartlow. At the church take a path SE of the churchyard and follow between fences and over the old railway line to the Roman tumuli of Bartlow Hills. Retrace your steps.

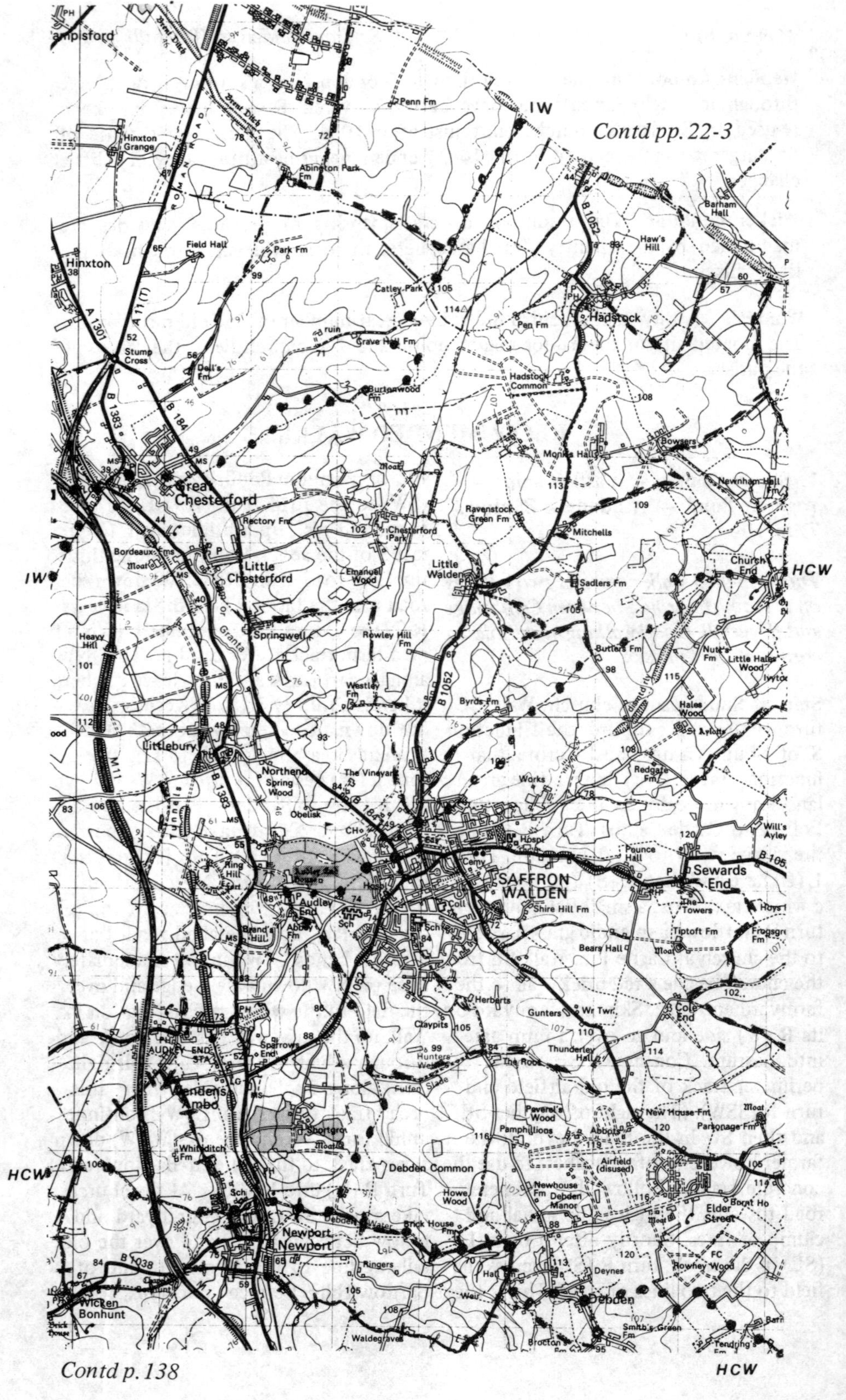
Contd pp. 22-3
IW
Hinxton Grange
Abington Park Fm
Penn Fm
ROMAN ROAD
Field Hall
Park Fm
Hinxton
A 11(T)
A 1301
Catley Park
Haw's Hill
Barham Hall
Hadstock
Pen Fm
Grave Hall Fm
ruin
Stump Cross
Dell's Fm
Burtonwood Fm
Hadstock Common
B 1383
B 184
B 1052
Bowsers
Monks Hall
Great Chesterford
Rectory Fm
Chesterford Park
Ravenstock Green Fm
Mitchells
Newnham Hall Fm
Bordeaux Fms
Moat
Little Chesterford
Emanuel Wood
Little Walden
Sadlers Fm
Church End
HCW
IW
Heavy Hill
Springwell
Rowley Hill Fm
Butlers Fm
Nutt's Fm
Little Hales Wood
Granta
Westley Fm
Byrds Fm
Hales Wood
Littlebury
Northend
Spring Wood
The Vineyard
Works
Redgate Fm
M11
Tunnels
Obelisk
Will's Ayley
Ring Hill
Audley End House
Audley End
Brand's Hill
Abbey
Hospl
Pounce Hall
SAFFRON WALDEN
Sewards End
The Towers
Shire Hill Fm
Tiptoft Fm
Bears Hall
Frogsgre Fm
Herberts
Gunters
Wr Twr
Cole End
Claypits
Hunters Wells
The Roos
Thunderley Hall
AUDLEY END STA
Sparrows End
Wendens Ambo
Fulfen Slade
Peverel's Wood
Pamphillions
Abbots
New House Fm
Parsonage Fm
Whiteditch Fm
Shortgrove
Debden Common
Airfield (disused)
HCW
Howe Wood
Newhouse Fm
Debden Manor
Elder Street
Newport
Debden Water
Brick House Fm
Rowney Wood
Ringers
Deynes
B 1038
Wicken Bonhunt
Debden
Smith's Green Fm
Waldegraves
Broctons Fm
Tendring's Fm
Contd p.138
HCW

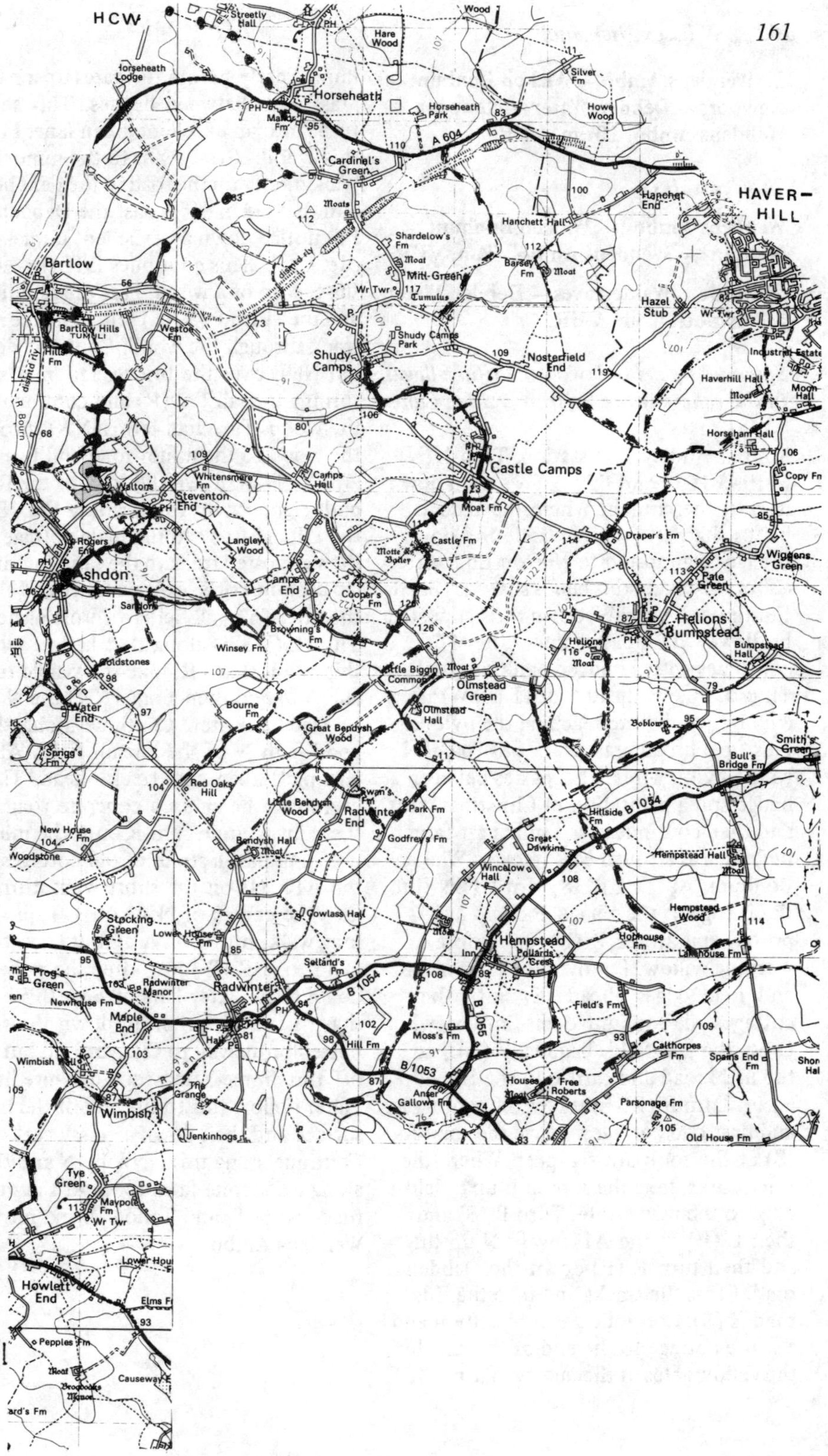

HCW
Streetly Hall
Hare Wood
Wood
Silver Fm
Horseheath Lodge
Horseheath
Horseheath Park
Howe Wood
Manor Fm
A 604
Cardinal's Green
HAVER-HILL
Hanchet End
Hanchett Hall
Moats
Shardelow's Fm
Moat
Barsey Fm
Moat
Mill Green
Wr Twr
Cumulus
Bartlow
Hazel Stub
Wr Twr
Bartlow Hills
TUMULI
Westoe Fm
Hills Fm
Shudy Camps Park
Shudy Camps
Nosterfield End
Industrial Estate
Haverhill Hall
Moat
Moon Hall
Horseham Hall
R. Bourn
Whitensmere
Waltons
Steventon End
Camps Hall
Castle Camps
Moat Fm
Copy Fm
Rogers End
Langley Wood
Castle Fm
Motte & Bailey
Draper's Fm
Wiggens Green
Ashdon
Camps End
Cooper's Fm
Pale Green
Sanpons
Browning's Fm
Helions
Helions Bumpstead
Winsey Fm
Goldstones
Little Biggin Common
Moat
Olmstead Green
Bumpstead Hall
Water End
Bourne Fm
Olmstead Hall
Boblow
Sprigg's Fm
Great Bendysh Wood
Smith's Green
Bull's Bridge Fm
Red Oaks Hill
Little Bendysh Wood
Swan's Fm
Radwinter End
Park Fm
Hillside Fm
B 1054
New House Fm
Woodstone
Bendysh Hall
Moat
Godfrey's Fm
Great Dawkins
Hempstead Hall
Moat
Wincelow Hall
Cowlass Hall
Hempstead Wood
Stocking Green
Lower House Fm
Moat
Hempstead
Inn
Pollards Cross
Hobhouse Fm
Lakehouse Fm
Prog's Green
Radwinter Manor
Radwinter
Setland's Fm
B 1054
Newhouse Fm
Field's Fm
Maple End
B 1055
Hall
Moss's Fm
Calthorpes Fm
Spains End Fm
Wimbish Hall
Hill Fm
B 1053
Houses
Free Roberts
The Grange
Anser Gallows Fm
Wimbish
Parsonage Fm
Jenkinhogs
Old House Fm
Tye Green
Maypole Fm
Wr Twr
Lower House
Howlett End
Elms Fm
Pepples Fm
Moat
Broccocks Manor
Causeway End

2. Wendens Ambo – Wicken Bonhunt – Newport – Debden Water – Newport – Wendens Ambo. 10½m. VHR.

Shorter walks:

Wendens Ambo – Wicken Bonhunt – Newport – Wendens Ambo. 5½m. VHR.

Newport – Waldegraves – Debden Water – Newport. 5½m. VHR.

Splendid tracks and two delightful villages in the valley of the Saffron Walden Cam.

Start at Audley End station. Turn L (N) to the B1039 and then L (W) again down it, past the church. Where the B road bends sharp R (W), continue SW down the lane signposted to Norton End. After a short distance, this bends sharp L (SSE). Continue ahead (SW) down the signposted bridleway. This passes under the M11 and continues with a hedged bank on the R to a line of pylons ahead. Turn L (SSW) along a hedge just before reaching the pylons. Pick up a broad grass track SSW parallel to the pylon wires. This passes between a hedge and a plantation of Christmas trees and then continues for a mile past farm buildings as a rough cart track to Wicken Bonhunt. At the B1038, turn L (ENE) to the E edge of the village. Pick up a signposted grass track R (E) just before a weeping willow. Follow the little stream and field edges ahead (E) until the cottages of Bonhunt come into view. Cross the last field diagonally (NE) to the little road and turn L to the B road again. Turn R (ENE) under the motorway and past two cottages. Leave the road R (S) at the footpath signpost. Where the track forks, take the L path E up a field edge to the new estate. Turn R (S) and then L (E) to the A11; walk N up this and then turn R (E) down the Debden road. Cross the tracks and take the side road R (S). Continue past the station and a white cottage to the end of the lane by the yellow gates of the quarry. Turn L (E) immediately before the gates up a narrow grass path between hedges. This soon turns into an excellent green lane. Follow this E and ESE for ¾m to the minor road. Walk briefly up the road to the next house and there turn off E past the Debden Hall Fm notice down an excellent unmetalled cart track. This continues ESE for ½m to the S edge of a wood. Pass the buildings and then turn L (NNE) following the main track through the wood. Continue downhill NNE over the bridge. Ignore a side turning to Hall Fm (R) and continue N to the wood. Turn half-left (NNW) through the wood to the minor road and turn L (WSW). Walk down the road to the footpath signpost by Brick House Fm. Take the L-hand track to the little cottage (not the signposted track to the farm buildings). Go past the cottage over a fence and along the side of a small field to a crossing hedge. Turn L (WSW) along that hedge. Where this bends sharp R, take the visible track ahead to and then along (NW) the N bank of Debden Water. Continue along the good path N of the stream ENE. After ½m pick up a cart track ahead. This eventually becomes a concrete road. At the railway arch, turn R onto the minor road and past a street of old cottages to the A11. (If on the short walk, turn L into the centre of Newport.) If on the long walk, turn L anyway but leave the main road R (W) just after the railway down Bury Water Lane. Where this bends sharp L, continue ahead down the signposted bridleway to Clanver End but turn off this immediately down Whiteditch Lane. Follow this to the end of the hard surface and then down a grassy cart track. Continue along this NNW by N and then along a concrete farm road. At the minor road, turn L and follow back into Wendens Ambo.

OTHER SUGGESTED ROUTES

Day Walks

1. Haverhill – Draper's Fm – Castle Camps – Winsey Fm – Sandons – Bartlow – Horseheath – Haverhill. 16m.
Can be ended at Horseheath with a bus.

2. Horseheath – Barsey Fm – Castle Camps – Winsey Fm – Sandons – Bartlow – Horseheath. 14m.
An excellent extension of the Recommended Walk.

3. Saffron Walden – Audley End – Wendens Ambo – Strethall – Icknield Way – Lt Walden airfield – Mitchells – Byrd's Fm – Saffron Walden. 15m.
Mostly good tracks in some deserted country.

4. Ashdon – Winsey Fm – Olmstead Hall – Radwinter – River Pant – Wimbish – Sewards End – Water End – Ashdon. 13m.
A mixture of good tracks and arable.

5. Saffron Walden – Wendens Ambo – Wicken Bonhunt – Debden Water – Fulfen Slade – Saffron Walden. 13m.
Excellent walking with many good views.

6. Saffron Walden – Fulfen Slade – Cole End – Sewards End – Water End – Butlers – Saffron Walden. 12m.
A great variety of paths and country.

7. Radwinter – Olmstead Gn – Hempstead Wood – Free Roberts – River Pant – Radwinter. 11m.

8. Linton – LDFP – Burtonwood Fm – Mitchells – Bowsers – How's Hill – Linton. 11¾m (starts p. 22).
Easy walking.

Medium Walks

1. Hadstock – Lt Walden airfield – Lt Walden – Butlers – Ashdon – How's Hill – Hadstock. 9m.
This can be reduced to two 7m walks by using the concrete airfield tracks of Mitchells and Bowsers.

2. Saffron Walden – Byrd's Fm – Butlers – Ashdon – Water End – Saffron Walden. 7¾m.
Check your direction at Byrd's Fm.

3. Radwinter – Godfrey's Fm – Olmstead Gn – Red Oaks Hill – Radwinter. 6¾m.
A lot of road on the return journey.

4. Saffron Walden – The Roos – Cole End – Sewards End – Saffron Walden. 6½m.
A variety of tracks.

5. Audley End – Wendens Ambo – Cuckingstool End – Debden Water – Fulfen Slade – Audley End. 7m.
Can be combined with a visit to the house.

Short Walks

1. Bartlow – River Bourn – Waltons Pk – Bartlow. 3¾m.
Broad tracks and views.

2. Olmstead Gn – Godfrey's Fm – Gt Bendysh Wood – Wigmore Pond – Olmstead Gn. 4½m.
Variable tracks but some pleasant wood.

3. Ashdon – Bowsers – Waltons Pk – Ashdon windmill – Sandons – Ashdon. 5m.
The first part follows airfield hard tracks.

4. Lt Walden – Cloptons – Mitchells – Lt Walden airfield – Lt Walden. 4½m.
Broad tracks taking in the centre of the old field.

5. Saffron Walden – Pleasant Valley – Fulfen Slade – Audley End house – Saffron Walden. 4½m.
Mostly good walking.

6. Saffron Walden – Pleasant Valley – The Roos – Cole End – Tiptoft Fm – Saffron Walden. 5¼m.
Likewise.

7. Wendens Ambo – Pylons – Cuckingstool End – Wendens Ambo. 3½m.
The easiest of strolls.

8. Wendens Ambo – Cuckingstool End – Debden Water – Debden Common – Audley End – Wendens Ambo. 5½m.
Some arable walking.

Saffron Walden to Royston

Predominantly arable, with comparatively small fields, often retaining their mature boundary hedges; some woodland; fairly easy walking.

Anstey A fine old village on the wooded slopes of the ridge, with a good pub and the remains of the medieval castle, by the church.

Arkesden Old and beautiful. A major find of metal weapons and moulds from the Bronze Age was made here. In the church is a monument to Richard Cutte and his wife, who died 1592-4. They lie on a stone six-poster bed, brightly painted, with six children around the base contemplating the thought: As ye now are, so once were we, As we now are, so shall ye be, When you remember us, forget not your selues. The church is beautifully positioned among trees, on rising ground at the end of the walk through the village. There is a stream, Wicken Water, many thatched cottages and a little village green. The village is shrinking, from a population of over five hundred in 1862, with three shops and as many pubs.

Barkway The name, the way over the hill, still describes the long, broad street with old houses and thatched cottages, including the Berg Cottage, owned by the National Trust. The pub is the Chaise and Pair, over three centuries old. The church had a rare system to amplify the preacher's voice – small acoustic jars set into the wall, unfortunately broken during the 19c restoration. A small hoard of Roman silver plates bearing votive figures of Mars and Vulcan was found in 1743 in Rokey Wood.

Chrishall Church in woods south of the village with a copy of Rubens' Adoration of the Magi, of which the original hangs in King's College chapel.

Clavering South of the main ridge, with cottages and houses on the high street and the road to the church. The extensive earthwork remains of the old castle lie immediately north of the church. Nearby Roast Green has two picturesque windmills.

Elmdon Entering the village from Park Wood, look left into a field with curious humps and hollows in the ground: this is the remains of Elmdonbury, the village's medieval moated site.

Heydon Heydon Ditch straddles the open chalk belt between forest and fens – in this case, the marshes three miles away at Fowlmere. Also around Heydon are some more earthworks of the same age – the terraced hillsides known as Strip Lynchets. Good views to the north.

Langley On the Roman road: 19c excavations of a large round barrow here have produced finds of Roman brick and glass. A fine pub, the Bull.

Nuthampstead The airfield here flew USAF Flying Fortresses in the daylight raids on Germany. One of these was forced to make a crash landing in the mound of Anstey Castle.

Reed A series of rectangular enclosure boundaries have been identified on the south-facing slopes here. These probably mark plots colonised by retired Roman legionaries. Reed's proximity to Ermine Street supports this conclusion and it may explain why even today the cottages are scattered over a square of roads and the village has no real centre. There is Saxon work in the church, and a ploughed-out site of a medieval castle at Periwinkle Hill. Good views before descent to Royston.

Royston A pleasant, bustling town where Cambridgeshire and Hertfordshire meet. Royston Cave is a cavern hewn out of chalk, reached by a winding passage leading 30ft under the road and ending in a chamber 17ft across with a large number of crudely carved reliefs upon the walls: saints and crusaders, kings and martyrs, the Virgin Mary, etc. The cave dates almost certainly from pre-Roman times, but the carvings are probably late medieval or Tudor. The church incorporates parts of the large 12c Augustinian canonry founded here. What remains is an interesting puzzle in ecclesiastical architecture, for the alterations of succeeding centuries have kept such a good likeness to the original style that even experts may be confused. Royston is on the railway, and an excellent place to start or finish a walk. James I coursed hares and hunted from the lodge; it was here that the warrant for Raleigh's execution was signed.

Strethall A deserted spot, with cottages and farmhouses hiding behind trees. In medieval days, however, this was a much larger and quite impressive village beside the green lane of the Icknield Way. Wool was the industry here, and the slopes must once have been covered with sheep. 1346 was the fateful year for Strethall, which perished almost to a single family during the first onset of the Black Death. The Saxon church now stands alone among the fields.

Therfield Old cottages, an interesting medieval church and a castle site. North of the village a splendid path runs to Royston, bypassing on the east side Therfield Heath. This rare patch of downland, now used as a golf course and training ground for racehorses, has five Bronze Age round barrows and a single Neolithic long barrow, the only one in Hertfordshire. The latter is 22yd wide and 40yd long, and up to 12ft in height. In prehistoric times, the heath must have been a major point on the Icknield Way route to Wiltshire, and possibly a centre for trade. Certainly the hoard of copper bars found in the Money Hill tumulus in 1861 would imply this.

RECOMMENDED WALKS

1. **Elmdon – Chrishall – Langley – Duddenhoe End – Elmdon. 7½m. VHR.**

Shorter walks:

Elmdon – Chrishall – Chiswick Hall – Upper Pond St – Elmdon. 4¾m. HR.

Langley Upper Green – Duddenhoe End – Chiswick Hall – Langley. 5m. HR.

Start at Elmdon church. Walk W out of the village to a sharp bend R (NNW) in the road just after Elmdonbury Moat. At that point, continue straight ahead (SW) down a broad bridleway skirting woods R and L. At the minor road S of Chrishall, turn L (S) and walk down to the church. The path leaves from the S side of the churchyard, as an old grassy field boundary to the B road. Cross and continue SSW along the pebbled farm road to Chiswick Hall. The path here turns sharp R back to its SSW bearing, along an excellent cart track leading to a belt of

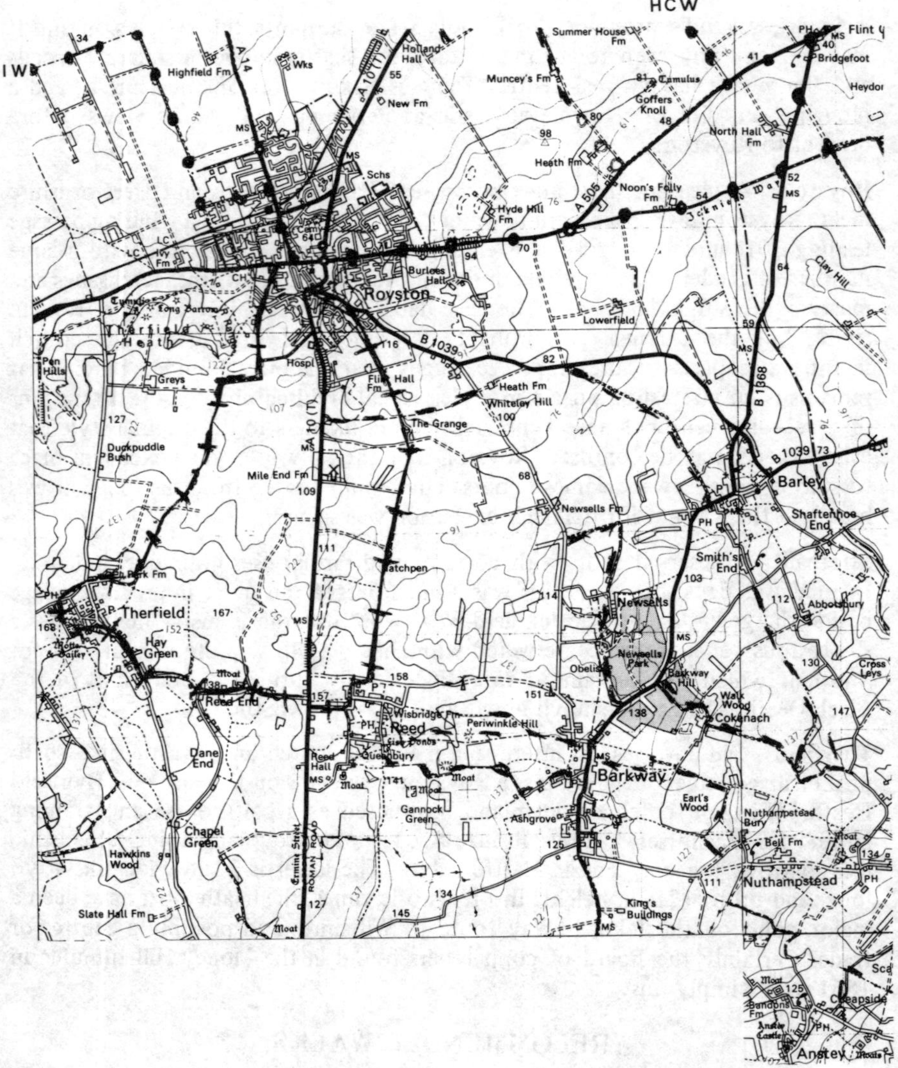

trees. The track continues on the L (E) side of this belt to Langley church. Walk L (SE) to the road and then round through Upper Green to Price's Fm. Pick up a signposted broad grass track L (NNE). This is the Roman Road. Continue along this magnificent path for a long mile. At the minor road, turn L (N) into Duddenhoe End. At the T-junction, turn L (W) briefly to the thatched cottage James Field. The

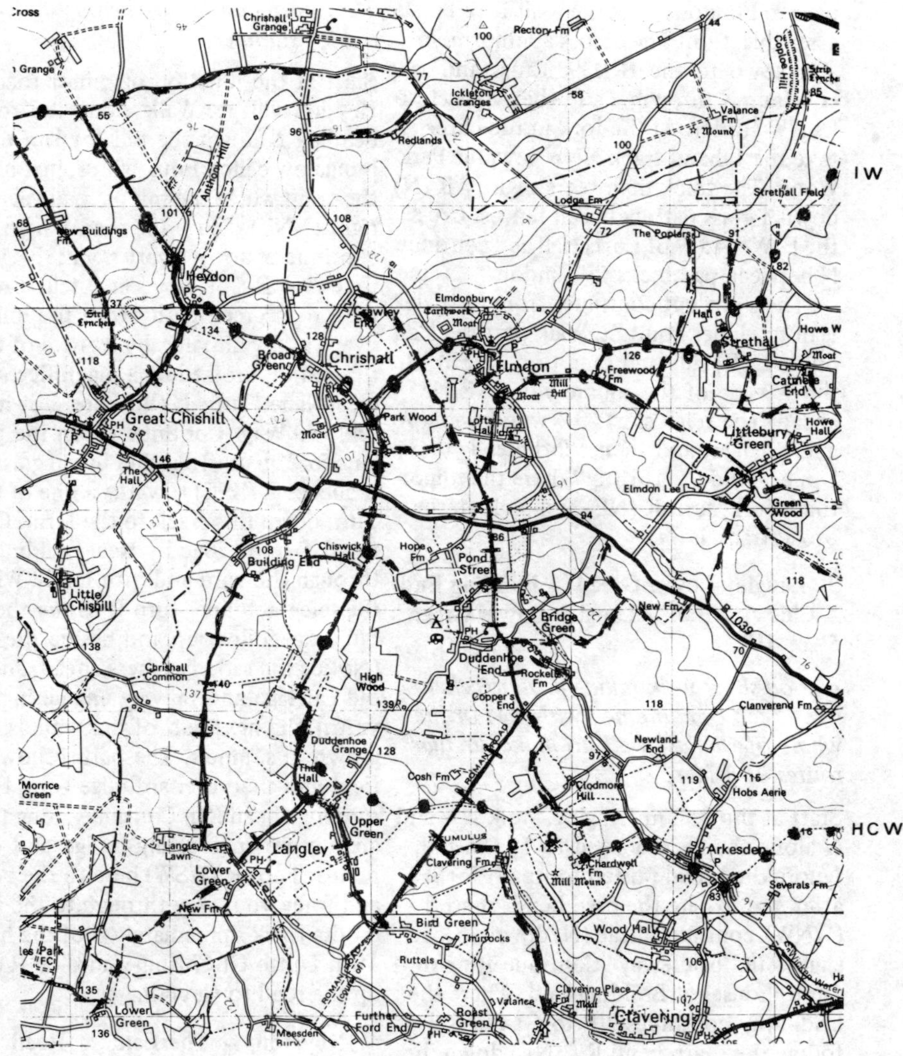
Chrishall Grange
Rectory Fm
Ickleton Granges
Redlands
Valance Fm
Mound
Anthony Hill
IW
Strethall Field
Lodge Fm
The Poplars
New Buildings Fm
Heydon
Elmdonbury
Earthwork
Moat
Strip Lynchets
Cawley End
Broad Green
Chrishall
Elmdon
Strethall
Freewood Fm
Howe W
Catmere End
Mill Hill
Great Chishill
Park Wood
Lofts Hall
Littlebury Green
Howe Hall
The Hall
Elmdon Lee
Green Wood
Chiswick Hall
Hope Fm
Pond Street
Building End
Little Chishill
Bridge Green
New Fm
Duddenhoe End
Rockell's Fm
Chrishall Common
High Wood
Copper's End
Clanverend Fm
Newland End
Duddenhoe Grange
Cosh Fm
Clodmore Hill
Hobs Aerie
Morrice Green
The Hall
Upper Green
HCW
TUMULUS
Arkesden
Langley Lawn
Langley
Clavering Fm
Chardwell
Mill Mound
Lower Green
Severals Fm
New Fm
Bird Green
Thurrocks
Wood Hall
Ruttels
ROMAN ROAD
Clavering Place
Lower Green
Valance
Roast Green
Further Ford End
Clavering
Meesden Bury

path to Elmdon leaves the road R (N) just after this. Continue across a minor road and down to the B1039. Cross and continue N through a strawberry patch to its NW corner. At the fork in the paths, take the L-hand track NNW towards Park Wood. The track then veers slightly R (N) down a grass path between fences. Cross the E-W road W of Lofts Hall and continue N between paddocks to Elmdon.

The short cut continues from Chiswick Hall to Upper Pond St. Walk past the Hall on its L (E) side and then turn R (SSE) to the W edge of the square wood visible ahead. The track skirts the wood on its W and S edges, and then continues E to Upper Pond St. Turn L. Where the minor roads fork, turn R (NE) and pick up the broad track L (N).

2. **Langley Lower Green – Building End – Chiswick Hall – Langley Lower Green. 5½m. HR.**

A good short walk taking in an excellent inn. It can be combined with part or the whole of the last walk to make circular routes of 8-10m.

Start at the Bull in Langley. Walk NW and N along the narrow road to Lt Chishill. Ignore the broad posted footpath R (SE) after ¾m. Where the road bends sharp L (WNW), continue ahead (N) down a broad signposted bridleway. Continue for over 1m to houses at Building End. Where the bridleway continues NE to Gt Chishill, follow the sharp bend R (ENE) down the lane past more buildings to the B1039. Turn R for ¼m past the side road L (N). Turn R (S) down the pebbled drive of Chiswick Hall and follow the route to Langley church as in the last walk. At the church, turn R (SW) down the road to the Bull.

3. **Heydon – Heydon Ditch – Icknield Way – Gt Chishill – Heydon. 4½m. HR.**

Much easy walking, with a great deal of historical interest and some good views. The return journey can be very agricultural in high summer.

Start at the junction of minor roads in Heydon village. Walk along the road heading N down the hill for ¼m to the bungalow called Four Winds, just before the point where the minor road veers half-right (NNE). Leave the road L here and continue N down a cart track; this is all that remains of Heydon Ditch. Follow the broad green path down the hill for over 1m. Eventually, by a grove of trees, this path is crossed by a magnificent E-W green lane. Turn L (W) here, down the Icknield Way. Continue down the green lane for ½m until another broad grass path branches L (SSE) towards a line of trees. Turn down this track to the farm. Cross the E-W farm road by New Buildings, go through the yard and turn L (E). Where the telegraph lines turn R (S) by the last building, follow up and beside the hill. (Notice the strip lynchets ahead, and the old carriage and railway engine in the yard.) The next part of this walk is overgrown in summer. The path follows a field and then orchard edge to a ditch running ahead (S). Continue along this to an overgrown crossing hedge and old ponds. Turn R (WSW) here to the house and force your way through to the road on the track immediately S of the house. Turn L into Gt Chishill and then R (NE) up the road to Heydon.

4. **Royston – Therfield – Reed – Royston. 8m. HR.**

Splendid paths and delightful scenery; only a long metalled section in the middle prevents me from giving it a higher recommendation.

Start at Royston station and walk S up the A14 to the centre of Royston. Turn R (W) down the main street (A505) but then very shortly afterwards bear L (S) up Briary Lane. Continue ahead past houses and a reservoir. Ignore a left fork a little later. Continue down the broad grassy cart track between hedges. This turns R (W) after a mile and crosses a Danger Area S of a rifle range: but the danger is normally non-existent since I have never known the range to be in use. The track then turns L (SSW) again and continues for 1½m up the hill to Therfield Park, bending R (W) just S of the park to the minor road. Turn L (S) through the village to Hay Green. A little diversion is necessary to the church and castle site. At Hay Green, turn L (E) down the road signposted to Reed. Follow for 1m to the A10. Cross half-right (take care) and turn L (E) down the next turning, also signposted to Reed. At the division in the roads, keep on E and round a bend L (N). Go N past another side track R (E) until the street ends in a T-junction. Turn R (E) here. Shortly afterwards, turn L (N) at the footpath signpost down a broad grassy path between crops. Follow this along field edges past Hatchpen Fm and then over a field (broad track). Go past the end of an E-W track and continue N to the L (W) edge of the belt of trees ahead. Continue from here down a narrow track between crops. Cross an E-W track and pick up the broad path ahead (N) to the Grange. Turn R before the house down a good grass path, normally roped and waymarked. Follow this round the E and N sides of the house and continue N down a lovely path. This goes through woods and along a field edge to the R of buildings (Flint Hall). Go through another belt of trees here and down (NNW by N) via houses into Royston.

OTHER SUGGESTED ROUTES

Weekend Walk

Wendens Ambo – Arkesden – Langley – Anstey – Nuthampstead – Barkway – Reed – Royston (overnight stop). Royston – Heydon – Chrishall – Elmdon – Strethall – Wendens Ambo. Day 1: 15½m. Day 2: 12½m.
Some excellent views and generally good paths.

Day Walks

1. Wendens Ambo – Strethall – LDFP – Elmdon – Duddenhoe – Arkesden – Wendens Ambo. 12m (starts p. 160).
Broad tracks almost all the way.

2. Gt Chishill – Langley – Duddenhoe End – Elmdon – Chrishall – Heydon – Gt Chishill. 11m.
An interesting variation on the Recommended Walk; it can be extended to take in Heydon Ditch (14m).

3. Royston – The Grange – Smith's End – Barkway – Reed – Therfield – Royston. 12m.
Variable.

Medium Walks

1. Arkesden – Clavering Fm – Clavering Place Fm – Clavering – Wicken Bonhunt – Arkesden. 8½m.
Some arable to be contended with.

2. Elmdon – LDFP – Chrishall – Heydon – Gt Chishill – Chiswick Hall – Pond St – Elmdon. 7½m.
Some good walking with excellent tracks.

3. Reed – Barkway – Barley – The Grange – Reed. 7½m.
Rather a lot of roadwork between Barkway and Barley.

Short Walks

1. Elmdon – Littlebury Gn – New Fm – Rockell's Fm – Elmdon. 5½m.
Variable paths.

2. Gt Chishill – Building End – Chiswick Hall – Chrishall – Heydon. 4½m.
Rather a lot of roadwork.

3. Barkway – Earl's Wood – Nuthampstead – Morrice Gn – Barkway Hill – Barkway. 5m.
The return journey is much easier than the first part.

10 LONG-DISTANCE FOOTPATHS

Icknield Way; Forest Way; Harcamlow Way; St Peter's Way; Three Forests Way

Icknield Way

Roudham/Knettishall Heath (Norfolk) – Ivinghoe Beacon. 107m.

Suggested daily stages
Roudham Heath – Brandon (including Grime's Graves). 14m.
Brandon – Dalham (bus to Newmarket). 22m.
Ashley – Gt Chesterford. 19m.
Gt Chesterford – Royston. 14m.
Royston – Letchworth. 14m.
Letchworth – Chalton Cross (bus to Dunstable). 14m.
Chalton Cross – Ivinghoe Beacon. 12m.

Maps 22 23 160 166

Official Status None. This is a route devised by the Ramblers Association a few years ago, for submission to the Countryside Commission to connect the Ridgeway and Peddars Way LDFPs. For a variety of reasons the scheme never materialised, although many walkers have already been using it as part of a Hunstanton-Avebury walk (221 miles). I have walked the Icknield Way myself in its entirety, and amended the route where I found better sections. Apart from very short sections explained in the text, it follows existing public rights of way.

Condition on the Ground The Icknield Way is not yet waymarked, though I hope to have this done eventually. Most of the paths are signposted, however, and it is difficult to get lost except in the section between Kentford and Willingham Green. This is the only major section where the route follows anything less than a broad green lane. There is very little road walking except through villages: the main sections otherwise being Thetford Forest-King's Forest (3 miles), Kentford-Gazeley (1½ miles), Dalham-Ashley (1 mile), Noon's Folly Farm-Royston (1¼ miles) and Houghton Regis-Sewell (1 mile). Of these stretches, the Royston road is busy, and I have included suggestions for avoiding this section.

Accommodation This is available at Brandon, Newmarket, Great Chesterford, Royston, Letchworth, Luton or Dunstable. The overnight stops at Newmarket, Letchworth and Luton/Dunstable require some diversion from the route; this can ordinarily be managed quite easily by public transport. Accommodation is also available at Tring, 6 miles from Ivinghoe Beacon, and connected by rail to London.

Access Roudham Heath and Knettishall Heath are both fairly difficult to get to. There are buses from Thetford, and Harling Road railway station can be used at a pinch for those beginning at Roudham Heath.
Ivinghoe Beacon: buses to Dunstable or walk on to Tring station, 6 miles from Ivinghoe Beacon and connected by rail to London. Tring also has accommodation.

Good Features The countryside is varied: forest, brecks, wooded arable and chalk ridge, with some good views. The paths followed are mostly broad and easy. Grime's Graves, Thetford Forest, the Devil's Dyke, the Roman Road, Ashwell Street, and the prehistoric camps and barrows on the route give it the added spice of antiquity. Finally, by linking the Peddar's Way and Ridgeway LDFPs, it makes it possible to walk the whole way along England's oldest right of way.

Bad Features The two stretches of major road walking are unfortunate, and there is some slackening in the quality of both signposting and footpaths between Ashley and Willingham Green.

Literature *Walks in East Anglia I* and *II* contain the only description of the Icknield Way so far available to the public. Volume I contains the small part to be found in Norfolk and Suffolk. This volume contains the remaining sections.

History of the Icknield Way

The Icknield Way in the popular imagination is a winding, enigmatic track along the great chalk belt, its origins lost in the mists of antiquity. But although it is impossible to date the Icknield Way with any certainty, the formation of the chalk ridge which bears it was completed by the end of the Ice Age. The ridge runs from Wiltshire to north Norfolk, and on beyond the Wash to Yorkshire and north-east England; it offered early man higher, less densely forested land which he could clear with his primitive tools and where he could graze his animals, and so it is back in this prehistoric period that the network of intercommunicating routes first sprang up.

Because the belt of chalk had a distinct direction, so these paths had an overall tendency to run from the south-west to the north-east. The Icknield Way should therefore be seen not as some prehistoric motorway, but as a band of easily negotiable countryside, with the few long-distance travellers being forced to make use of local paths between settlements. It is therefore in the best tradition of the Icknield Way that it should now require the same from the modern rambler.

Archaeological finds from all periods have confirmed the importance of the chalk belt as a settlement site and communications route. Neolithic sites have been found close by Dunstable, Galley Hill and Therfield Heath. The same age also produced Grime's Graves, the most extensive flint mines in Europe. Flints identifiably from Grime's Graves have been found throughout the country, and in great numbers at the Wiltshire end of the Icknield Way. Similarly, Neolithic stone axes from Cornwall and Wales have been found in East Anglia. The significance of the Icknield Way as a trade route seems to be beyond doubt even at this early stage in English history.

Shortly after 2000 BC, the Bronze Age began. The technique of working metal entered Britain, and new ideas circulated about the shape for pots and funerary monuments. In brief, this is the time of the beaker and the round barrow. Both are found in plenty along the Icknield Way.

In the 8th century BC, bronze gave way to iron with the arrival of Celtic peoples from the continent. They too settled mainly either in the river valleys or chalk belt, with only piecemeal clearances at the edge of the great forest heartlands. If the causewayed camp and the round barrow are the most visible proofs today of the New Stone and Bronze Ages, the hallmark of the Early Iron

Age is undoubtedly the hill fort. Superimposed on the old Neolithic camp at Maiden Bower is a Celtic hill fort, still visible despite the chalk quarries threatening its northern edge. Less than a mile to the west is Totternhoe Castle, where just such a fort has been neatly converted by a Norman baron into a motte-and-bailey. At the East Anglian end, there are two main hill forts, at Ring Hill near Saffron Walden, and Wandlebury, near Cambridge.

The arrival of the Romans inevitably removed some of the emphasis from this archaic route, simply because they were so adept at building their own long-distance roads. However, certain of the Icknield Way routes were metalled then, including Ashwell Street and the Peddars Way, and there were Roman settlements at several places en route, including Icklingham in Suffolk, Ashwell, and above all at Great Chesterford, whose very name proclaims the size of their camp upon the Cam crossing.

Even after the arrival of the Romans, the Icknield Way continued to be a major route for both trade and invasion. The Anglo-Saxons undoubtedly used it in their initial penetration into England, as did the Danish invasion of 871. The Cambridgeshire chapters of this book describe the great defensive earthworks that the East Anglians found it necessary to erect against armies striking north-eastwards up the chalk belt, the largest of which is the Devil's Dyke – not a single fortification to guard a single route, but designed to block the several different paths through the narrow gap separating forest and fen in eastern Cambridgeshire. Even in the middle ages and later when the Icknield Way was used by drovers transporting their sheep and cattle across the country, it is clear that there were two or three different routes that could be taken.

In drawing up the Icknield Way route, I have tried to marry good paths as closely as possible with what is generally agreed as being the most common of the different Icknield Way routes. Throughout the chalk belt, there are certain places which are traditionally linked with the way. These include Grime's Graves, Icklingham and Kentford, Ickleton on the crossing of the Saffron Walden Cam, Royston, Letchworth and the Dunstable Downs. I have also included some paths, often now metalled, which are considered by local people to be *the* Icknield Way; these stretches include the broad central track through King's Forest, the green lane between Ickleton Grange and Royston, and the series of unmetalled roads from Pirton to Luton. Moreover, I have adopted the generally accepted belief that the main Icknield route should follow the lower slopes of the chalk ridge rather than its summit or the flatlands below.

The route generally satisfies these criteria. Of the places linked with the Icknield Way by tradition, only Ickleton lies off the path, and then only just so. All the traditional paths mentioned above are part of the Icknield Way as laid out in the book. There are minor qualms: the stretch between Kentford and Linton undoubtedly lies a mile or so south of the main original track; between Royston and Letchworth, the route along Ashwell Street correspondingly may be a little far north. In both cases, the most likely route for the largest of the tracks has been turned into a trunk road; and the paths selected as an alternative lie well within the belt of Icknield Way settlement.

The places between the Peddars Way and Royston which are considered in this book or in *Walks in East Anglia I* appear in the route description in **bold** type. They include the villages mentioned below and not otherwise featured.

Cambridgeshire

Ashley The name means a clearing among the ash woods. There is an excellent pub, the Crown.

Cheveley A long street-village, with as many old as modern buildings. The pub is the Red Lion.

Hertfordshire

Litlington The village has been inhabited since Roman times; a sumptuous villa was excavated here in 1936, with thirty rooms and a fine mosaic pavement. The curiously rectangular shape of the village suggests that the plan of the original Roman settlement has been maintained ever since.

Steeple Morden Ashwell Street misses Steeple Morden entirely, but does go briefly onto one of the old concrete roads of the Second World War airfield. This was a satellite of Bassingbourn, and flew Wellingtons as a training unit. In 1942 the USAF arrived, concreting the grass runways and constructing the hangars. P-47s, P-51s and Mustangs flew from here over Belgium and France, and later to the Ruhr and Berlin. On D Day, it gave the Allies fighter cover, and then was abandoned as 355 Group left for escort and interdiction duties on the Continent. The airfield closed officially on 1st September 1948, and was sold for agriculture in the early sixties.

Ashwell A large and charming village, with many good cottages from all periods. Roofs are thatched or tiled, walls timbered or (in one case) pargeted, while some have overhanging storeys. The pargeted building is St John's guild hall in the High Street. The 16c museum south of the church contains relics of Old Ashwell. Once Ashwell held four great fairs a year and merchants flocked to it along Ashwell Street. This traffic brought the plague here: 14c graffiti on the wall of the tower reads 'Miserable, wild, and distracted, the dregs of the people alone survive to bear witness'. South of the village lies Arbury Banks, an Iron Age hill fort west of our route out of Ashwell, in the shape of a horseshoe 300 by 220yd. It can be reached by a brief diversion up an arable track (see map).

Letchworth Letchworth is interesting as the New Town that worked. It is the oldest of these planned urban communities, and its success directly influenced the architects and politicians who pressed after the Second World War for the construction of towns like Harlow and Stevenage. The idea for Letchworth belonged to Ebenezer Howard, a visionary whose antipathy to the slum life of London caused him to invent the idea of the Garden City in his book of 1898, but also with a dozen friends to found an Association, purchase the land around Letchworth village, and construct it stone by stone. The town shows many of the features which have since been introduced into communities old and new: a planned green belt about the town, new estates with curving roads, conscious division into housing, public and industrial areas laid out in an axial scheme, and so on. There is a town museum, south of the railway station, with excellent natural history and curiosity collections. Wilbury Hill, a small remnant of an Iron Age hill fort, just off the route, is bounded by Stotfold Road to the west and the cemetery to the north.

Ickleford The church is at one end of a splendid avenue of cedars. Nave, chancel and tower are the work of Gilbert Scott, the Victorian architect. In the churchyard lies a former traveller of the Icknield Way – Henry Boswell, king of the gypsies in the 18c.

Pirton On the common are the unmistakable earthwork remains of the original Norman castle. The walking from here to Luton is particularly good, both in the breadth of the paths and the beautiful wooded countryside.

Bedfordshire

Galley Hill Before reaching Luton itself, after a great deal of spectacular climbing and falling, the walker reaches Galley Hill, mercifully unincorporated with the surrounding golf course. At the top, with good views to all sides, stand two almost flattened round barrows dating back to about 3500BC. To the south-west are the (rather poor) remnants of Dray's Ditches. Excavations show that these ditches originated in the Bronze Age, and were greatly extended in the early Iron Age (about 700BC) to form a boundary across the line of the Icknield Way. The original ditches consisted of three parallel, V-shaped ditches about 5ft deep, 14ft wide, and a mile long. The last part of our route before the A6 lies directly along the top of one of these ditches. There have been Roman finds here, including a mass burial in the barrows on Galley Hill.

Maiden Bower The most important earthwork in Bedfordshire. What remains now is a fairly modest circular Iron Age plateau camp, with good views across to Ivinghoe Beacon. The fort is 700ft across, with earthen ramparts still over 8ft high in places, at the top of the modern chalk quarry. The 11ft deep ditch that surrounded it has almost entirely silted up. Its only entrance lay to the south-east, shaped like a funnel with a rampart walk above it. It was inhabited into Roman times. Beneath the camp lie relics of much older settlement, including ditch sections, pottery and an antler-comb from about 3500BC.

Totternhoe The village has mostly 20c buildings, but there is a splendid motte-and-bailey on Castle Hill, probably built on the site of a prehistoric earth work.

Dunstable Downs Our route passes through Dunstable itself with the greatest of ease, penetrating to the heart of the city down a beautiful green lane. Across the road rises Dunstable Downs Country Park. At the top of the hill stand the Five Knolls – Bronze Age round barrows still in a remarkable state of preservation. They command enormous views – west to Ivinghoe Beacon, north over Totternhoe Castle and the great plain, east over the cities of Dunstable and Luton. The ridge-top walk that follows is exhilarating.

Buckinghamshire

Edlesborough St Mary's church is picturesquely sited on an isolated spur overlooking the western slopes of the Chiltern Hills. The village itself is mostly modern.

Ivinghoe Beacon The Icknield Way ends on Beacon Hill at the start of the Countryside Commission's Ridgeway. It is a magnificent place, with views to the north and west across the valleys of the Ouzel and Thame. Beacon Hill, like Maiden Bower and Galley Hill, is another Icknield Way hill fort. Most experts date the earthworks to the Late Bronze or Early Iron Age, about 700BC. The ridge is scattered with barrows, and it is the atmosphere of great antiquity and the commanding position which make so strong an impact on the walker – particularly the walker who has covered the length of the Icknield Way.

ROUTE DIRECTIONS

DAY 1: **Roudham Heath – Brandon. 14m.**
Walks in East Anglia I

1:92 Access to Roudham Heath is fairly obscure except for those walking down the Peddars Way. I will therefore describe the start of the Icknield Way in a little detail. Those being driven to the start up the A11 should stop the car at the E edge of Bridgham Heath, immediately before the forest and ½m after a side road had left the A11 to the R (ESE). There is a large Peddars Way notice on one side of the road, and an unmade lane to the L (N). Go down this lane and under the railway line. This brings you into a little clearing that is the start of the Icknield Way. To the E is a field and the open space about the railway line. To the N (ahead) is the Peddars Way, a broad forest ride. To the W is a white cottage, two covered pools with Danger – Deep Water notices, and two forest rides. Turn down the northern of these rides, heading WNW. This is the Old Drove Road, and the start of the Icknield Way. Where this forks shortly afterwards, take the N ride ahead (WNW); continue under an old railway bridge after a further 300yd and then between belts of silver birch. Go past the S edge of an open field with a low white building to your R (N) and along the broad ride to the W edge of the forest (1¼m from the start). At this point, the main track turns half-right (NNW) to skirt the W edge: ignore this. Instead, go ahead through the Forestry Commission gate and down a broad grass track between typical Breckland scenery of rough sheep pasture and clumps of gorse. Cross the A1075 by the parking space and East Wretham Heath Nature Reserve notice-board, and pick up the drove road on the other side. This broad unmade lane goes past Lang Mere (and **Ring Mere**), and eventually re-enters the forest. After a further ⅔m, the ride forks. Keep on the main, N ride (WNW) and follow to the minor road (3m from Roudham Heath.) Turn L (SSW) for 100yd and then R (WNW) at the T-junction down the narrow road signposted to Mundford. Go past Fowlmere on its L (S) side and turn L (S) down the forest track to Punchbowl Picnic Place. This is a Forestry Commission
leisure area based on the **Devil's** 1:91
Punchbowl. The Icknield Way continues down the N edge of the Punchbowl and then ahead (S) down a broad grass ride through the forest. At the minor road, turn R (SSW) and follow until it ends at a T-junction with the B1110. Cross and pick up the broad dirt track opposite by the footpath signpost. Follow this for 1¼m to and through the forest to the A134. Turn R (NW) up the main road for a long ½m to a picnic place on the R (NE) of the road. At this point, turn L (W) down a broad cart track into the forest (this was numbered 21 when I was there). Keep on this for 2m, going past the little flint church of Santon after 1m. The track ends in a minor road by a level crossing and another large grassy area used for picnics. Cross and pick up the broad unmetalled lane ahead (WNW) on the other side. We are now on the Forestry Commission's long-distance forest path, waymarked with red-topped logs. After ½m, look out R (N) for ride 63, so waymarked. Turn R (N) up this ride, go over an immediate crossing ride and ahead for ¼m. Where the main drove bears slightly L (NNW), continue ahead (NNE by N) down a narrower forest track waymarked with the red-topped log. Continue ahead along the waymarked route until you come to a huge open clearing within the forest. This is **Grime's Graves**. Go over the gate and down a broad grass track to the building at the centre of the clearing. Turn L (WNW) here and cross the clearing to the weather

station (water pump just to the S). Continue W from the station to the N edge of the forest. There is a broad track skirting this edge W to the B1108, but the right of way lies a little to the N on a WNW bearing through the heath. Turn L (WSW) down the B road and then R (N) up the A1065 for a short distance. Leave the road L (W) down a broad unmade track just after Emily's Wood cottage. This goes ahead (W) through the wood for ½m and then down a sandy cart track WSW by W between the forest (N) and open fields (S). After ½m, just after a sandy track has joined from the L (S), the main path turns R (N). Follow this bend but turn L (WSW) 30yd later down a rubble track. Follow this SSW to Weeting church. For the **castle**, pick up the signposted path L (E) over the field, and then return. Continue down a metalled lane and past a playground on your R (W) side to the B road and post office. Turn R (W) here down Rectory Lane. Follow around a sharp bend L (S). At the next bend R (W), continue ahead down the unmade lane signposted to Fengate Fm. Go past the farm driveway, between fields and round a bend L (ESE) to the sawmill in Brandon. Continue to the B1106 and turn R (S) into the centre of the town. (Accommodation.)

DAY 2: **Brandon – Dalham. 22m.**
Walks in East Anglia I

The Icknield Way leaves the B1106 in Brandon down the unmade White Hart Lane (E). This starts just N of the Bell inn. After a long ½m, turn R (S) back to the B1107 and then L (E) along it. After ⅓m, a minor road forks L (ENE) from the B1107 signposted to Santon Downham. Keep on the B road for about 20yd to Green Road and pick up a green path R (S) immediately beyond it. Go down this path to its end. Cross the clearing ahead (S) and enter the forest on a narrow grass ride by a notice saying Danger Deep Holes (I never found any). After ¾m, this track ends in a broad gravel ride. Turn R (SSE) along this. You are now back on the long-distance forest path, and will be guided for the next 3½m by its excellent waymarking. After ½m, the path takes a decisive turn R (S) down Ride 12; after 1¼m, it turns L (E); after 1½m, it veers R (S) again down Ride 10; after 2½m, it swings L (ESE) and continues generally on that bearing to the A11.

The long-distance forest path resumes on the other side of the road and continues for 2½m to the N edge of King's Forest, which is also our aiming point. However, the paths it follows are governed by an oral agreement between the Forestry Commission and the Elveden Estate, and are only open to walkers on the long-distance forest path. The Icknield Way must therefore regretfully make a 3½m detour along the A11 and B1106, as shown on the map.

After 1¼m along the B1106, the long- 1:8
distance forest path crosses the road and immediately turns L (SSE) down a waymarked grass path behind the trees. We, however, continue down the road to the large triangle of grass with a stone pillar in the centre. Cross this triangle and pick up an immensely broad straight drove road heading SSW into the Forest. This is the Icknield Way. Continue ahead (SSW) for 3½m to the S edge of the Forest and then ahead to a minor road. Turn R (WSW) down this past Rampart Field picnic place to the A1101 and turn R (NW). After 100yd, turn R (NNE) at the footpath signpost down the track to Weatherhill Fm. Follow this around a bend L (WNW) to the farmhouse. The farmer here believes that the right of way stops at the E side of the yard and resumes at the W side, with no right of passage between. He is however mistaken, according to an oral query that I made to Suffolk County Council. In any case, the farmer is happy to let walkers go round his farmyard by the obvious track on its

N side. Pick up the broad cart track WSW from the W side of the yard. Where it bends sharply L (SSW), walk R (N) through the trees and turn immediatley L (WNW) along the mature hedge to the corner of the field. Turn briefly R (NNE) here to the S end of the belt of conifers and cross the stile L (WNW). Pick up the indicated field edge path ahead (WNW). This brings you to a broad SSW-NNE crossing track. Cross this and pick up the broad grass path between fences ahead. Continue WNW to the next crossing lane. Turn R (NNE) here for 100yd to its end and then L (WNW) down another excellent sandy cart track. After a long ½m, this
:78 ends by a bend in the A1101. Turn L (S) down the road for 200yd to a sharp bend L (SE). At this point, pick up a narrow byroad R (W) signposted to Temple Bridge. Go down this to the bridge and cross. Continue down the broad sandy lane for the next 1½m, through the nature reserves of Tuddenham and Cavenham Heaths. This later becomes a narrow metalled lane into Tuddenham.

Cross the road by the telephone box on the green. Pick up a grass path opposite, by the footpath signpost. Follow this WSW over the stream, and then half-left (SSW). After ½m, the track enters a field and continues across it. At this point, turn half-right (WSW) down a broad field edge track towards farm buildings. This ends in farm roads L (S) and ahead (WSW). Continue ahead to the village street in Herringswell. Turn L (S) at the post office and telephone box down a very narrow road. This soon becomes a broad cart track ahead (S) through the woods and then along the W side of a belt of trees. Continue for a further 1m SSW by S to the quarry at Slade Bottom, where the path bears L (SE) to a minor road. Turn R (SSW) here under the bypass. At the road beyond, turn briefly L (E) and then R (S) down the narrow road signposted
152 to Gazeley. After 1m, this is joined by a wider road and turns L (SSE) into the village. Go past a side road R (W) to the church. Pick up a narrow but good path W from the NW corner of the churchyard to a minor road between Gazeley and Moulton. Continue ahead (WNW by W) down this for ⅔m, to a footpath signpost on your L just after and opposite the private road to Primrose Hall Fm. The path ascends a small rise. At the top, pick up a hedgeside path WSW down the hill towards **Moulton** church. Cross the stand of trees and pick up a broad path to the church.

Accommodation is available in Newmarket, by bus from Moulton.

DAY 3: **Moulton – Gt Chesterford. 20m.**
Walks in East Anglia I* and *II

Start at Moulton church. Pick up the pebbled track by the entrance and walk ESE down the E bank of the river Kennett. A lovely little path continues under trees for ⅓m. At its SE edge, bear half-left (SE) along an old hedge boundary cutting off an arc of the river. This leads to the NW tip of a belt of trees beside the river. Continue down a broad bridleway to the minor road. Turn R (SW). Follow this road over the B1085 and past junctions with other minor roads from the L (E) and R (N) into the centre of Ashley. At the B1063, turn L (S), signposted to Clare. After 200yd, at the footpath signpost, turn R (WSW) down a broad grass path. Continue for 1m along this into Cheveley. Turn L (S) down the village street. Continue past the church and on to a large wooden shed and a notice saying Fittock's Stud on your R (W). (If you reach the pub, you have gone too far.) Pick up an excellent little grass track R (WSW) at this point, and follow to a narrow road. Cross by the footpath posts and go over the stile. Continue WSW down the meadow and through the belt of trees onto a broad, chalky cart track. Continue WSW down this; after ½m, it becomes metalled. Continue to the road junction and then turn R (WNW). Where this road ends in a

T-junction, turn very briefly R (N) and then L (WSW) down a cart track signposted to Devil's Dyke. After ½m, this ends in an excellent crossing track, Dane Bottom. The right of way crosses the arable field ahead diagonally half-right (W) to the trees ahead. Most walkers however walk R (NNW) up Dane Bottom to the first field boundary, L (WSW) along the trees to **Devil's Dyke**, and then L (SE) along the Dyke for 300yd to the end of the trees on its W side. At that point, pick up a good track WSW along the belt of trees separating Stetchworth Park (N) from the open fields. Continue to the bungalows ahead. At the estate road, cross half-right to the fenced path ahead between bungalows. This continues to a minor road by a T-junction and pub.

Turn L (SE) here along the Woodditton road. Where this bends L (E), two footpaths leave the road. The signposted track under the hedges is not the Icknield Way, which continues half-right (S) from the bend up a hedgerow to the edge of the wood visible on the hill. Turn R (SSW) to skirt its W edge, and then L (SE) along its SW side. At the S corner of the wood, turn R (SSW) down a deep ditch between crops. Where this ditch ends halfway across the field, turn briefly L to the end of the line of trees and then R (SSW again) to the red-tiled cottage and the road. Cross the road by the cottage and pick up a narrow cyclepath just L (S) of the modern bungalow. This continues SSW beside orchards. Where the path bends R (W) by the white cottage and poplars, continue ahead (SSW) along a path under telegraph poles. This soon turns L (SSE) behind houses and then R down a lane beside the Bull inn. Cross the road and village green to Sherriff's Court and pick up a footpath signposted to **Brinkley**. After one field, the path bends R and then quickly forks. Take the L-hand broad grass track across the field. Go over a gate into pasture and cross it diagonally (SW) to the far gate. Go over this and then a third gate in the same corner of the next field. This brings you into a large field with trees in it and a white house on its R (W) side. Cross this to the L (E) of the green hut and towards the poplars. Exit onto the road by a telephone box. Turn R (N) for 30yd to the village green and footpath post. Walk L (SSW) down a lane and then a broad grassy path. Where this ends after the first field, continue across the next field down a track under the telegraph poles. This ends in a minor road at **Willingham Green**. You have negotiated the most difficult part of the Icknield Way.

Turn briefly R to the B road and then L (WSW) along the B1052 to a sharp bend L (SSW). At this bend, continue ahead (WNW and then NNE) down a broad cart track. (The official right of way in fact crosses the field from the B1052 to join this cart track, but I assume that the farmer would prefer walkers to take this diversion.) Follow the track around a bend L (NW) to the cow sheds. Continue from here down a beautiful broad cart track WNW for 1m to a minor road. Turn L (SSW) along this to the first bend L (ESE). Turn R (WNW) here up a broad green lane. This almost immediately turns L (SSW). We follow it for the next 2½m into **Balsham**, past two minor roads and the S end of **Fleam Dyke**. At the Queen's Head, turn L (SE) along the B1052 through Balsham. Follow this past the village sign and a sharp bend R (S). At the next bend L (ESE), continue ahead down Wood Hall Rd (No Through Rd). After ½m, this passes Wood Hall Fm and becomes a broad green lane. It wiggles L (ESE) and R back onto its SSW bearing, and then continues downhill, ending in an even broader crossing green lane. This is the **Roman road** or **Via Devana**. Turn R (WNW) up the road for ⅔m. At the B road, turn L (SSW). Where this bends sharp L (SE), continue past the bridleway post and up the lane towards the water tower (SSW). At the tower, continue ahead down a grassy (and often muddy) downhill track between trees. At the N edge of **Linton**, go up steps L into Rivey Close, go down the road onto the B1052 and turn R. Continue along the B road through the village to the Dog and Duck inn. Where the road bends L, continue down Meadow Lane. This soon becomes a grass path ahead past the Village College park and through meadows NW to a hard track at Lt Linton. Turn L (SSW) here to the A604. Cross and pick up a broad cart track under an old railway arch. Follow the track uphill to the derelict farm buildings. Bear L (S) through the buildings and then through a small wood. Take the field boundary ahead (SSW) to the large wood. Turn half-right (SW) into the wood and cross it down a broad, sometimes muddy path. Continue ahead along the foot of a field of pasture and onto a broad cart track. Walk down this SW to the sheep pens. Turn L (SSE) here down a side track. This soon swings R (S and then SW) to the farm. (The right of way lies to the S, among field paths; but the farmer told me that he preferred walkers to use this route.) Go through Burtonwood Fm and down the driveway to the point where it bends R (NW) to the trees. The right of way continues from here across the field WSW to pick up an excellent hedgeside path. Most walkers however continue NW and then WSW down the farm road to the point where it bends R (WNW) to join Cow Lane. At that bend, a good cart track goes up the hill L (SSE) to the hedgerow and then turns R (WSW) beside it. Continue WSW to the A130. Walk a few yards R (NNW) up the road to the footpath signpost opposite and there turn L (SW) down a well-used field edge path into Gt Chesterford. (Accommodation at Crown & Thistle.)

DAY 4: **Gt Chesterford – Royston. 14m.**
Walks in East Anglia II

Walk through the village to the A11 and turn L (SW). Where the main road swings L (SE), turn R (WNW) instead down the B1379. Go over the level crossing (not under the bridge) and turn L (SSE) down an unmade lane. This passes houses and then swings R (SW). Continue down this and then a grass track between hedges ahead (SW) to the M11. Cross the motorway on the bridge provided to your L (S). Once across, turn R (N) to the hedgeside. The Icknield Way follows this L (SSW) for ⅔m past three crossing hedges towards a gap in the line of trees visible on the hillside. After a short distance, the right of way cuts diagonally SSW over the field to the minor road. Turn L (SSW by S); go over a crossroads and on for ¼m. At that point, turn R (WSW) up a broad track. This soon swings L (SSW) to **Strethall** church and then continues SSE to a crossing lane. Turn R (W) here. After a short distance, the track turns half-right (WNW) into and beside the trees. Follow this along the S edge of one wood and then the N and W edges of the next to the Freewood Fm road. Turn R (W) down this to the minor road. Turn R (WNW) down this into the village. Follow the main street between the pub and church and L (W) past Elmdonbury. Where the road bends R (NW) again, continue ahead (SW) down an excellent grassy lane. This skirts the SE edge of one wood and then the NW edge of Park Wood to another minor road. Turn R (NW) into **Chrishall**. Go over the crossroads and pick up a signposted path half-left (W) across meadows to Broad Green. Turn R and pick up a signposted path L (W) after Camps Cottage. This goes past farm buildings and pasture to a footbridge; turn L briefly and then R (W) up a broad track to the wood. Turn slightly R (NW) here down to the minor road at **Heydon**. Turn L (WNW) here around two bends. At the next T-junction, take the side road R (N) going down the hill. After ¼m, by the bungalow called Four Winds, the road veers half-right (NNE). Leave the road L here and continue N down a cart track.

This is all that remains of **Heydon Ditch**. Follow the broad green path down the hill for over 1m. Eventually, by a grove of trees, this path is crossed by a magnificent green lane. Turn L (W) here. Follow the lane for 2¾m, going over the B1368 after 1¼m. Eventually, the grass lane terminates in a layby of the A505. There is unfortunately no other route into **Royston** except to walk along this road for 1½m: please take great care. (Accommodation is available in Royston.)

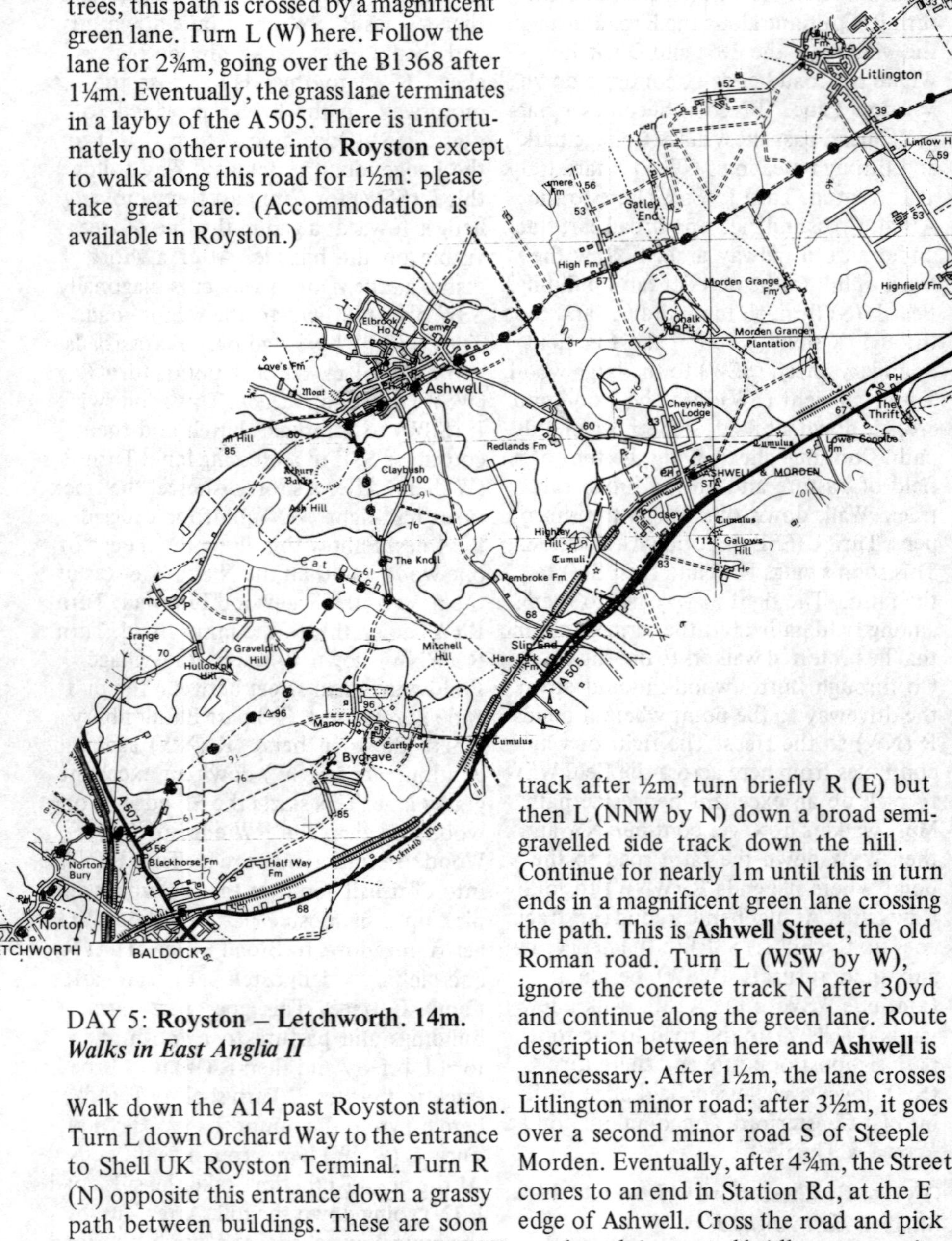

DAY 5: **Royston – Letchworth. 14m.**
Walks in East Anglia II

Walk down the A14 past Royston station. Turn L down Orchard Way to the entrance to Shell UK Royston Terminal. Turn R (N) opposite this entrance down a grassy path between buildings. These are soon left behind, and the track continues NNW by N between fields with some excellent little views. Where this ends in a crossing track after ½m, turn briefly R (E) but then L (NNW by N) down a broad semi-gravelled side track down the hill. Continue for nearly 1m until this in turn ends in a magnificent green lane crossing the path. This is **Ashwell Street**, the old Roman road. Turn L (WSW by W), ignore the concrete track N after 30yd and continue along the green lane. Route description between here and **Ashwell** is unnecessary. After 1½m, the lane crosses Litlington minor road; after 3½m, it goes over a second minor road S of Steeple Morden. Eventually, after 4¾m, the Street comes to an end in Station Rd, at the E edge of Ashwell. Cross the road and pick up a broad signposted bridleway opposite. This soon becomes a metalled road (also called Ashwell Street). Continue to the R

(N) of Cooke Engineers and pick up an unmade road ahead (WSW) by the new bungalows – including one with an encouraging name, The Ridgeway. This road ends in a broad crossing track by a red brick house with a slate roof, and another house called High Acre. At this point, turn L (SSE) up the hill along a broad cart track. After a short distance, and before the top of the hill, a much lesser track branches R (SSW) to **Arbury Banks**: this can be visited, but the main Icknield Way continues up the broad track to the top of the hill and then down to the road at Chalkman's Knoll. Turn R (S) down the road to a footpath signpost on its L side pointing ESE. At this point, leave the road R (WNW). The right of way lies on the R bank of the ditch, but it is the L bank that would appear to be the more used. Continue WNW for ⅓m, to the first hedge on the L bank of the ditch. Turn L (SSW) along this hedge. The field edge path is indeed followed for the next 2¼m, along hedges and ditches. There is only one crossroads of field edges, and the route goes straight over that and down beside a ditch WSW. Eventually, the narrow path becomes a pleasant farm track going SW to the road. Turn briefly R (NNW) along the A507 but take the first turning L (W) down Nortonbury Lane, under the A1. Continue round a bend half-left (SW) past the mill to a junction in the road by farm buildings. At this point, go through a little gate opposite and pick up a grass track SSW up the hill. Cross over the road by the **Letchworth** city boundary board, go over a stile by the footpath signpost and follow a good track to the church. Go out of its S gate and turn L (ESE) down the lane to the houses at its end. At this point, turn R (SW) past a No Horses notice and onto a broad track to a road. Turn R up this to the T-junction and then L onto Norton Rd. Walk down this to a roundabout. Go straight over into Wilbury Rd. After ¼m, turn R down a broad grassy avenue between trees crossing Norton Common to the Icknield Way and the centre of Letchworth.

DAY 6: **Letchworth – Sundon Park. 13m.**
Walks in East Anglia II

Leave Letchworth WSW along the Icknield Way to where it ends by the cemetery and Wilbury Steak House. Turn L (S). Very shortly afterwards, leave the road by a speed derestriction sign and pick up an excellent unsignposted path down the hill (WSW). Continue down this past the sewage works and over the railway line. Negotiate the muddy stretch by the pond WSW and continue under the old railway bridge and into **Ickleford**. Walk WSW through the village exiting onto the A600 by Turnpike Lane. Cross the road and continue ahead down Westmill Lane until you see a footpath signpost to Holwell pointing R (N). Turn down this broad track. Where this bends half-right by a junction in telephone wires, about 300yd later, turn half-left (WNW) down a good field edge path. The squat tower and typical Hertfordshire spike of Pirton church soon becomes visible ahead. Continue down the track for over 1m. Cross the N edge of Pirton playing fields and continue down the gravelled drive to the road. Turn L here and skirt the green on its S side (or go straight across it on a right of way to the timber-framed brick house). Continue W along the street to a T-junction at the SW corner of the green and turn R (WNW). After a short distance turn L (WSW) down a broad unmetalled lane signposted Pegsdon 1. This continues quite steeply uphill for 1m to the corner of Tingley Wood. Where the track ends in a field and two diverting hedgeside paths, take the L hedge S to the B655. Turn R (W) along the road for a short distance and then L (SW) by a footpath signpost just inside the Bedfordshire border. This broad grassy lane continues for 2m to a

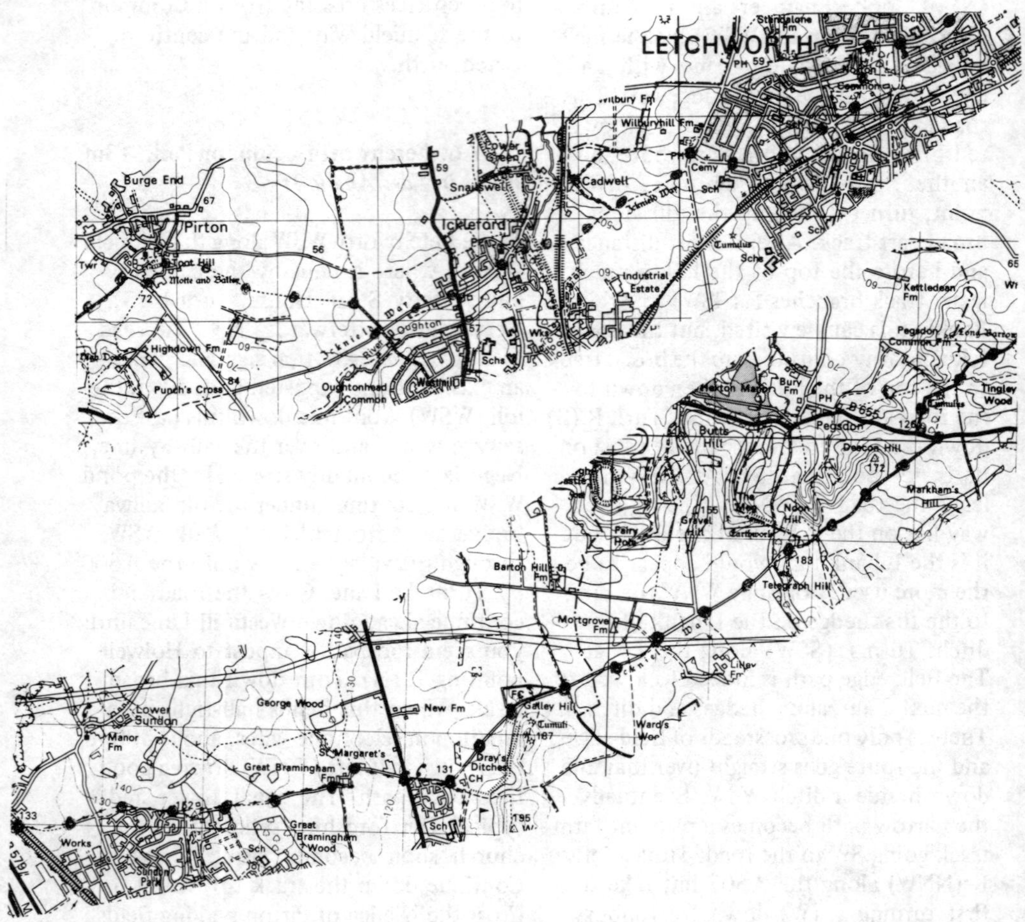

minor road; after 1m, where the track opens out into a field, keep to the R (N) of the field alongside the scrub. Otherwise, it is unmistakable. Follow the track down to the minor road and continue ahead (WSW) along it to the next bend L (SE). At this point, by Mortgrove Fm, continue ahead (SW) down the broad, partly cindered lane. Continue for 1m over a crossing track onto **Galley Hill**. There is a right of way for those wishing to ascend the hill; otherwise, continue down the lane SW skirting the golf course until the track ends in a group of footpath signposts by the edge of an estate. Turn half-right (W) here down the broad track under trees skirting the estate to the A6. Cross and pick up the metalled No Through Road opposite. Go past St Margaret's Hospital and round the bend to Gt Bramingham Fm. At the barn, turn R (W) down a broad grassy cart track. This continues down several field edges toward the R (N) of the new estate and water tower. After 1m, pick up a back path behind the new houses and exit onto Hampshire Way. Follow Hampshire Way to the water tower and then pick up the back path again past the trig point and immediately R (N) of the last housing estate into Sundon Pk. This ends in Chestnut Avenue. Walk down the avenue to Chestnut Rd. If staying in Luton for the night, turn L and catch a bus.

DAY 7: **Sundon Park – Ivinghoe Beacon.** ***Walks in East Anglia II***

Start at the end of Chestnut Avenue. Cross the road half-right and continue W down Camford Way. After 200yd, pick up the line of the hedge on the N side of the road and follow it to the railway line; then turn half-right (NW) along a broad field edge path to the road. Turn L and follow the road over the M1. At the B road, turn L (SSE) but then R (W) down the next side road. Walk down this road for ½m, going round a bend half-left (SW) and ignoring a footpath signpost on the bend. Eventually, turn R (WNW) at the second footpath post just before the road is crossed by the second line of pylon wires. Pick up a broad grass path between fields here. This soon picks up the S bank of a little stream. After ½m, the path switches to its N bank as a narrow track through the scrub. Shortly afterwards, it is crossed by a broader path SSE under telegraph poles. The Icknield Way, however, continues ahead along field edge paths N of the stream to the A5120. Turn L and follow this briefly SW to the next minor road R (WSW) signposted to Thorn. Turn down this past a little wood L (S) and round a gentle bend R (W). Where the road bends back L (WSW), go through a gap in the hedge and cross the field SSE up a tractor path toward a solitary tree. Cross the ditch here and continue along a good field edge path past a red brick farm away to your L (E) side. Where this path swings sharp R (WSW) over the fields towards the works, continue instead half-right (S) over the field toward a concrete road. Go onto the road but do not enter the fenced area; instead, turn R (SW) down a narrow track under bushes immediately N of the boundary fence. When the trees end, continue ahead (SW) along the field edge past the sewage works and allotments. Turn L (S) at the minor road onto the A5 and continue S past the pub for 30yd. Then cross by the Luton Crest Motel and go down the minor road signposted to Sewell. Continue through the hamlet to the end of the lane by the old railway bridge. Go under the arch to the quarries and turn sharp L (E) up the hill along a broad track. This quickly bends half-right (SE) past **Maiden Bower**. After ¼m, it turns R again (SSW). Continue along the green lane (views of Ivinghoe Beacon) to a crossroads of tracks. Turn L (ESE) here. Follow the green lane past houses to the B489, by the Windsock pub. Cross the road to the open green space and pick up

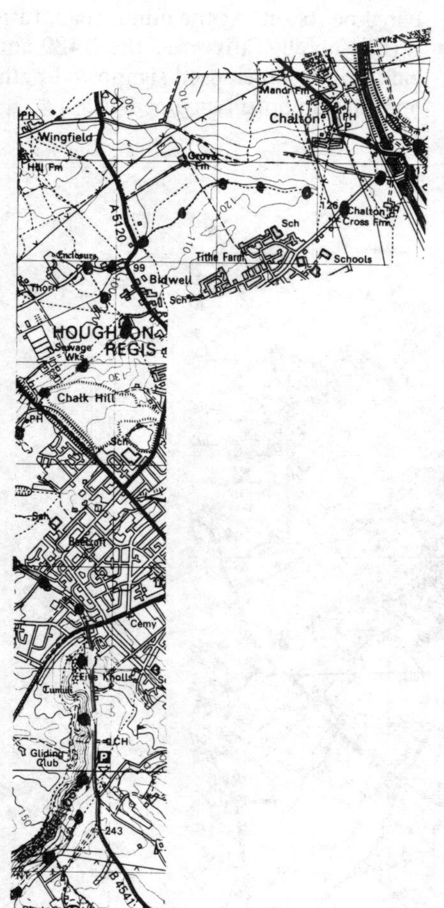

a well-worn path under the avenue of trees. This climbs steeply up to the **Five Knolls** on the top of Dunstable Downs. The next ²/3m lies in Dunstable Country Park, rather than along rights of way. Pick up the well-trodden path just below the top of the ridge. Go past the pyramidal-roofed building (away to your L) and immediately W (downslope) of the glider emergency landing area. Continue through scrub and on until the park ceases in an arable field. The right of way lies across the middle of the field, but there is a broad track along its top edge which is used by everybody. Skirt the wood at the top of the field along its W edge and continue along the top of the next field (views of Dunstable White Lion). Continue SSW through a third grass field (owned by the National Trust) to the B road. Turn R (NNW) down this but immediately turn R (N) onto a well-trodden little path into the scrub. This winds through trees and then comes out for one more spectacular view (including the best sight of the White Lion) before plummeting down to the road again WNW through the trees. Turn R (NW) down to the Plough pub.

For those walking the Icknield Way only, this is the best end. Those continuing down the Ridgeway should however pick up the minor road immediately W of the Plough. This continues WNW for ⅓m; then turn L (WSW) down the first side road; follow past two side roads R but take the third (NNW) into Edlesborough. At the T-junction, turn L (SW) past houses until it in turn comes to an end in the A4146, opposite Edlesborough church. Pick up the broad signposted track L of the church; this continues for 1¼m SW into Ivinghoe Aston. At the minor road, turn L (SE) uphill. Cross over the B489 and pick up the much-used signposted path opposite up onto Ivinghoe Beacon.

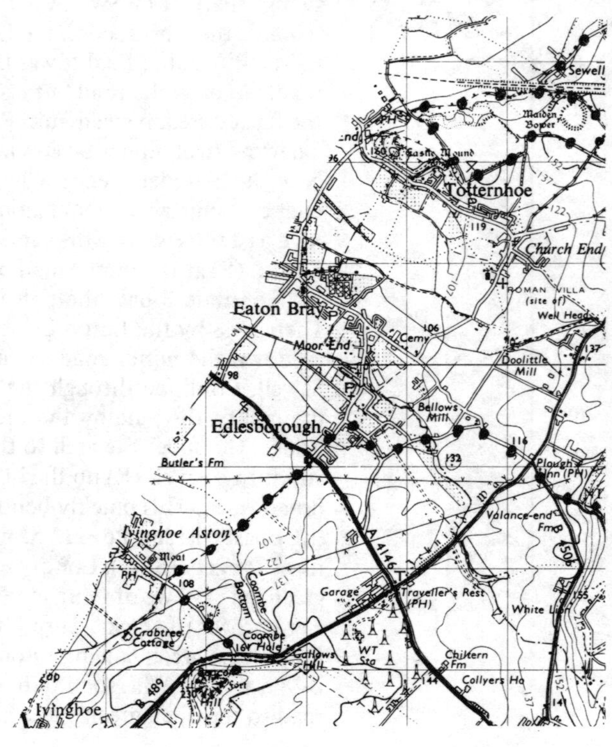

Three Forests Way

Epping Forest – Hatfield Forest – Hainault Forest. 60m.

Suggested daily stages
Loughton – Sawbridgeworth. 19m.
Sawbridgeworth – Chipping Ongar. 19m.
Chipping Ongar – Loughton. 22m.

Maps 121 128 144

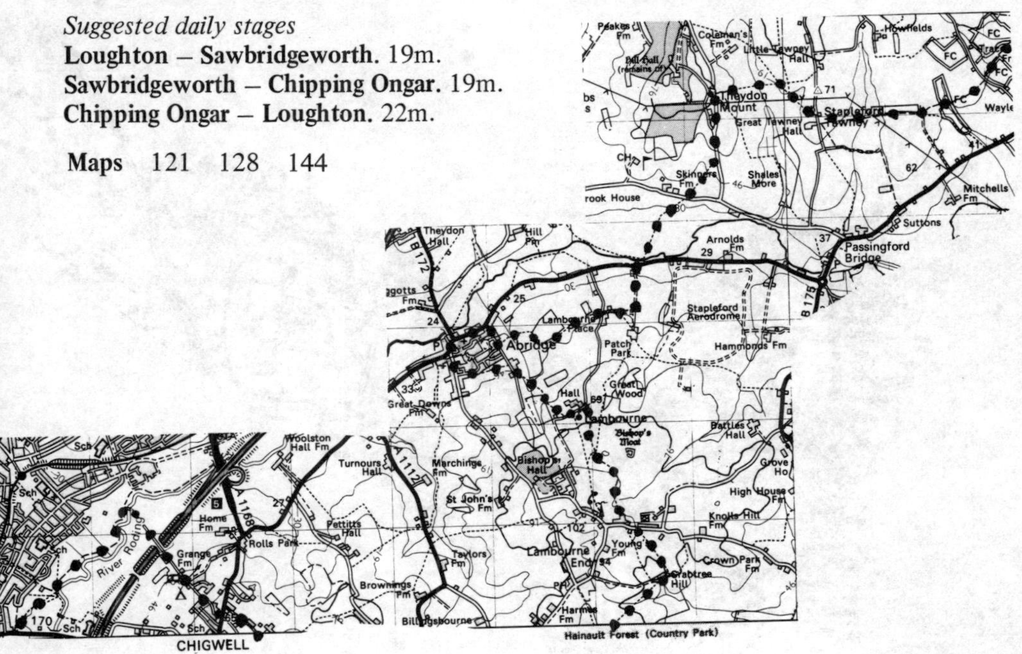

Forest Way

Epping Forest – Hatfield Forest. 20m.

Suggested daily stages
To be completed in one day.
Epping Forest – Harlow, Harlow – Hatfield Forest.

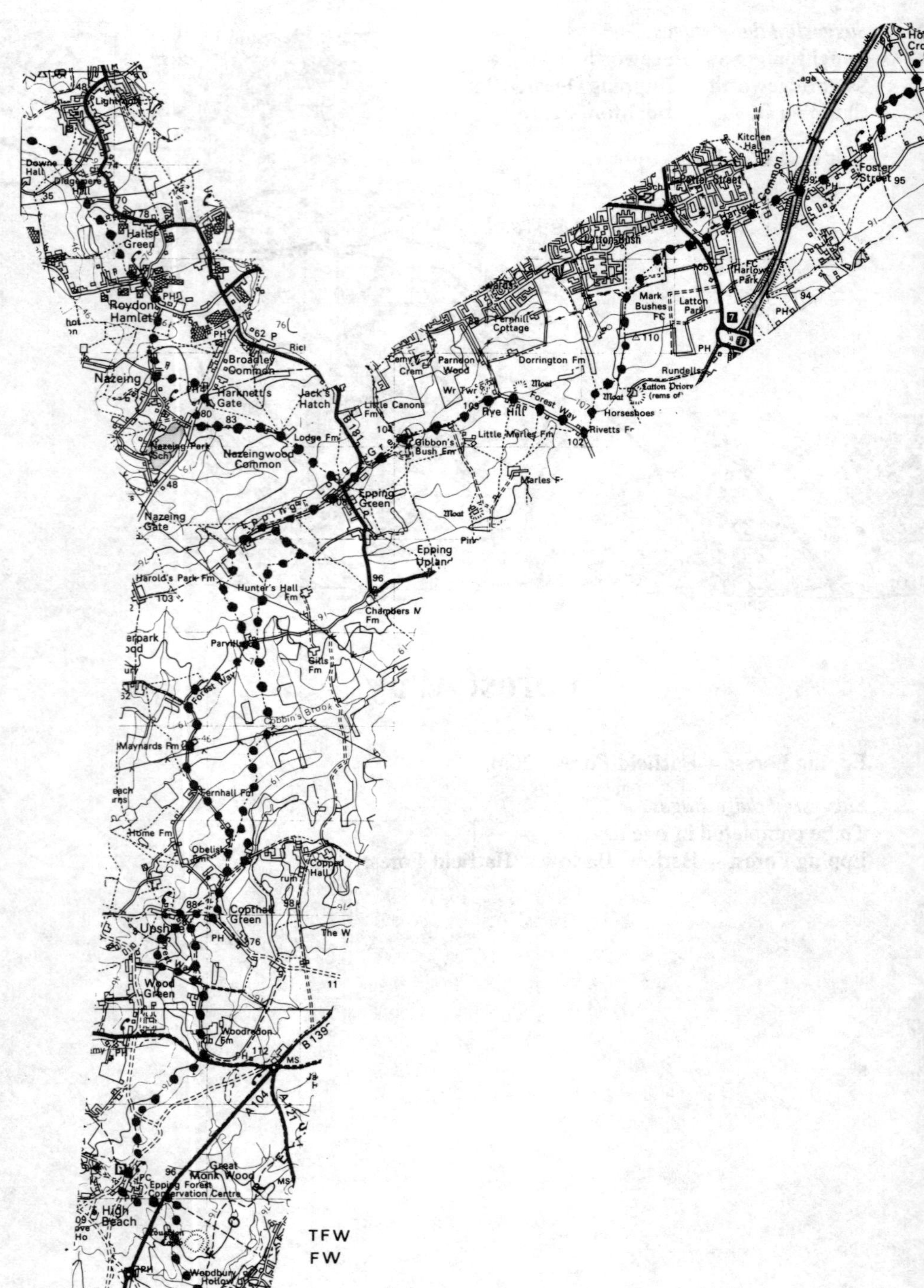
Hobbs Cross
Kitchen Hall
Foster Street
Potter Street
Harlow Common
Latton Bush
Mark Bushes
Latton Park
Harlow Park
Fernhill Cottage
Parndon Wood
Dorrington Fm
Rundells
Latton Priory
Moat
Rye Hill
Forest Way
Horseshoes
Rivetts Fm
Little Canons Fm
Gibbon's Bush Fm
Little Marles Fm
Marles Fm
Lodge Fm
Jack's Hatch
Broadley Common
Harknett's Gate
Nazeing
Nazeingwood Common
Roydon Hamlet
Halls Green
Downe Hall
Epping Green
Epping Upland
Nazeing Gate
Harold's Park Fm
Hunter's Hall Fm
Chambers Fm
Gills Fm
Cobbin's Brook
Maynards Fm
Fernhall Fm
Home Fm
Obelisk Fm
Copped Hall
Copthall Green
Upshire
Wood Green
Woodredon Fm
B181
B1393
A104
A121
Great Monk Wood
Epping Forest Conservation Centre
High Beach
Woodbury Hollow
TFW
FW

ESSEX WAY

Epping – Dedham. 53m.

Suggested daily stages
Epping – Good Easter. 17m.
Good Easter – Coggeshall. 17m.
Coggeshall – Dedham. 19m.

Maps 108 121 128

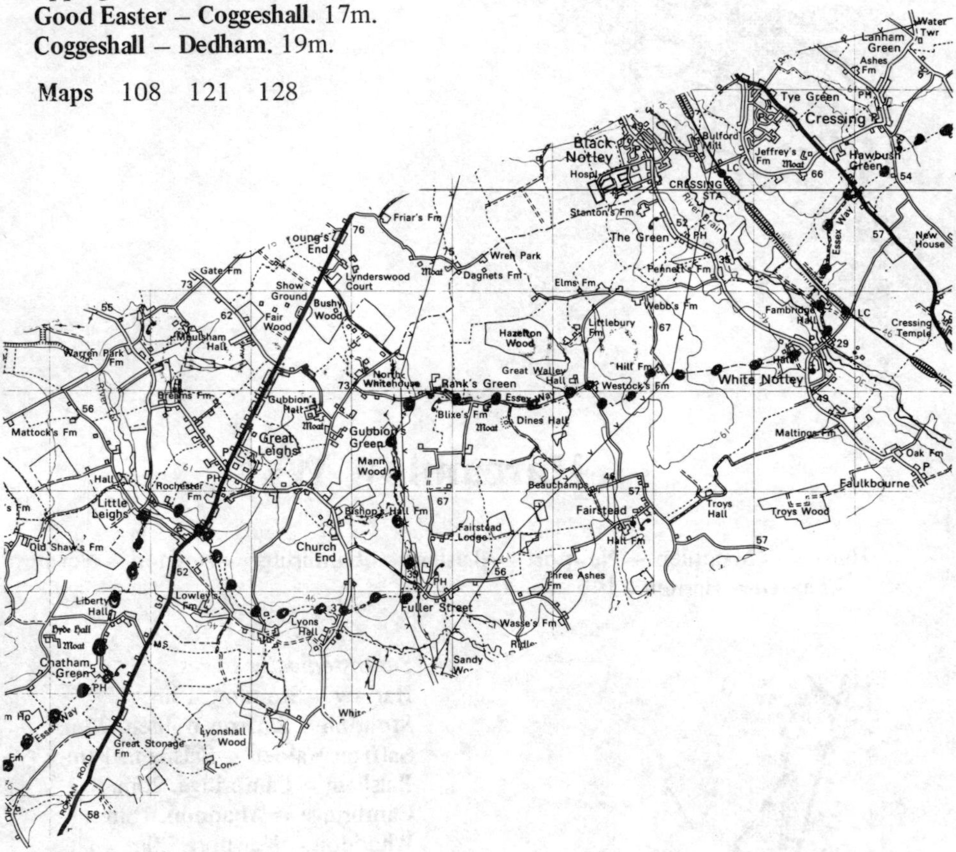

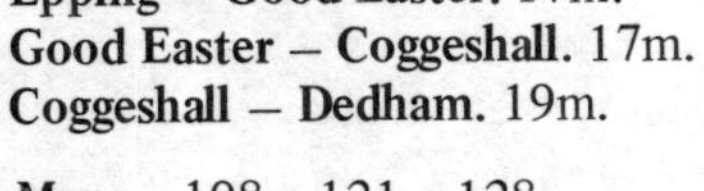

Harcamlow Way

Harlow – Manuden – Newport – Balsham – Cambridge – Heydon – Newport – Thaxted – Harlow. 140 m

Suggested daily stages
Harlow – Stondon. 15m.
Stondon – Saffron Walden. 22m.
Saffron Walden – Balsham. 14m.
Balsham – Cambridge. 20m.
Cambridge – Whaddon. 18m.
Whaddon – Newport. 20m.
Newport – Takeley. 17m.
Takeley – Harlow. 14m.

Maps 17 22 30 144 138 168

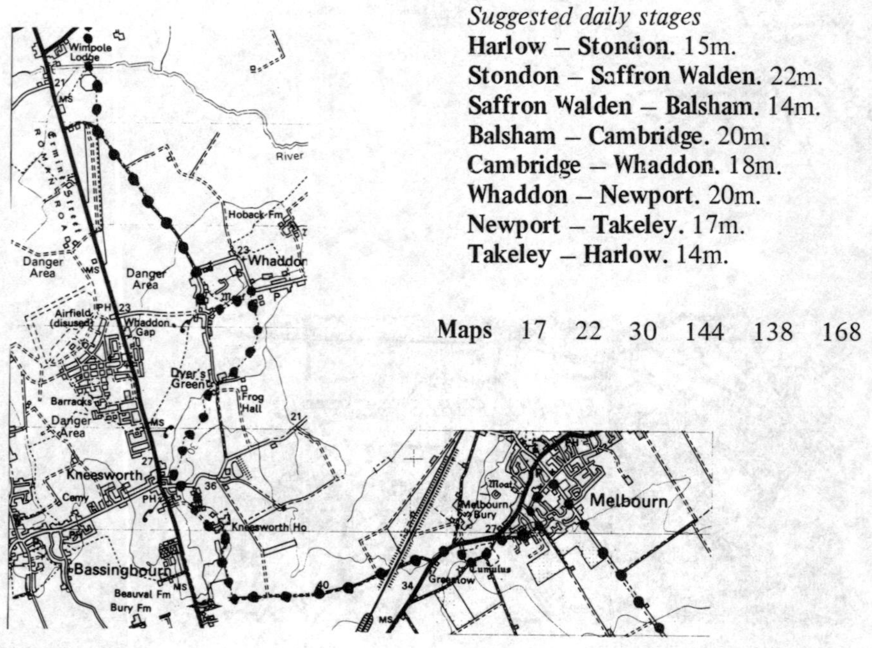

St Peter's Way

Chipping Ongar – St Peter-on-the-Wall, Bradwell-on-Sea. 39m.

Suggested daily stages: two-day walk
Chipping Ongar – Purleigh. 20m.
Purleigh – St Peter's Chapel, Bradwell-on-Sea. 19m.

Three-day walk
Chipping Ongar – Stock. 12m.
Stock – Lower Mayland. 14m.
Lower Mayland – St Peter's, Bradwell-on-Sea. 13m.

Maps 94 121

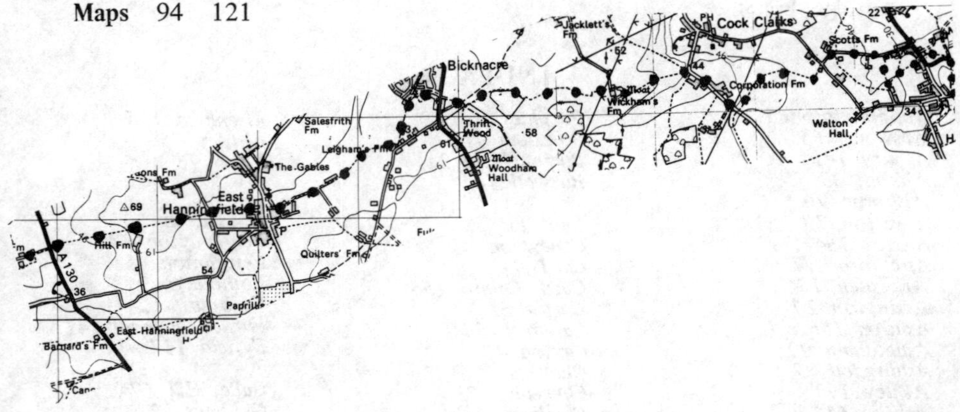

BIBLIOGRAPHY

Long-Distance Footpaths

Three Forests Way
The Harcamlow Way
St Peter's Way all three by and from Fred Matthews, Glenview, London Rd, Abridge, Essex.
Essex Way, East Anglia Tourist Board, 14 Museum St, Ipswich, Suffolk.
Forest Way, Essex County Council Planning Department, Chelmsford, Essex. Free.

A variety of booklets, leaflets and maps covering walks in different parts of Essex and Cambridgeshire are available. Unfortunately, these come and go out of print with great frequency and irregularity. Readers wishing to have a complete list of publications on walking in the area would be well advised to obtain a copy of the fact sheet for the area from the Ramblers Association, 1/5 Wandsworth Rd, London SW8 2LJ.

WALKING ORGANISATIONS

Area RA Secretary and Cambridge RA Group Secretary – George Smith, 5 Garlic Row, Cambridge.

Huntingdon RA Group – Mrs M. Gillian, Rose Cottage, Cotterstock, Cambs

Peterborough RA Group – Mrs J. Laws, 32 Fitzwilliam St, Peterborough, Cambs.

Brentwood RA Group Secretary – Miss A. Ebsworth, Cob Cottage, Lower Stock Rd, West Hanningfield, Essex.

Colchester RA Group Secretary – Mrs R. Clarke, 54 Shelley Rd, Colchester,

S.E. Essex RA Group Secretary – Miss B. Kirsh, 5 Imperial Lodge, Imperial Avenue, Westcliffe-on-Sea, Essex.

West Essex RA Group Secretary – Fred Matthews, Glen View, London Rd, Abridge, Essex.

INDEX